Praise for

Unlocking Literacy, Second Edition

"The field of reading will benefit once again from Marcia Henry's unparalleled knowledge of literacy development and instruction. This updated edition, like its predecessor, is the most authoritative text on the origins of English orthography and the development of decoding and spelling skills. A stellar contribution that is a must read for anyone engaged in teaching children to read."

—**G. Reid Lyon, Ph.D.**
Distinguished Professor and Chairman, Department of
Education Policy and Leadership, Annette Caldwell Simmons
School of Education and Human Development, Southern
Methodist University, Dallas, Texas

"Since the first edition was published, I have referred to and recommended this wonderful book over and over again. Its unique strength is its organization of word study (word recognition, vocabulary, and spelling) around morphology and the history of English. The specific topics make sense in relation to a coherent whole—the 'deep' structure of orthography—and all the teaching strategies Marcia Henry advises are practical and powerful. No teacher, especially of intermediate and middle grade students, should be without this book."

—**Louisa Moats, Ed.D.**
President, Moats Associates Consulting, Inc.

"Once again Marcia Henry has created a treasure chest of practical teaching tips for helping students coordinate the sound, spelling, and word parts for meaning in learning to read and spell. Research shows this approach works!"

—**Virginia Berninger, Ph.D.**
Professor of Educational Psychology, Director of University of
Washington Brain Education and Technology—Education Site,
and Coordinator, Research Area on Learning Disabilities, Eunice
Kennedy Shriver Intellectual and Developmental Disabilities
Research Center (IDDRC), University of Washington

"Another masterful contribution to the professional literature by one of education's leading literacy experts. This book provides the practical tools needed to build fluent readers—this will be embraced by practitioners."

—**Donald D. Deshler, Ph.D.**
Williamson Family Distinguished Professor
of Special Education and Director, Center for
Research on Learning, University of Kansas

UNLOCKING *Literacy*

UNLOCKING *Literacy*

Effective Decoding & Spelling Instruction

2nd EDITION

by

Marcia K. Henry, Ph.D.

·P A U L·H·
BROOKES
PUBLISHING C?.®

Baltimore • London • Sydney

Paul H. Brookes Publishing Co.
Post Office Box 10624
Baltimore, Maryland 21285-0624
USA

www.brookespublishing.com

"Paul H. Brookes Publishing Co." is a registered trademark of
Paul H. Brookes Publishing Co., Inc.

Typeset by Integrated Publishing Solutions, Grand Rapids, Michigan.
Manufactured in the United States of America by
Sheridan Books, Inc., Chelsea, Michigan.

The individuals described in this book are composites or real people
whose situations are masked and are based on the author's experiences.
In all instances, names and identifying details have been changed to
protect confidentiality.

Library of Congress Cataloging-in-Publication Data

Unlocking literacy : effective decoding and spelling instruction / by Marcia K. Henry.—2nd ed.
  p.   cm.
Includes bibliographical references and index.
ISBN-13: 978-1-59857-074-8 (pbk.)
ISBN-10: 1-59857-074-9
1. Reading—Phonetic method.   2. English language—Pronunciation—Study and teaching.
3. English language—Orthography and spelling—Study and teaching.   I. Title.

LB1050.34.H46   2010
372.46'5—dc22   2010023552

British Library Cataloguing in Publication data are available from the British Library.

2014   2013   2012

10   9   8   7   6   5   4   3   2

Contents

About the Author

Marcia K. Henry, Ph.D., brings 50 years of experience working in the field of reading and dyslexia as a diagnostician, tutor, teacher, and professor. Dr. Henry received her doctorate in educational psychology from Stanford University. Prior to her retirement in 1995, she was a professor in the Division of Special Education at San José State University, where she taught and directed the Center for Educational Research on Dyslexia. Dr. Henry taught as a Fulbright Lecturer/Research Scholar at the University of Trondheim, Norway, in 1991.

Dr. Henry is a frequent speaker at regional, national, and international conferences on topics related to intervention strategies for learners with dyslexia. She also writes for a variety of professional journals and serves on the editorial boards of *Dyslexia* and *Annals of Dyslexia*, the journals of The British Dyslexia Association and The International Dyslexia Association (IDA), respectively.

Since her retirement, Dr. Henry has taught at the University of New Mexico, the University of Pittsburgh, and the University of Minnesota–Duluth. She provides teacher training related to the teaching of reading and related language arts and consults with several school districts and states on informed reading instruction. Dr. Henry is the author of teaching materials for integrated decoding and spelling instruction. She is a past president (1992–1996) of The Orton Dyslexia Society (now known as IDA). She is a fellow of the Orton-Gillingham Academy and received the Margaret Byrd Rawson Lifetime Achievement Award from IDA in 2000.

Dr. Henry now lives on Madeline Island in Lake Superior, where she spends much of her time writing. She volunteers as a tutor at the island's two-room elementary school when needed. She compiled and co-edited *Dyslexia: Samuel T. Orton and His Legacy* for IDA's 50th anniversary in 1999.

Foreword

As the late, wonderful elementary teacher Merryl Pisha rhetorically asked all of her first graders, "Why is it that the hardest thing you will ever have to learn is the first thing you have to learn?" It's a good question. It took our species more than 2,000 years to move from the first writing systems to a true alphabetic principle, and we give our children 2,000 days to grasp these same concepts in order to learn to read.

From both a neurological standpoint and a historical one, learning to read is a semimiraculous achievement. This is in large part because, unlike language or vision, reading is a human invention, not a biological capacity that comes from our genetic endowment. Because human beings were never born to read, it means that the brain has to do some remarkable handiwork to go outside its own repertoire of skills. Basically, to learn to read, the brain must also learn to rearrange itself to form a brand new circuitry that connects some of our most complex and sophisticated areas in vision, language, and cognition. Very important for every teacher, this requires a whole new circuit to be built afresh with each new reader. Within this context, cognitive psychologist Steven Pinker once remarked that speech is programmed by our genes, "but reading is an optional accessory that must be painstakingly bolted on."

We who teach are the "bolters," and there is no better teacher of bolters, I believe, than Marcia Henry in her new edition of *Unlocking Literacy*. With this book she provides an elegant, cogently written summary of what educators need to know about how reading is learned and how it is best taught.

A brief summary of the first 500 milliseconds of the reading act illumines the way the brain's reading circuit works. It also provides a fair approximation of what teachers must bolt, which, in turn, provides a rather unusual conceptual backdrop for the chapters in this book. For example, when reading even a single word, the first milliseconds of the reading circuit activate extensive areas of the cortex and subcortical regions that are necessary for "decoding" the word's visual information about the features of letters, the common orthographic patterns in the language, and the visual conventions in text (see the first two chapters). This information is then connected to *all that we know about the word.* This latter knowledge, which is described in the book's early and middle chapters, requires the input from regions responsible for everything from the word's phonemes to its multiple possible meanings and associations, to its morphological information, to its varied grammatical and pragmatic functions. Over the first years of learning, this early set of cognitive and linguistic operations becomes virtually automatic or "fluent," thus allowing the reader in the next milliseconds to go beyond the decoded text to connect the decoded information to the "deep reading" comprehension processes. Ultimately, our capacity to understand the text and to think new thoughts is the generative, cognitively transformative platform at the heart of literacy and what "unlocks" the potential of every expert reader.

What Marcia Henry knows better than almost anyone in the field of reading research is how important knowledge of the structure of the English language is to the optimal functioning of this reading circuit. For example, for two decades she has helped both researchers and educators understand the pivotal contribution of morpheme knowledge by the reader. Most teachers of reading have little formal work in linguistics and never realize how much of a contribution explicitly taught morpheme knowledge makes in the development of a reader. To take the smallest example from this book's title, *unlocking* can be either nine long letters for a child to decode or three very reasonably sized morphemes: *un* + *lock* + *ing.* Recognizing and knowing the meaning of these morphemes provide three pieces of information that hasten decoding and facilitate comprehension. First, the morphemes provide a very quick orthographic chunking strategy that helps fluent identification; second, they present important semantic information for comprehension; and third, they give syntactic information about how the word is used.

Marcia Henry's emphasis on the development of morphemic knowledge in our readers has been one of the pivotal contributions to the field. This book provides one of the single best examples of how knowledge about morphemes and other aspects of the structure of the English language should inform the teaching of literacy. At the same time the structure of the book, like the structure of the reading circuit itself, embeds this pivotal knowledge inside the whole of a very complex set of operations that Marcia Henry, somehow, makes simple to understand and noble to teach.

Maryanne Wolf
John DiBiaggio Professor of Citizenship and Public Service
Director, Center for Reading and Language Research
Tufts University

Preface

The second edition of *Unlocking Literacy: Effective Decoding and Spelling Instruction* coincides with what we know about effective reading instruction today. Much of the current research validates work that has intrigued me for most of my professional life. Thus, this book was revised to share insights gained during 50 years of working in the field of reading and specific reading disability, which is often called dyslexia. My own education in this field began when I began tutoring students at the Rochester Reading Center in Rochester, Minnesota, in 1959. Encouraged by the center's directors, Paula Dozier Rome and Jean Smith Osman, I began to learn more about reading acquisition and instruction—an entirely new field for me at that time.

It was in Rochester that I learned the actual teaching techniques that are recommended today for all children learning to read. I learned the importance of giving children strategies that empower them to read and spell, including the use of phonology and understanding the role it plays in learning to read and the significance of morphology, and the importance of teaching morphemes (the meaningful units of language, e.g., prefixes, suffixes, and Latin roots and Greek combining forms) to older students. I found that although teaching the structure of the language is important with all children, it is essential with those who have dyslexia or need explicit instruction to acquire the alphabetic code.

I discovered that almost all children appear to benefit from a multisensory approach in which all modalities used in learning—visual, auditory, and kinesthetic-tactile—are linked and sound, letters, and letter formation all play important roles.

I continued more formal education at Santa Clara University and Stanford University, where I took more courses related to reading acquisition, psycholinguistics, and psychology. All of this experience prepared me for my work with children and with preservice and in-service educators and for the writing of this book.

Only one component of the reading/language arts curriculum, the decoding–spelling continuum, is featured in this book. Before students can comprehend text, they must be able to decode words fluently and accurately. Before they can compose stories, they must spell accurately. Acquiring adequate vocabularies and learning sentence structure and construction, paragraph elements, and comprehension of narrative and expository text are also important components of any child's reading/writing instruction, but these topics are not covered in this book. (See Birsh, 2005, for a research summary on all components of reading.)

In Chapter 1, along with the rationale for the ideas expressed in this book, current research on decoding and spelling is summarized. The implications of this research are clear: Instruction cannot be piecemeal or scattershot. It must be cohesive, systematic, explicit, and direct. This instruction allows students to understand the structure of English orthography (the spelling system) and provides numerous strategies for decoding and spelling.

Chapter 2 presents a brief history of written English. Knowledge of the historical factors inherent in English words provides useful clues for accurate decoding and spelling. Written English took years to form and is still changing, as all artifacts do. Children enjoy learning about the history of words and especially about the English words they are learning to read and spell.

Chapter 3 describes the structure of English orthography based on both word structure and word origin. I discuss the structure of English words, focusing on the letter–sound correspondences, syllable patterns, and morpheme patterns of English words of Anglo-Saxon, Latin, and Greek origins.

In Chapter 4, reading fundamentals, including lesson concepts, lesson format, and lesson procedures are discussed. Lessons take place as dynamic discussion sessions with the teacher acting as facilitator as well as instructor. The multisensory approach of these lessons encourages active learning through metacognitive strategies, introduction of useful patterns found in thousands of words, and numerous opportunities for practice. Lessons are connected to real reading and writing in context.

Chapter 5 discusses prerequisites for effective decoding and spelling, including preliteracy events, readiness skills, and phonological awareness tasks. Informal assessment as well as lessons and activities beneficial in preschool and kindergarten are presented.

The last three chapters of the book include sample lessons along with content and opportunities for practice. Chapter 6 introduces patterns and rules needed by primary grade students, including letter–sound correspondence patterns and related rules, compound words, syllable patterns, and common prefixes and suffixes. Examples of possible supplemental activities are provided.

Chapter 7 focuses on specific instructional lessons and activities useful for upper elementary and middle school students. The Latin and Greek layers of language are introduced. Latin word roots and their corresponding affixes, along with the common Greek combining forms found frequently in science and math texts, are emphasized. In Chapter 8 additional, less common Latin roots and Greek combining forms are presented. Teachers will gain information related to activities useful in high school content area classes.

This book also contains substantial back matter. The appendixes begin with surveys of language knowledge for teachers that were developed by Louisa Cook Moats (2003). In addition, there are appendixes of common nonphonetic words, compound words, prefixes, suffixes, Latin roots, and Greek combining forms. Words often found in elementary and secondary content area textbooks are also presented. The glossary defines terms that are used in the book (see boldface terms in text) and that are beneficial for teachers and their students to learn.

McGuinness (2005) noted that "reading and spelling are easy to teach if you know how to do it" (p. xii). *Unlocking Literacy: Effective Decoding and Spelling Instruction, Second Edition,* will help teachers in general or special education, tutors, and therapists working with small groups or individuals learn "how to do it." Parents, too, will enjoy knowing more about effective decoding and spelling instruction. I hope that students will discover the joy of language as they acquire reading accuracy and fluency in decoding and spelling words.

REFERENCES

Birsh, J.R. (2005). Research and reading disability. In J. Birsh (Ed.), *Multisensory teaching of basic language skills* (pp. 1–21). Baltimore: Paul H. Brookes Publishing Co.

McGuinness, D. (2005). *Language development and learning to read.* Cambridge, MA: The MIT Press.

Moats, L.C. (2003). *Speech to print workbook: Language exercises for teachers.* Baltimore: Paul H. Brookes Publishing Co.

Acknowledgments

My profound thanks go to the wonderful team at Paul H. Brookes Publishing Co. Among them, special thanks to Production Manager Mika Sam Smith, who was invaluable during the first edition, and to Acquisitions Editor Sarah Shepke for her helpful assistance in this second edition. Project Editor Jan Krejci provided important queries and suggestions in the copyediting phase. I am grateful to Louisa Moats and to Brookes Publishing for allowing me to include several of Louisa's language knowledge surveys.

I am deeply grateful that Paula Dozier Rome and Jean Smith Osman of the Rochester Reading Center started me on this journey 50 years ago. Robert Calfee and several other Stanford professors provided opportunities for learning, teaching, and research in the fields of education and psychology. I am extremely appreciative of their confidence in me. I also consider the late Norman Geschwind, Isabelle Y. Liberman, and Margaret Byrd Rawson, with whom I served on The Orton Dyslexia Society (now The International Dyslexia Association [IDA]) board of directors, among my best teachers.

I am indebted to Susan Brady and Keith Stanovich for supporting the writing of the first edition of this book as they reviewed the original prospectus. Appreciation also goes to my colleagues at San José State University and at other universities where I taught and to members of IDA who continue to influence the field of reading disabilities with enthusiasm and professionalism.

I acknowledge with loving memory my parents, Bob and Margaret Kierland, who inspired me in many ways. I am grateful to my brother Pete, who first made me aware of the struggles of children who do not learn to read easily. To all my children, who are "30- and 40- and 50-something," thanks for continuing to make life diverse and eventful. My hope is that my eight grandchildren will enjoy the gifts that books provide. Finally, I thank my husband Burke for his steadfast support of all my endeavors and for his constant love. Without his encouragement, this book would never have been written or revised.

*To my students of all ages, from whom I continue to learn.
And to the teachers who know how important reading
and spelling are for their students
and who persist in learning more about written language.
They make it all worthwhile!*

SECTION I

Preparation

CHAPTER 1

Decoding and Spelling

Keys to Unlocking Literacy

L iteracy ranges from the basic ability to read and write (or functional literacy), required in everyday life, to advanced literacy, reflecting knowledge of the significant ideas, events, and values of a society. For many children, literacy comes easily, but others need help unlocking the complexities of reading and writing. Two significant factors in acquiring literacy are **decoding** (or **word identification**) and spelling.

Reading is probably the most important scholarly activity a person masters. Every subject in school requires at least grade-level reading ability. Just as important is the ability to read for pleasure. Much of what we learn about the past and present is found in books and magazines. Thus, reading adds to our knowledge of the world and our understanding of human relationships. Cunningham (2009) reported that speech is lexically impoverished compared with print and noted that print offers more rare words, even in children's books, than does adult speech.

Reading has two major elements: decoding and comprehension. Decoding comprises the skills and knowledge by which a reader translates printed words into speech. More simply, *decoding* is the ability to pronounce a word subvocally in silent reading or vocally in oral reading. *Comprehension,* in contrast, is the ability to understand the words, sentences, and connected text that one reads. Perfetti asserted, "Only a reader with skilled decoding processes can be expected to have skilled comprehension processes" (1984, p. 43). Gough and Tunmer (1986) urged educators to consider decoding a necessary part of reading because print cannot be understood (comprehended) if it cannot be translated into language (decoded). When children have access to words important to the gist of a story or to the meaning of text, the children's understanding is enhanced. Butler and Silliman (2002) contended that researchers are uncertain exactly how decoding affects comprehension, but they know that without decoding one cannot comprehend. We need to decode words in order to assign meaning to words, sentences, and texts. We now know the importance of **fluency.** Decoding must be accurate and automatic in order to be fluent (Wolf, 2007).

In this book, I deal with the integrated teaching of decoding and its linguistic counterpart, *encoding,* or spelling. Note the **base word** here is *code.* I am reminded of the *Dennis the Menace* cartoon in which Dennis sees his mom and dad whispering and says to his chum, "They're spelling things around me and I haven't been able to break the code yet." That is the purpose of this book. To unlock the code surrounding decoding and spelling.

Decoding is a receptive language process in which letters on the page are received by the reader. The **alphabetic principle,** the systematic correspondence between spoken and written forms of words, informs the reader. Spelling, in contrast, is a productive language process; the speller hears sounds and must translate them to alphabetic symbols by writing or by speaking letter names.

The decoding of unfamiliar words requires that children recognize the common symbols, or letters, of the language. These symbols have corresponding sounds. Instruction in letter–sound correspondences is called **phonics.** In order to develop adequate decoding and spelling skills, children need explicit instruction in phonics that is systematic, structured, sequential, and multisensory (McIntyre & Pickering, 1995).

Two themes flow through this book: word origin and word structure. The first theme comes from an examination of the history of written English and the way this history has influenced the English **orthography,** or spelling system, over centuries (see Chapter 2).

Word origin reflects the historical and geographic origin of a word. This second dimension of this book comes from three major structural components: 1) letter–sound correspondences, 2) **syllable** patterns, and 3) **morpheme** patterns (*morphemes* are the units of meaning in words such as **prefixes, suffixes,** and **roots;** see Chapter 3). An understanding of the historical forces influencing written English, along with an understanding of the structure of the English spelling system, provides teachers and their students with a logical basis for the study of English. Yet, few teacher preparation programs include these knowledge bases in the curriculum (for examples of texts that do cover these domains, see Berninger, 2000; Berninger & Wolf, 2009; Moats, 1994, 2000, 2003, 2009a, 2009b). Berninger concluded that reading problems are more related to the instructional program than to the child because teachers often do not use systematic, explicit instructional strategies. In addition, teachers may have an insufficient understanding of the structure of language at multiple levels (e.g., **phonology, morphology,** syntax) and may not understand the ways in which phonology is represented in the orthography.

Appendix A provides an opportunity for teachers to check their language knowledge before proceeding through this book.

The framework for the **decoding–spelling continuum** in this book is based on word origin and word structure (Henry, 1988a, 1988b). This framework provides a structure for presenting and organizing information, allowing teachers to avoid presenting skills in isolation. The three languages of origin most influential to English are Anglo-Saxon, Latin, and Greek. Students who recognize letter–sound correspondences, syllable patterns, and morpheme patterns in words of Anglo-Saxon, Latin, and Greek origin hold the strategies necessary to read and spell most unfamiliar words.

Figure 1.1 illustrates the framework undergirding the integrated decoding and spelling instruction. The cells in the blank 3 × 3 matrix shown in Figure 1.1

	Letter–sound correspondences	Syllables	Morphemes
Anglo-Saxon			
Latin			
Greek			

Figure 1.1. Blank word origin and word structure matrix. (*Source:* Henry, 1988b.)

refer to the origin and structural categories of language. Both word origin and word structure guide what is to be taught. The great majority of English words come from Anglo-Saxon, Romance (primarily Latin), and Greek origins. Brown (1947) noted that 80% of English words borrowed from other languages come from Latin and Greek and make up 60% of words used in text. By receiving instruction in all of the components in this framework, students will learn the significant patterns found in English words. A completed matrix appears in Chapter 3 (see Figure 3.1), where the specific word origin patterns are presented. As the patterns are introduced, teachers and their students will become familiar with terms in the Decoding–Spelling Instruction Register (see Chapter 4) that are necessary in discussing decoding and spelling concepts.

THE RELATIONSHIP OF READING TO SPELLING AND SPELLING TO READING

Decoding and spelling share a common orthography, or writing system, so it makes sense to teach the two in conjunction. The patterns useful in decoding are reinforced by spelling and vice versa. In addition, readers who have difficulty in reading usually have difficulty in spelling (Bruck & Waters, 1990; Ehri, 1987; Henry, 1988b, 1989; Moats, 1995; Templeton, 1995). Bruck and Waters observed that "although spellers of all ages and skill levels use sound–spelling information for spelling, accurate knowledge of these correspondences differentiates the more skilled from the less skilled speller" (pp. 165–166).

Moats concluded, "For young children, research clearly indicates that spelling supports learning to read, and for older children, it's likely that learning about the meaningful relationships between words will contribute to vocabulary growth and reading comprehension" (2005–2006, p. 42).

McGuinness (2004) stated that reading and spelling are structurally reversible processes and should be taught in tandem. Psychologically speaking, however, reading and spelling draw on different memory skills. Decoding involves recognition memory, with letters as the prompt. Spelling, in contrast, involves recall memory, without any prompts as clues. She noted that spelling is therefore considered the more difficult task.

Ehri (2006) noted that a key ingredient in learning to both read and spell is knowledge of the alphabetic system. This includes the following capabilities: knowing the shapes, names, and sounds of letters; having **phonemic awareness;** recognizing mapping relations between **graphemes** in the spelling of words and **phonemes** in their pronunciations; and knowing **spelling patterns** and their relationship to syllabic units in speech.

Treiman also concluded that children's phonemic awareness and knowledge of letter names and corresponding sounds "[help] them make the connections between speech and sounds" (2006, p. 581).

Herron (2008) recommended that students construct words before they try to read them; that is, spelling first, reading second. She cited research studies pointing to "the fact that the foundation of reading is speech and that the organization of reading skills in the brain must be built on this foundation" (p. 78).

Moats concurred with this view when she wrote the following:

> One of the most fundamental flaws found in almost all phonics programs, including traditional ones, is that they teach the code backwards. That is, they go from letter to sound instead of from sound to letter. . . . The print-to-sound (conventional phonics) approach leaves gaps, invites confusion, and creates inefficiencies. (1998, pp. 44–45)

My own preference, based on many years of teaching and the practicalities of classroom instruction, is to teach the alphabetic principle, the connection of sound to symbol and symbol to sound, simultaneously. Patterns taught for spelling and for decoding—those letter–sound correspondences, syllable patterns, and morpheme patterns—can be taught for both decoding and encoding. Students need to be aware of phonological, orthographic, and morphological aspects of words.

THE CONTINUUM OF INTEGRATED DECODING AND SPELLING INSTRUCTION

The decoding–spelling continuum across the grades is supported by the work of several researchers in the field of reading and spelling who have theorized that learners move through developmental stages as they begin to read and spell (Bear, 1992; Chall, 1983; Ehri, 1985; Frith, 1980; Henderson, 1990; Perfetti, 1984, 1985). These stages generally move from prealphabetic, to partial alphabetic, to mature, and then to consolidated alphabetic phases for reading multisyllabic words. Chall (1983) proposed the following stages of reading development. In Stage 0 (prereading), children develop the prerequisites of visual, visual-motor, and auditory skills. This stage contains many of the skills we now know as **phonological awareness,** or understanding of the role that sounds play in language. During Stage 1 (initial reading or decoding), first and second graders learn the **alphabetic code** and recognize **sight words.** In Stage 2 (confirmation, fluency, or ungluing from print), second and third graders gain fluency and pay less direct attention to spelling–sound relationships. In Stage 3 (reading for learning new information), fourth through eighth graders become more efficient readers as they relate print to ideas, although they read text that is limited in technical complexity. Stage 4 (multiple viewpoints) strategies, which come into play in high school, include the ability to deal with layers of facts and concepts added to previous knowledge. Stage 5 (construction and reconstruction) is found at age 18 and beyond. Stage 5 readers depend on analysis, synthesis, and judgment as they construct abstract knowledge.

Henderson (1990) and Bear (1992) described similar developmental stages for spelling as 1) preliterate, 2) letter name, 3) within-word pattern, 4) syllable juncture, and 5) derivational principles. During the preliterate stage, 1- to 7-year-olds begin to scribble, identify pictures, and draw. They listen to stories and identify some symbols. These children may pretend to read, even holding a book upside down. By the letter-name stage, between 5 and 9 years of age, children use "invented" spellings, know most common sight words, recognize initial and final sounds, and read orally but disfluently. The within-word pattern stage, from 6 to 12 years old, finds students recognizing short (**lax**) and long (**tense**) **vowel** markers. Readers are comfortable with silent reading. Oral reading becomes more fluent, with appropriate expression. During the stage of syllable juncture, between 8 and 18 years old, students understand the **consonant** doubling principle (e.g., *boat/boated* but *pat/patted*). Errors are common at the juncture where syllables come together and in **schwa** positions. (A *schwa* is the neutral vowel in an unaccented syllable, such as the sound that corresponds to the grapheme *a* in *asleep*.) Students in the syllable juncture stage begin using prefixes and suffixes. Although students in this stage prefer silent reading, oral reading becomes even more fluent, with good expression. The final stage, that of derivational principles, occurs from age 10 through adulthood. Students in this stage understand etymological principles and know roots and bases, predominantly from Latin and Greek. These students have "new control and correctness in regard to polysyllabic words" (Henderson, 1990, p. 74). Metalinguistic reasoning and classical vocabulary expand rapidly.

Even those students who learn phonics for decoding and spelling short, **regular words** often have difficulty at a more advanced level because they have only learned rudimentary rules of sound–symbol association. The decoding–spelling continuum illustrated in Figure 1.2 begins with an introduction to phonological awareness and continues through Latin and Greek morphemes. The term *phonological awareness* is generally used to indicate awareness of and facility with all levels of the speech sound system, including word boundaries, stress patterns, syllable patterns, onset–rime units, and phonemes.

Phonemic awareness, the most advanced level of phonological awareness, requires the conscious awareness of individual phonemes in a given word, along with the ability to manipulate these sounds. Students with phonemic awareness understand that *sand* and *sick* begin with the same sound /s/ and that *told* and *laid* end with the same sound. These students are able to complete the more difficult task of removing one sound from a **consonant blend,** such as deleting /l/ from *plant* to get *pant* and removing /m/ from *blimp* to get *blip*.

After phonological awareness training, in which children learn to rhyme, segment, and blend orally (described in Chapter 5), children begin learning the upper- and lowercase alphabet letters and letter–sound correspondences while continuing to improve their phonological awareness skills. Students need to automatically name each letter and give the sound(s) each letter makes. Children learn a variety of patterns found within the domain of letter–sound correspondences (see Chapters 3 and 6). By second grade, children need exposure to common patterns of syllable division, **compound words,** and frequently used prefixes and suffixes (see Chapter 6). Third grade is a transition year in which more multisyllabic words are introduced. These longer words are not necessarily harder to read once children know the common prefixes and suffixes.

In the upper elementary grades, many words found in text are multisyllabic and often contain Latin roots and **affixes** and Greek **combining forms.** Thus, ad-

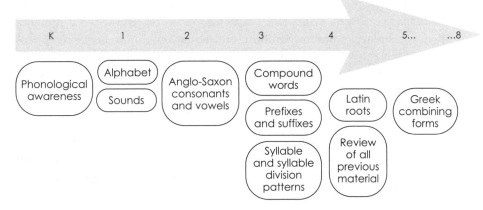

Figure 1.2. The decoding–spelling continuum. All of the topics should be taught by eighth grade. (*Source:* Henry, 1997.)

ditional strategies must be taught to those students who have not acquired an automatic level of **word recognition** for longer words. By fourth grade, children begin learning common Latin roots, along with additional prefixes and suffixes. Greek word parts come next, early in fifth grade. By the end of sixth grade, most common Latin roots and Greek combining forms should have been taught (see Chapter 7). For students in middle school or high school, review of all patterns should continue. Less common roots and combining forms and other linguistic concepts must be acquired in middle school and high school (see Chapter 8).

APPROACHES TO DECODING AND SPELLING INSTRUCTION

Several strategies have been used in the teaching of decoding, including looking for context clues, memorizing whole words, learning letter–sound correspondences (or phonics), and using literature and children's own language as in the whole-language approach. Spelling has usually been taught as a rote memory task. Students study a list of words and take a weekly test. These words are usually unrelated in their structure.

Decoding

The teaching of decoding and spelling has undergone numerous changes over the years. A pendulum appears to swing between the phonics side and the sight-word side of instruction. Chall and Squire (1991) summarized the history of readers and textbook publishing. They found that the first widely used reader was *The New England Primer,* with alphabetic rhymes, pictures, and religious content. The most popular reader through the early 1800s was Noah Webster's *American Spelling Book,* which emphasized the "sounding out" of words and "standard" American pronunciation and spelling. McGuffey's readers, with their focus on the alphabetic/phonetic method, were popular between 1836 and 1920. By the 1930s the *Dick and Jane* series by William S. Gray introduced the whole-word method, controlled vocabulary, word recognition, and stress on comprehension. In this whole-word (or sight-word) approach, students memorized words by seeing them over and over again. For example, students saw the word *Jane* over and over again. Students did not learn that *J* sounds like /j/, that *n* sounds like /n/, and that *a* represents a **long vowel sound** because of the final silent *e*. This approach was the basis for the later whole-language instruction.

Whole-language instruction assumes that through exposure to good literature and opportunities to read and write, children will pick up the alphabetic code and make their own phonics generalizations. In the whole-language approach, any phonics instruction is embedded in "real," predictable text. Unfamiliar words are to be guessed from the context, not sounded out. Stanovich and his colleagues (Stanovich, West, & Feeman, 1981; West & Stanovich, 1978) found that reading was not a "psycholinguistic guessing game" as proposed by Goodman (1967, 1976); rather, only poor readers guess words from context, whereas good readers do not. Stanovich and his colleagues inferred that skilled readers did not need to rely on context information because their word recognition processing was so rapid and automatic. It should be noted, however, that in the case of heteronyms, context is essential for the correct pronunciation of words.

After careful examination of many studies and her own research, Adams concluded, "The single immutable and nonoptional fact about skillful reading is that it involves relatively complete processing of the individual letters of print" (1990, p. 105). She noted that skilled readers of English process individual letters with comparative ease and speed as they recognize, at an automatic level, many of the ordered sequences of letter patterns. She provided this conclusion as one of the reasons that phonics instruction is so important.

Chall (1967) encouraged a move back to phonics for beginning reading instruction. During phonics instruction, students learn to connect letters with sounds. Instruction in phonics in the 1970s and early 1980s centered on a drill-and-practice format, often with worksheets guiding the practice. In this type of instruction, students rarely heard the sounds they were to practice; rather, they might look at a picture of a boy and write the letter related to the first sound of the word *boy*. In contrast, the type of phonics advocated in this book is based on frequent discussion of sounds and corresponding letters and provides practice in actual reading and spelling from dictation. Beginning phonics instruction usually is accompanied by the reading of decodable text or text based primarily on patterns that have been or are being taught. (*Note:* Whereas *phonics* refers to the teaching approach, *phonetics* refers the nature and articulation of speech sounds and their representation, and the systematic classification of speech sounds in a language.)

In the late 1980s and early 1990s, opposing camps advocated either phonics or the whole-language approach. Stahl and Miller (1989) suggested that the whole-language approach is not very effective in developing decoding skills and found nothing to favor the use of whole language beyond kindergarten. Many teachers, reading researchers, and teacher educators support an informed and balanced approach to teaching reading based on research outcomes (Brady & Moats, 1997; Pressley, 1998). Ehri (2004) concluded that systematic phonics programs help children learn to read more effectively than do programs with little or no phonics instruction. Moreover, she found that **synthetic phonics,** an approach in which children blend sounds to make words, is especially effective in teaching beginning reading in classrooms. Johnston and Watson concurred and noted that in addition to accelerated letter–sound learning, "synthetic phonics develops phoneme awareness, and gives rise to word reading, reading comprehension, and spelling skills significantly above children's chronological ages" (2006, p. 679). Pressley concluded that upon finding an unfamiliar word, "sounding out a word is the preferred strategy of good readers" (1998, p. 23). Many teachers find that teaching explicit phonics is useful, but they also know the value of having students read good literature, work on comprehension, and receive instruction in composition.

More school districts throughout the United States are reemphasizing the teaching of specific skills such as phonics, especially in the primary grades. The goal set by Presidents Bill Clinton and George W. Bush is that by third grade, all students will read at grade level. Although this goal is laudable, it assumes that all of the necessary skills can be taught by third grade. Yet many of the content area words required in fourth grade and beyond contain elements that are not taught in a lower elementary grade reading/spelling curriculum. In the early grades, children need to read few words beyond two syllables. Children study few of the prefixes, suffixes, and roots important for upper-grade success in reading. Without recognizing the value of syllabic and morphological patterns, however, students are constrained from using clues available to identify long, unfamiliar words found in upper-grade text. Unfortunately, most decoding instruction largely neglects syllable and morpheme patterns, perhaps because these techniques are only useful for the longer words found in literature and subject matter text beyond second and third grade, at which point decoding instruction becomes virtually nonexistent in most schools.

Spelling (or Encoding)

Bourassa and Treiman (2007) noted that until the late 1960s, spelling was a form of rote memorization because of the impression that the English writing system was complex and illogical. As language researchers and cognitive psychologists pointed out regularities between spoken and printed English, views of spelling development changed.

Yet spelling instruction has changed little since the 1950s in most classrooms. A typical procedure is that children receive a list of 20–25 words on Monday. They go over the words with the teacher and are expected to memorize the sequence of the letters in each word. Children practice during the week, often having a pretest on Wednesday or Thursday. The real test comes on Friday. Most children, even those with reading and language problems, do well on the Friday test but often cannot write the word correctly in context 2 or 3 weeks later.

During the height of the whole-language movement, children were encouraged to use invented spelling that was based on what they thought was correct. Although this practice makes sense developmentally for kindergartners and first graders, children soon need to spell correctly. They benefit from explicit and direct instruction in the alphabetic code. Carney (1994) emphasized that spelling errors distract the reader from the message. Poor spellers are often thought to be careless or unintelligent. Carney contrasted errors of competence with performance errors. Errors of competence are fairly consistent misspellings, whereas performance errors tend to be temporary. Children with reading and spelling problems are consistent in their misspellings. Teachers need to analyze carefully the error patterns displayed by their students.

Carney also urged teachers to be aware of the part that **dialects** play in spelling. For example, a child who pronounces *saw* as "sore" and *law* as "lore" may tend to spell the words as they sound to him or her. The closer a person's dialect is to standard English pronunciation, the easier it is for that person to spell. The United States has many dialects. *Bury, berry,* and *Barry* are pronounced the same in the Midwest but not necessarily in the Northeast or South. In addition, English language learners often have difficulty pronouncing English words, especially if the sounds are not found in their native languages.

Ehri (1989) encouraged teachers to provide beginning readers with a full knowledge of the spelling system, including its orthographic and phonological connections. She urged teachers to perfect the way they teach children to read and spell.

Templeton and Morris (1999) pointed out that although memory plays an important role in learning to spell, it is not the only role. Students must also learn to understand how words work. Knowing word structure and how this structure signals both sound and meaning is important. Templeton and Morris concluded that instructional emphasis should be placed on exploration of patterns as opposed to memorization of the 5,000 most frequently occurring English words.

Berninger and Wolf (2009) noted that good spellers need only one or a few exposures to a word to remember it. Unfortunately, students with **dyslexia** often lack this "fast mapping" of sounds to symbols. Berninger and Wolf stated, "Reading involves creating maps between written words, based on visual inputs, and spoken words, based on auditory inputs" (p. 64).

Melvyn Ramsden (2001) discussed the importance of knowing the meaning of a word before it is spelled. Although reading the words *mist* and *missed* is not so difficult, one must know the meanings of these **homophones** in order to know which one to use in a given context. Students must understand meaning to know which of the following homophones to write in a certain situation: *meet* or *meat, here* or *hear, pail* or *pale, maid* or *made,* and numerous others. As noted later in this chapter, a computer spell checker cannot help correct spelling if the writer does not know the correct meaning of the words that he or she wants to use.

CURRENT RESEARCH AND IMPLICATIONS FOR INSTRUCTION

Numerous studies over the past three decades have investigated both reading and spelling development. Both neurobiological and psychoeducational research evidence informs instruction. (See Birsh [2005] for a summary of research-based intervention strategies.)

Elementary Grade Instruction

Research sponsored by various educational institutions has focused on prerequisites for reading acquisition and the specific literacy tasks that influence future reading ability. Historically, educators have looked at the maturity and readiness of future readers. Children's use of oral language, fine and gross motor skills, general intelligence, concepts of print, and basic perceptual-motor skills all play a part in reading readiness.

In the mid- and late 1990s, Scarborough (1998) studied the prerequisites for reading acquisition. Four factors stood out as the strongest predictors of reading: expressive vocabulary, general language ability, sentence/story recall, and phonological awareness. Scarborough noted that

> Not surprisingly, measures of skills that are directly related to reading and writing—including knowledge about letter identities, about letter–sound relationships, and about the mechanics and functions of book reading—have yielded the highest simple correlations with subsequent reading scores. (p. 91)

Somewhat weaker effects were obtained for all measures of general ability and various narrower facets of language skill. Even weaker average correlations were obtained for the other kindergarten abilities examined, including speech production and perception, visual and verbal short-term memory, and other nonverbal abilities.

Research initiated by Liberman and her colleagues (Liberman, 1973; Liberman & Liberman, 1990; Liberman & Shankweiler, 1991; Liberman, Shankweiler, Fischer, & Carter, 1974) found that children's phonological awareness is extremely important in learning to read. Results from many studies suggest that the common trait running through the reading ability of children and adults with reading disorders appears to be impairment in phonological, and primarily phonemic, awareness. Samuel T. Orton (1937) remarked on the fact that even in the 1920s many of the children under his care lacked an understanding of the role that sounds play in words and had difficulty understanding letter–sound relationships.

Since the early 1990s, the U.S. Department of Education and the National Institute of Child Health and Human Development (NICHD) of the National Institutes of Health have conducted numerous studies on reading acquisition. Many research network center sites and many noncenter research sites funded by the NICHD have focused on prerequisites for learning to read and factors necessary in early reading instruction. More than 42,000 children have been involved in prevention and intervention programs in more than 300 schools in the country (Lyon, 2004; Lyon, Fletcher, & Barnes, 2003). Scientific advances from these studies are described in more than 2,600 peer-reviewed publications for the following areas of investigation:

- Behavioral/linguistic predictors of reading disorders in children ages 5–6 years

- Early identification of reading disorders in children ages 5–6 years

- Prevention and early intervention programs for reading disorders

- Remedial treatment of reading disorders

- Developmental course of reading disorders

- Cognitive profiles/subtypes of reading disorders

- Causal mechanisms in reading disorders: genetics and neurobiology

- Definitional model of dyslexia

- Epidemiology of reading disorders

- Disproving of the developmental lag hypothesis, which states that some children have delayed maturity for typical reading acquisition

- Gender differences in reading disorders

- Genetic and environmental contributions, including development of pediatric structural and functional neuroimaging methods

- Development of neural circuitry for children and adult readers without impairments and for children and adults with reading disorders

NICHD research concluded that approximately 20% of children in the United States have substantial difficulties learning to read (Lyon, 1995). Research in numerous studies converges on the importance of phonological awareness in learning to read (see Chapter 5). Although phonological awareness may be a necessary condition for learning to read, it is not sufficient. Ehri found that orthographic knowledge has a profound influence on phonological awareness (Ehri, 1998, 2004; Ehri & Soffer, 1999). She proposed that graphophonemic awareness is a prerequisite of learning to read. As children learn *graphemes* (the written symbols that represent speech sounds) such as *ch* and *tch,* they must reconcile the sounds with the appropriate spellings. Ehri suggested that graphophonemic analysis is central for retaining sight words in memory and contributes mainly to early reading and spelling acquisition: "The big chore is grappling with the correct spelling of individual words and figuring out how the graphemes and phonemes come together in a systematic way" (1998, p. 108). This task is so critical to learning to read that, as Lyon stated,

> Unless identified early on and taught by expert teachers using detailed and intensive approaches emphasizing teaching both in phonological awareness and

phonics instruction, children who learn poorly in the third grade can be expected to learn poorly throughout middle- and high-school grades. (1996, p. 71)

Seidenburg and McClelland (1989) noted that children must come to understand at least two basic characteristics of written English as they acquire word recognition skills. First, children must understand the alphabetic principle. Second, they must learn about the distribution of letter patterns in the lexicon. That is, children must learn that only some combinations of letters are possible in English and that the combinations differ in frequency. Of all of the possible combinations of 26 letters, only a small percentage yield letter strings that are permissible in English. In addition, Seidenburg and McClelland noted that skillful word reading depends on the coordinated and interactive processing of the appearance or orthography of the words, their meaning, and their pronunciation.

Stanovich noted that children with little phonological awareness have trouble acquiring skill in alphabetic coding and thus have difficulty recognizing words: "When word recognition processes demand too much cognitive capacity, few cognitive resources are left to allocate to higher level processes of text integration and comprehension" (1996, p. 281).

Adams (1990) noted that students with **specific reading disability,** or *dyslexia,* do not easily discover the alphabetic code and therefore exhibit considerable difficulty in learning to decode and spell (see also Ehri, 1991; Perfetti, 1985; Stanovich, 1986). Students must be able to apply this knowledge when reading and spelling. Knowledge of the alphabetic code is useful not only in attacking new words but also in storing words in memory as students build a sight vocabulary, read words by analogy, and make informed predictions about words in text. This working knowledge grows and changes as beginning readers become more fluent.

Several prevention and intervention studies support the need for explicit teaching of patterns and rules for successful decoding and spelling (Berninger, 2000; Berninger et al., 2005; Ehri, 2004; Felton, 1993; Foorman, Francis, Beeler, Winikates, & Fletcher, 1997; Scanlon & Vellutino, 1996; Torgesen, 2000; Torgesen, Wagner, & Rashotte, 1997). Barbara Foorman and her team in Houston concluded that second and third graders "who received an Orton-Gillingham, synthetic phonics approach [Alphabetic Phonics] outperformed children receiving a combined synthetic/analytic phonics approach or a sight-word approach in the development of literacy related skills" (p. 63).

When students receive appropriate instruction, changes in brain activation while reading can be shown using functional magnetic resonance imaging (fMRI) (see Berninger et al., 2005; Berninger & Wolf, 2009; Shaywitz, 2003; Wolf, 2007). Shaywitz discussed the "patient-friendly" aspects of fMRI and noted that this imaging makes it possible to map the neural circuitry for reading. These images show markedly different brain activation patterns in readers with dyslexia and in good readers. Shaywitz concluded that "Appropriate intervention provided startling results. Activation patterns were comparable to those obtained from children who had always been good readers. We had observed brain repair. And the children improved their reading" (p. 86).

Other studies have concluded that the ability to read and comprehend also depends on rapid and automatic recognition and decoding of single words. Fluency and **automaticity** should not be confused as identical constructs. *Fluency* is the speed of decoding that is gained as one masters the alphabetic code (Stanovich, 1980). Wolf and Katzer-Cohen noted, "After it is fully developed, reading fluency refers to a level of accuracy and rate, where decoding is relatively effortless; where oral reading is smooth and accurate with correct prosody; and where attention can be allocated to comprehension" (2001, p. 219). The National Reading Panel (NICHD, 2000) suggested that practice and exposure to print are essential to fluency.

Automaticity, in contrast, is the immediate recognition of words. Improvements in fluency and automaticity appear to be harder to obtain than improvements in decoding and word reading accuracy (Wolf, 2007; Wolf & Katzer-Cohen, 2001). In fact, according to Wolf (2009), "Fluency is the most overlooked aspect in the field of dyslexia." Interventions for both fluency and automaticity are discussed in Chapter 6.

Rapid automatized naming (RAN) has also been investigated since the mid-1970s as a correlate to reading acquisition. The rapid naming of colors, numbers, and objects appears to have a significant effect on later reading ability (Bowers, Sunseth, & Golden, 1999; Denckla & Rudel, 1976; Wolf, 1991). The most difficult task for young poor readers is naming common objects, colors, and symbols. By second grade, problems with letter and number naming are more reliable markers of poor reading ability. In fact, Adams (1990) noted that one of the best predictors of first-grade reading ability is the fast and accurate skill of naming and recognizing shapes of letters. Naming speed is thought to be a marker for processes sensitive to precise and rapid timing requirements.

The "double-deficit hypothesis" predicts that children with problems in both phonological awareness and RAN will have more trouble learning to read and spell than other children (Badian, 1997; Bowers & Wolf, 1993; Wolf, 2007). Children with dyslexia who have phonemic awareness weaknesses and few problems with RAN show relative orthographic strength. Those with RAN impairments have poor orthographic skill and poor text reading speed.

Hammill, Mather, Allen, and Roberts (2002) noted that it is not yet possible to say specifically which predictors (e.g., semantics, grammar, phonology, RAN) are most meaningful for accurately identifying children who will have trouble learning to read and spell. Hammill et al. encouraged more research and more explanations to predict who will and will not be good at word identification.

Numerous researchers now conclude that decoding and spelling should be taught explicitly, at least through eighth grade (Snow, Burns, & Griffin, 1998). This instruction is important for all children but is essential for children who do not readily acquire reading and spelling skills. These children may be identified as having learning disabilities, and 80% of them have a specific reading disability or dyslexia. Others who do not learn to read and spell easily may include children whose first language is not English and children without any special category label who need explicit instruction in learning the alphabetic code. Students who do not master the alphabetic code prior to secondary school may need direct instruction in reading and writing throughout and perhaps even beyond their formal schooling.

Upper-Grade Instruction

Studies of older students have found that many who are identified as having learning disabilities read and spell at a second- or third-grade level (Henry, 1988b). Even those students who learn rudimentary sound–symbol association rules for decoding and spelling short regular words often have difficulty at a more advanced level. In the upper elementary grades, many words in text are multisyllabic and often contain Latin and Greek parts. Thus, additional strategies must be taught to those students who have not acquired an automatic level of word recognition for longer words.

Just as awareness of the sounds of language provides clues for accurate decoding and spelling, knowledge of morphemes (the smallest units of meaning in language) provides additional information (Aaron, Joshi, & Quatroche, 2008; Berninger & Wolf, 2009; Carlisle, 1987, 1995; Carlisle & Stone, 2005; Carreker, 2005; Henderson, 1990; Henderson, 1982, 1985; Henry, 1988a, 1989), such as knowing that the addition of -s to nouns makes them plural (e.g., *cat, cats*). Prefixes and suffixes provide additional meaning. Prefixes tend to hold specific meaning (e.g., *re-* means *back* or *again*), whereas suffixes provide grammatical distinctions (e.g., *-ous* signifies an adjective ending). **Roots,** the base elements of words, provide consistent patterns used in thousands of words.

Studies suggest that proficient readers and spellers use morphological knowledge as they read and spell, whereas poor readers and spellers "lack awareness of the presence of base forms within derived counterparts, and they lack specific knowledge about how to spell suffixes and how to attach suffixes to base words correctly" (Carlisle, 1987, pp. 106–107). Henry (1988b) found that even good readers lacked morphemic awareness and often could not use knowledge of prefixes, roots, and suffixes while reading and spelling.

Singson, Mahony, and Mann (2000) investigated upper elementary students' knowledge of derivational suffixes. *Derivational suffixes* are morphemes that are added to roots or base words and that usually change the grammatical category of a word (e.g., the suffixes *-ion* and *-ive* can be added to the verb *instruct* to make the noun *instruction* and the adjective *instructive,* respectively). Singson et al. concluded that the upper elementary grades are an important time for the development of derivational morphology in both written and oral language and that this understanding of morphology contributes to decoding and spelling ability.

Scandinavians Elbro and Arnbak (1996; Arnbak & Elbro, 2000) found that morphological awareness training significantly increased comprehension and spelling of morphologically complex words in fourth- and fifth-grade children with dyslexia. In one study with secondary students, Elbro and Arnbak indicated that "dyslexic adolescents use recognition of root morphemes as a compensatory strategy in reading both single words and coherent texts" (1996, p. 209).

Carlisle and Stone (2005), Henry (1989), and Nunes and Bryant (2006) investigated the effects of explicit instruction about morphology and provided experimental evidence that morphological instruction improved word reading and spelling. Yet they noted that this type of instruction is rarely found in schools.

Researchers are investigating the effects of teaching morphology for vocabulary development. Bowers and Kirby (2010) and Bowers, Kirby, and Deacon (in press) found that teaching about morphological structure led to gains in vocabulary learning after the initial vocabulary knowledge of fourth and fifth graders was controlled. Ebbers (2008) found that even second graders need to access both inflectional and derivational morphemes in narrative and especially in informational text.

Ebbers and Denton (2008) described an outside-in procedure (based on the work of Baumann) in which students look for context clues not only outside the target word but also inside the word in morphemic units such as prefixes, roots, and suffixes. (See also Nunes & Bryant, 2006; Pressley, Disney, & Anderson, 2007; and Templeton, 2004, for research related to morpheme instruction and vocabulary acquisition.)

Abbott and Berninger (1999) found that older underachieving readers benefited from learning structural analysis, for example by studying syllable structure and morpheme patterns. One experimental group focused on structural analysis based on the *Words* curriculum (Henry, 1990, 2010) as they learned a core group of Greek combining forms. The researchers noted that had all students mastered beginning word recognition skills, including phonological awareness, orthographic knowledge, and application of the alphabetic principle to phonological decoding, prior to the study, training might have provided stronger effects.

In 1997 the director of the NICHD, in consultation with the U.S. Secretary of Education, convened the National Reading Panel, a team of leading educators, reading researchers, teachers, educational administrators, and parents to assess the status of research-based knowledge and the effectiveness of various approaches to teaching children to read. Major findings from the National Reading Panel (NICHD, 2000) included the importance of teaching phonemic awareness skills; teaching systematic synthetic phonics skills; assisting students in gaining fluency, accuracy, speed, and expression in reading; and applying reading comprehension strategies to enhance understanding and enjoyment of reading material. The panel also concluded that teachers need to understand how children learn to read, why some children have difficulty learning to read, and how to identify and implement the most effective instructional approaches. The panel also noted that although silent reading is an accepted practice, research demonstrates that it is not as effective as guided oral reading in helping children become fluent readers. In addition, the panel encouraged rigorous research on the potential of computers in reading instruction.

Use of Technology

What role should technology play in reading instruction? Clearly, technology can be a powerful tool in reading instruction, especially for children with reading problems. Improved software and devices for speech production and recognition make possible the reading of text on the computer screen or the conversion of speech into electronic text (Elkind & Elkind, 2007; Wise, 1998). Wise and Raskind (2007) noted that computer technology provides at least three kinds of help to children with reading disabilities. A computer can be used 1) as a compensatory tool to bypass slow reading, 2) for support and social networking on the Internet, and 3) for remediation and instruction in both reading and writing. Wise, Olson, and Ring (1997) found that children benefited from reading stories with accurate computer speech feedback for difficult words. Wise et al. acknowledged that the gains were enhanced with intensive training in phonological awareness without the computer.

Elkind (1998) reported on specific programs (the Kurzweil 3000 and the WYNN Arkenstone software) that offered increased accuracy of character recognition and fidelity of speech. Children using this technology increased their reading rate and also enhanced comprehension on timed and untimed tasks. The children also increased endurance for the reading task. These machines can show an electronic image of an actual page with pictures, graphics, page layout, and text formatting faithfully reproduced in color. West (1998) discussed how technology moves verbal literacy to visual literacy, or a "world of images," which is important in the lives of children.

Elkind and Elkind (2007) discussed text-to-speech software that allows students to scan in text and hear it read aloud by a computerized voice. They cited research that shows that the simultaneous highlighting of print while software reads it aloud often improves reading ability and provides accommodations that allow poor readers to read texts at the same levels as their peers.

There are, however, some caveats to the use of technology in reading instruction. Catts and Kamhi (1999) concluded that children need language skills, world knowledge, and metacognitive and self-regulatory strategies to perform computer tasks. Catts and Kamhi noted that some children are poorly prepared in these prerequisite areas. Macaruso and Hook concluded that computer programs "may be especially beneficial for low performing students by providing the opportunity for ample practice of skills" (2007, p. 43). However, they suggested three important challenges to effective implementation: Schools must provide sufficient technical support, ensure that software programs are integrated properly into the reading curriculum, and establish sufficient use of software programs by students.

For children in the primary grades, computer programs developed for reinforcement and drill and practice appear to be motivational. In addition, these programs require no special keyboarding skills. Once computers are used for writing assignments, however, upper elementary and secondary students need to learn effective keyboarding skills through direct instruction (Berninger & Wolf, 2009).

Wise and Van Vuuren (2007) discussed several areas of consideration for teachers and parents when choosing reading software. They suggested looking for a program that

- Meets the particular reading needs of the child

- Teaches reading

- Has a strong pedagogical base

- Engages the child with interesting activities that are simple to perform and do not distract from the task at hand

- Gives the child clear expectations and knowledge of what he or she is learning

- Uses time wisely

- Supports the curriculum taught by teacher or tutor

- Gives evidence of effectiveness

More studies need to be designed for different settings, not only the lab but also pull-out situations and the classroom. One meta-analysis of 42 studies involving computer-assisted instruction concluded that these programs generally have a positive, although small, effect on beginning readers (Blok, Oostdam, Otter, & Overmaat, 2002). The National Reading Panel (NICHD, 2000) report noted that few systematic studies exist of computers and other technologies related to reading instruction. The panel did find that the talking computer (i.e., the addition of speech to print) may be a promising instructional option. The panel concluded that a great deal of additional exploration must be undertaken.

Students often rely on spell checkers to correct spelling errors. Yet consider this explanation from an anonymous professor with dyslexia:

> The computer spell check is a wonderful invention. However, there are a number of ways the process can go awry. The spell checker leaves me with many spelling errors. Computers are considerable help in catching such errors as *worgn* for *wrong, apirently* for *apparently, wemon* for *women, alian* for *alien* and such garbles as *inderrent* for *indifferent*. A common problem comes when I type a correctly spelled word but with a meaning not intended and often humorously alien in my sentence—for example, *impalement* for *impairment*. The spelling program gives me a pass on spelling the word and I am not aware that an error remains. Often what I type are nonwords. Sometimes the word is so far off the mark that the spelling program can think of no possible words to suggest. I sit there frustrated.

The professor gives more examples of his errors, with incorrect word choices (each of which is *spelled* correctly and would not be caught by a spell checker) in italicized type and the intended words in brackets:

I remember being in a small *rome* [room].

. . . a place where ships at *see* [sea] were located.

My typing teacher *latterly* [literally] took me by the hand.

In *collage* [college] my reading difficulty . . .

Finely [finally] I found . . .

. . . and *low* [lo!] I missed every word on the spelling test.

Male (2003) suggested that computers can function as a tool to help a child perform. But human "communication partners," in the form of peers or teachers, are essential to the process of developing spoken and written language skills. Nothing gives children the feeling of success like independently reading a book and writing a story. For that, instruction is usually necessary. (See Engstrom & Hecker, 2005, for information on assistive technology for children with learning disabilities.)

SUMMARY

By teaching the concepts inherent in the word origin and word structure model across a decoding–spelling continuum from the early grades through at least eighth grade, and by using technology when it serves to reinforce these concepts, teachers ensure that students have strategies to decode and spell most words in the English language. This framework and continuum readily organize a large body of information for teachers and their students. Not only do students gain a better understanding of English word structure, but they also become better readers and spellers (Henry, 1988b, 1989).

CHAPTER 2

A Brief History of Written English

Language is one thing that differentiates mankind from any other species of animal. Linguists continue to try to discern the beginnings of vocal language and look for a universal ancestral tongue. The vocal system for oral language was present with first man. *Ethnologue: Languages of the World* (Lewis, 2009) catalogues 6,909 known living languages throughout the world. Linguists predict that 90% of these languages are at risk, as only 600 are being taught to children (Sampat, 2001). Over time the major languages have surpassed many regional tongues.

English is one of approximately 130 languages composing the Indo-European linguistic family. Indo-European is the common ancestor of many languages, including Latin, French, Norwegian, Dutch, and Spanish. Although English is the first language of more than 320 million people and is spoken as a second language by approximately 350 million people, Mandarin Chinese is the most common tongue, spoken by nearly 900 million people (Sampat, 2001). King (2000) estimated that perhaps as many as 1 billion people are learning English as a foreign language. Students throughout the world study English, as it is the common language for global communication in business, primarily via the web.

Estimates of the number of English words hover around 1 million but vary greatly, ranging from 450,000 words to about 1.3 million (AskOxford Online Dictionary, 2009; Claiborne, 1983; Crystal, 2006; McCrum, Cran, & MacNeil, 1992). The second edition of the *Oxford English Dictionary* (*OED*) contains 231,100 main entries, plus combinations and derivatives, and phrases. When we ask the question "How many words are there in English?" we must determine what we mean by *word*. For example, is *set* one word or many words, as it has so many meanings? In fact, the *OED* describes *set* using 60,000 words, detailing more than 430 senses. The third edition of the *OED* will go online in 2018 and will contain more than 300,000 main entries, not including entries with senses for different parts of speech and different meanings. (In the third edition, which is now in preparation, *put* has the longest entry so far.)

The term *language* refers to both spoken and written language and to the use of words. Human language, both oral and written, must be learned; it is not just acquired. The language learner must be born into a linguistic community in which the relationship between sound and meaning is prescribed by local customs. By listening to the world around them, young children learn the meanings of words already understood by adult speakers (Barnett, 1964). In those cultures with written languages, children begin formal written language instruction when they are between 5 and 7 years old.

English is a dynamic, constantly changing language, and numerous historical forces shape its development. The historical perspective is of primary importance to the study of word formation in English and explains some of the consistencies and inconsistencies in English words. By giving students an understanding of how words entered the language, we can dispel some of the difficulties surrounding the exceptional spellings of some common English words. When understood from this perspective, English orthography begins to make sense.

It is difficult to say when early writing systems were first established, but early cave paintings at Lascaux, France, were made approximately 30,000 years ago. Other findings suggest that modern human written communication developed in Africa as early as 77,000 years ago (Henshilwood et al., 2002). The Blombas Cave, located east of Cape Town in South Africa, holds etchings on numerous ochre stones that contain intricate geometric patterns and chiseled lines. Henshilwood et al. assumed that these symbols were drawn to be interpreted by other cave dwellers or nomadic peoples. Such early drawings were not considered language but usually represented agricultural or religious symbols important to the culture.

The advent of written language marked the beginning of civilization and the start of history. The first written languages began with visual symbols impressed in clay or inscribed on papyrus scrolls 5,000 years ago by people in Sumerian and Egyptian cultures. These *cuneiforms* (meaning "wedge-shaped" because of the triangular shape left by the reed or stick on the clay) or pictographs were a form of logographic writing in which each symbol stood for a whole word or syllable. These forms were often difficult to interpret and took considerable space and time to create; furthermore, making them required some artistic talent. They became the writing system of the Middle East.

Other pictographs include the Scandinavian Stone Age and Bronze Age carvings frequently found in Norwegian fields and the drawings found on the teepees of 19th-century Native Americans. As life became less nomadic and as people began to own property, written accounts became necessary. Language as a medium for drama or narrative came somewhat later.

Around 3200 B.C.E. (Before the Common Era) or earlier, hieroglyphics developed in ancient Egypt. This earliest writing was often connected with religion or magic. These pictograms connected symbols and sounds and represented associated ideas, abstractions, or metaphors. Even in ancient societies, writing was taught systematically through educational systems and transmitted to successive generations.

Runic alphabets first appeared among Germanic tribes in central and Eastern Europe and spread across northern Europe by 400 C.E. (Common Era). Up to 38 straight-line symbols made these alphabets easy to carve into wood or stone. They were used by early Norse peoples, including the Vikings.

The Chinese language uses a form of logographic writing. Literate Chinese writing requires 6,000 characters representing 40,000 words. Even more characters must be learned by those in the professions. Thus, well-educated Chinese people must learn a significant number of characters. Contrast the thousands of Chinese characters necessary to become literate with the 26 letters of the Roman alphabet used in English writing.

In phonetic writing, the final major type of writing, written language corresponds to spoken language, and signs represent sounds. Semitic writing usually represented consonants only. It was considered a *syllabary*, or a writing system whose characters represent syllables (a consonant followed by a vowel sound). Both syllabaries and alphabets correspond to spoken language and use signs to represent sounds. Japanese Hiragama and Katakana are both syllabaries, as their symbols stand for the sounds made when words are separated into syllables. The Cherokee syllabary was invented in 1819 by Sequoyah. Each of its 85 symbols represents a syllable rather than a single phoneme.

Alphabet writing is easiest to master and the most economical means of writing, as it uses fewer symbols. Coulmas (1996) noted that having as few symbols as possible keeps memory load manageable. The very first alphabets contained only consonants. Although the vowels were sounded in speech, they were considered unnecessary in writing. Arabic and Hebrew alphabets made up entirely of consonants still exist.

Early writing went from right to left on the page. In the sixth century B.C.E., the Greeks changed to the boustrophedon order, which alternates right to left and left to right (as an ox plows a field). The Greeks created the first true alphabet by reassigning some early Semitic and Phoenician consonant symbols to symbols that represented vowel sounds. The Greeks also modified letters to signify other sounds they needed. The Etruscan alphabet evolved from the Greek alphabet and contained 23 letters.

The Roman alphabet, which is the basis for the English alphabet, developed between 700 and 500 B.C.E. as the Romans adapted Etruscan script and wrote left to right. By the first century B.C.E., letter formations had been refined and mastered. Capital letters were used exclusively; uncial letters (precursors of modern lowercase letters) appeared in the fourth century C.E. The English alphabet reached 26 letters after medieval scribes added *w* and Renaissance printers distinguished *i* from *j* and *u* from *v*.

The alphabet has been crucial to mankind since its invention. Indeed, Logan (1986) noted that

> Of all mankind's inventions, with the possible exception of language it-self, nothing has proved more useful or led to more innovations than the alphabet. . . . The alphabet is one of the first things that children learn once they are able to speak. It is the first thing that is taught in school because it is the gateway to learning and knowledge. (pp. 17–18)

Samoyault (1996) estimated that the Roman alphabet is now used by half the people in the world.

HISTORICAL MILESTONES

Among the important languages of the world, English is one of the youngest. The original inhabitants of the English Isles, the Celts, spoke a different language in the Indo-European family. They were conquered by Julius Caesar, a Roman, in 54 C.E. The Britons continued to speak Celtic, whereas the Romans spoke Latin. The Romans departed and returned almost a century later and stayed for nearly 400 years. During this second stay, Celtic and Latin were spoken side by side. Many place names, especially city names ending in *-chester* and *-caster,* such as *Manchester, Winchester, Rochester,* and *Lancaster,* still exist based on the Latin root *castr,* meaning "camp." About 175 early Latin loanwords such as *chalk, dish, kettle, pepper,* and *coin* survive today (Pyles & Algeo, 1982).

Table 2.1 highlights important events contributing to the changes in written English over the years.

Old English: 450–1150 C.E.

During the fifth century C.E.,[1] Germanic groups—the Angles, the Saxons, and the Jutes—began to settle in different parts of England after terrorizing the inhabitants of the land during the Teutonic invasions. They did not adopt the Celtic language and did not practice the religion of the Celtic people (Balmuth, 1982). Rather, Anglo-Saxon (also called Germanic or Teutonic) became the dominant language, and the vocabulary stressed the people, objects, and events of daily life. The Roman alphabet, which the Romans had adapted from Greek via Etruscan, was reintroduced to the British Isles by Christian missionaries at this time.

Five major segments of evolution shaped the English language during this period. First, the language was influenced by Teutonic invasion and settlement. Sec-

---

[1]Dates of the periods of the development of English vary by author. The dates used in this chapter are those of Nist (1966). See Table 2.1 for a chronological listing of language-related events.

Table 2.1. Periods of the English language

Period	Year	Event
Pre-English (54 B.C.E.–450 C.E.)	ca. 200 B.C.E.–200 C.E.	Germanic tribes begin their migrations.
	54 B.C.E.	Julius Caesar defeats the ancient Britons (or Celts). Roman Emperor Claudius I colonizes Britain, and the Celtic and Latin languages coexist.
Old English (450–1150)		The Romans leave Britain as the Teutonic tribes (the Jutes, Angles, and Saxons) invade.
	ca. 600	St. Augustine arrives in Britain and introduces Christianity, bringing more Latin words.
	ca. 600	England divides into seven kingdoms; Northumbria emerges as the dominant Christian kingdom affiliated with the Roman Catholic Church.
	ca. 700	*Beowulf* is orally composed.
	ca. 731	St. Bede the Venerable chronicles the violence of these times.
	878	The Vikings (generally called Danes or Norsemen) invade and pillage England and are defeated by King Alfred the Great.
	ca. 900	Old English reaches its literary peak under the West Saxon kings.
	ca. 1000	Anglo-Saxon continues as the dominant language, although the Danes successfully invade and triumph.
	1066	The Norman Conquest. William the Conqueror, Duke of Normandy, invades Britain. Norman French becomes the official language of the state while English remains the language of the people.
Middle English (1150–1500)	ca. 1350	English again becomes the official language of state as Edward III takes control.
		English replaces Latin as the medium of instruction in schools except at Oxford and Cambridge, which retain Latin.
	1400	Geoffrey Chaucer dies, leaving his classic *The Canterbury Tales*.
	ca. 1400	The Great Vowel Shift begins, bringing changes in consonant and vowel pronunciations.
	ca. 1420	Henry V becomes the first English king to write in Middle English.
		During the Renaissance and its classical revival, English borrows heavily from Latin and Greek.
	1476	William Caxton prints with the first English printing press.
	1492	Columbus discovers the New World.
Modern English (1500 to Present)		
Early Modern English (1500–1650)		Queen Elizabeth I and William Shakespeare write in English.
	1604	Robert Cavdry develops the first English dictionary.
	1607	Jamestown, the first English settlement in the New World, is founded.
	1611	The King James Bible (or Authorized Version) is published.

(continued)

Table 2.1. *(continued)*

Period	Year	Event
Authoritarian English (1650–1800)		The Industrial Age begins in Britain, and words are modified or created as a result of rapid changes in technology.
	1702	The first English daily newspaper, *The Daily Courant*, is established in London.
	1755	Samuel Johnson compiles the first comprehensive dictionary of English.
	1768	Samuel Johnson and Benjamin Franklin support spelling reform.
	1776	Thomas Jefferson writes the Declaration of Independence.
Mature Modern English (1800–1920)	1806	Noah Webster urges spelling reform.
	1828	Noah Webster compiles a dictionary of American English.
	1857–1920	The *Oxford English Dictionary* is developed and published in parts.
World Power American English (1920 to Present)		The 20th century brings a communications and globalization revolution, and with it new terminology.
	1922	The British Broadcasting Company is founded.
	1928	The *Oxford English Dictionary* is published in full.
	mid-1970s to present	Linguistic diversity increases with new waves of immigrants.
	2009	The third edition of the *Oxford English Dictionary* is almost complete.

Period categories and several events are taken from Nist (1966). Other events are from Henderson (1990), Kemmer (2009), and Boyanova (n.d.).

ond, Northumbria, in what is now northern England, emerged as the dominant Christian kingdom affiliated with the Roman Catholic Church around 600 C.E. Third, with poetry such as *Beowulf*, a national English culture began to emerge. Fourth, Scandinavians from primarily Norway and Denmark invaded, bringing with them political adjustment and racial assimilation, but these people were defeated by King Alfred in 878. English and Old Norse came from the same ancestral Germanic language. The Norse brought words such as *dream, skirt, crawl, bleak, root,* and *trust,* which were Anglicized.

Finally, the Norman Conquest, led by William the Conqueror, Duke of Normandy, brought the decline and subjugation of Old English (Nist, 1966). During the Old English period, Germanic, Celtic, Latin, Greek, Anglo-Saxon, Norse, and French words entered the language. Words in the Old English period were phonetically very regular, as they almost always followed letter–sound correspondence. For example, *why* was spelled *hwy,* and *where* was spelled *hwær.* Sounds and symbols had even more of a one-to-one correspondence than they do in English today. Only the Christian priests, monks, and nuns were able to write using the Roman alphabet, which was the language of the Roman Catholic Church.

King (2000) estimated that about 4,500 words from Old English survive in some form today, including *freond* (*friend*), *cild* (*child*), and *hus* (*house*). Other Old English words include *be, water, month, dog, swine,* and *strong.* Note that prefixes and suffixes, which together are called affixes, entered the language during the period of Old English. For example, the Old English suffix *-scipe* has been passed down as *-ship*. Thus, *freondscipe* translates as *friendship*. Some Old English suffixes remain in use today, such as *-ness, -less,* and *-ful*. Most of these words are short, everyday, down-to-earth words.

The Norman Conquest in 1066 was the transition point to Middle English. William the Conqueror and his troops set out to claim the English throne and finally defeated the British at the Battle of Hastings. The Normans brought their own words to describe their laws, their feudal system, architecture, knightly conduct, hunting, cooking, and fashion (King, 2000).

According to Nist, at the end of the Old English period, "that language was no longer the basically Teutonic and highly inflected Old English but the hybrid-becoming, Romance-importing, and inflection-dropping Middle English" (1966, p. 107). Stress on the root syllable became fixed during the Old English Period (e.g., love, love'r, love'ly, lov'ing, love'liness, love'less, and love'lessness). As Latin-based words entered the language, stress became more flexible and resourceful in word formation processes (e.g., confer', con'ference, conferee').

New spellings entered the language during this time of transition. Coulmas (1996) deduced that the Normans brought the *ou* vowel spelling to English and inserted *g* in front of *h*, as in *night*, which had been spelled *niht*. They replaced *u* with *o* before *m, n,* and *v,* as in *come, son,* and *love,* because a series of arcs was difficult to read. The Normans also introduced *qu-* to replace *cw-*, as in *queen*, which had been spelled *cween*.

Middle English: 1150–1500

The period of Middle English brought great changes in the native tongue of Britain. Early Middle English (1150–1307) sounded much like present-day German and was the language of the commoners and the uneducated. This period also brought words spelled with less phonetic regularity, such as *rough, cough, although,* and *through,* which use one spelling (*-ough*) to represent different sounds.

Claiborne estimated that after the Norman Conquest, "more than ten thousand French words passed into the English vocabulary, of which 75 percent are still in use" (1983, p. 112). Anglo-French compounds and affixed words (e.g., *gentlewomen, gentleman; faithful, faithfulness*) appeared during this period. Words borrowed from French became increasingly important, especially words related to government, law, and the arts, such as *parliament, justice,* and *prologue.* As a result of the Norman Conquest, England was actually a bilingual country, as the upper classes spoke French and the rest of the country spoke English at home and in the community. By 1300, nearly everyone in England spoke English rather than French because of antagonism by native-born English and strong nationalism by landowners (Claiborne, 1983). In addition, by the mid-1300s, the mayor and aldermen of London ordered that all court proceedings there be held in English.

A renewed Latin influence penetrated the language during the period of Mature Middle English (1307–1422) in the 14th and 15th centuries. Chaucer, regarded by many as the first great master of the English tongue, wrote his *Canterbury Tales* in the late 1300s. This was the time of the Renaissance, which brought a wave of cultural advancement. Hanna, Hodges, and Hanna observed that

> The Latin vocabulary was felt to be more stable and polished and more capable of conveying both abstract and humanistic ideas than was a fledgling language like English. Further, Latin was something of a lingua franca that leaped across geographical and political boundaries. (1971, p. 47)

Many of the words used in English today are borrowed from the Romance languages of the Mature Middle English period. The use of the term *Romance* implies Latin-based terms that come primarily from France, Italy, Portugal, Romania, and Spain.

At this time, too, Latin affixes entered the language in great numbers. The affixation of roots greatly expanded the number of words formed by any one Latin root (e.g., *rupt: rupture, ruptured, disrupt, disruptive, abrupt, erupt, eruption, interrupt, interruption*). Prefixes and suffixes were added to roots to form words such as *adjacent, inferior, lunatic, moderate, necessary, prosecute, rational, solitary,* and *testimony.* Thus, through affixation, English words grew in length and English vocabulary grew at an astounding rate (Claiborne, 1983). During this time, prefixes such as *counter-, dis-, re-, trans-, sub-, super-, pre-, pro-,* and *de-,* along with suffixes such as *-able, -ible, -ent, -al, -ous,* and *-ive* entered the language.

The period of Late Middle English (1422–1500) is known for the growing importance of the written word. English became the language of private and public and informal and formal correspondence. Gutenberg developed the first printing press in 1452 and printed 200 copies of his 42-line Bible (in Latin) in 1456. Soon other printers advanced his work by using illustrations and printing stories and poems. The English pressman William Caxton introduced the printing press to England using the English spoken in London by the well-to-do. Caxton's translation of *Recuyell of the Historyes of Troye* in 1475 was the first book printed in English. The advent of printing in English encouraged new spelling conventions. For example, the spelling of *gost* became *ghost* when Dutch and Belgian printers inserted *h.* The letters *u, v, l, n,* and *m* were once written very similarly, and Burridge (2004) suggested that many spellings occurred as blunders by printers and scribes. By the year 1500, more than 1,000 printers throughout Europe had printed millions of books (Krensky, 1996).

Modern English: 1500 to Present

English, then, is a polyglot, with Anglo-Saxon, Latin, and Greek all playing a role in establishing the words read and written today (Balmuth, 2009; Hanna et al., 1971; Nist, 1966). Indeed, Claiborne, in *Our Marvelous Native Tongue,* noted,

> The truth is that if borrowing foreign words could destroy a language, English would be dead (borrowed from Old Norse), deceased (from French), defunct

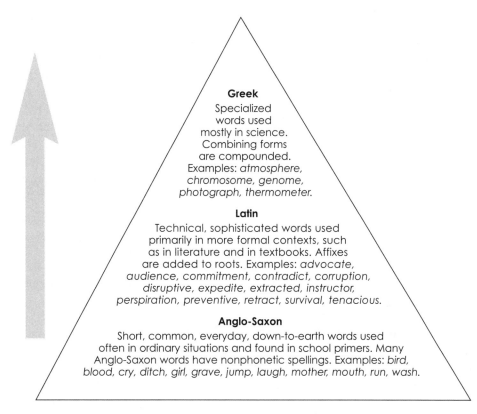

Greek
Specialized words used mostly in science. Combining forms are compounded. Examples: *atmosphere, chromosome, genome, photograph, thermometer.*

Latin
Technical, sophisticated words used primarily in more formal contexts, such as in literature and in textbooks. Affixes are added to roots. Examples: *advocate, audience, commitment, contradict, corruption, disruptive, expedite, extracted, instructor, perspiration, preventive, retract, survival, tenacious.*

Anglo-Saxon
Short, common, everyday, down-to-earth words used often in ordinary situations and found in school primers. Many Anglo-Saxon words have nonphonetic spellings. Examples: *bird, blood, cry, ditch, girl, grave, jump, laugh, mother, mouth, run, wash.*

Figure 2.1. Layers of the English language. (From Calfee, R.C., et al. [1981–1984]. *The book: Components of reading instruction.* Unpublished manuscript, Stanford University, California; adapted by permission.)

(from Latin) and kaput (from German). When it comes to borrowing, English excels (from Latin), surpasses (from French) and eclipses (from Greek) any other tongue, past or present. (1983, p. 4)

Figure 2.1 summarizes the three major languages that have influenced English and provides a brief description and examples of the types of words that have come from these languages. But other cultures also added to the English language, especially to American English. American English differs from British English primarily in its vowel sounds and orthography (e.g., *organizing* versus *organising; color* versus *colour; traveled* versus *travelled*); the vocabularies in both are almost identical, and the syntax remains virtually the same. Claiborne (1983) emphasized that most early British immigrants to America were barely literate. He noted, "Their language, therefore, was not, as has sometimes been said, the tongue of Shakespeare, but the plain, homely English of the King James Bible, at its best capable of eloquence but seldom marked by elegance" (p. 200).

Modern English is typically described as comprising three periods: Early Modern English (1500–1650), Authoritarian English (1650–1800), and Mature Modern English (1800–1920).

Early Modern English: 1500–1650

Even more of English orthography was locked into convention during the period of Early Modern English. During this period, the sound patterns of the language were changing, especially the vowel sounds. This shift in vowel sounds was so marked that it is often referred to as the "Great Vowel Shift" (Jespersen, as cited in Nist, 1966, p. 221). In Chaucer's time, the vowel sound in *house* was pronounced /ōō/ as in "hoos"; by Shakespeare's time in the early 1600s it had shifted to /ō/ as in "hose"; and by the Mature Modern English of T.S. Eliot's time in the 20th century it had become /ou/. Pronunciation of consonant and vowel spellings often changed. For example, in the word *sweord* in Old English, both the /s/ and /w/ sounds were pronounced. The Modern English spelling, *sword*, retains the *w*, although it is no longer pronounced. In Old English, all five letters in *cniht* were pronounced. The Modern English spelling *knight* includes the silent letters *k*, *g*, and *h*.

Crystal (2006) stated that Shakespeare coined 1,700 words and that at least half of them exist today. Shakespeare often made up words as he wrote. Among those seen first in his writings are *bandit, daunting, dwindle, eyeballs, leapfrog, laughable, scuffle, swagger,* and *epileptic.*

Authoritarian English: 1650–1800

During the periods of Authoritarian and Mature Modern English, vocabulary continued to expand, especially with the use of Greek and Latin morphemes in scientific terms. In fact, many Latin roots came directly from Greek. Nist (1966) called the time from 1607 to 1789 the Colonial Period in American English. This era ran from the settling of Jamestown to the ratification of the Federal Constitution in 1789.

Few books were available during colonial times, but new terms were needed, especially to describe the natural wildlife, such as plants, trees, crops, and animals. From the Native Americans, British immigrants took names for the land, such as *Penobscot, Merrimac, Passaic, Susquehanna,* and *Savannah,* along with words for animals, such as *chipmunk, moccasin, skunk,* and *moose.* Dutch settlers provided names such as *Breukelyn* (*Brooklyn*) and *Haarlem* (*Harlem*) and words such as *brandy, golf, duck, wagon,* and *uproar.* Words from African slaves in the 1600s included *gam, chigger,* and *goober* (peanut). English colonists used words that were already in their language but assigned them new meanings, such as with the words *underbrush, clearing, log cabin,* and *corn crib.*

American English became partly standardized through the diligence of Noah Webster. From 1783 to 1785 he published a speech book, a grammar, and a reader. Webster followed in the footsteps of Samuel Johnson and Benjamin Franklin in urging spelling reform.

Mature Modern English: 1800–1920

Nist (1966) wrote of three stages of American English in these years: Continental Expansion (1790–1860), Independent Status (1860–1890), and Nationalist (1890–1920). Changes continued throughout the Mature Modern English period to bring about today's pronunciations.

Noah Webster's *American Dictionary of the English Language,* published in 1828, reflected American and British English usage in terms of vocabulary and definitions. Webster tried to simplify spellings somewhat. If two spellings were current in England, he picked the simpler of the two. Thus, *musick* became *music* and *risque* became *risk*. It was Webster who dropped the *u* in such English words as *honour, favour, colour,* and *labour*. He also changed to *-er* the spellings of words ending in *-re,* such as with *theater* for *theatre* and *center* for *centre*. The *OED* was developed and printed sequentially in several volumes during this time.

In 1848, John R. Bartlett published his *Dictionary of Americanisms,* in which he collected terms from prairie culture and frontier life. During the same year James Russell Lowell issued *The Biglow Papers,* "fashioning a new and native style based upon the mastery of a regional dialect" (Nist, 1966, p. 349).

Many great writers of American literature lived and wrote during this period. These included Washington Irving, James Fenimore Cooper, Ralph Waldo Emerson, Henry David Thoreau, Nathaniel Hawthorne, Henry Wadsworth Longfellow, John Greenleaf Whittier, Herman Melville, Edgar Allan Poe, William Cullen Bryant, Samuel Clemens, Henry James, and Walt Whitman. **Neologisms,** such as *boom, cuss word, hoodlum, grubstake, crook, joint, spellbinder,* and *side-track,* abounded. After the Civil War, "clipped" words such as *photo, phone, gas, auto, Coke, pen* (for penitentiary), *beaut, combo,* and *flu* became popular. College slang brought words such as *prof, grad, medic, dorm,* and *plebe* (Nist, 1966).

Many new words formed during the westward movement. Words such as *cantankerous, rambunctious,* and *caboodle* became part of the daily vocabulary of settlers in the American West. Words from other cultures also entered the American English lexicon during the 19th and 20th centuries. Immigrants and international trade brought new words such as *caravan* and *shawl* from Persia, *divan* and *turban* from Turkey, and *harem* and *elixir* from Arabia. Consider all of the foods from various countries that are now familiar to most Americans, such as Mexican *burritos* and *tacos,* French *bouillabaisse* and *Brie,* and Chinese *chow mein* and *won ton* soup.

World Power American English: 1920 to Present

World Power American English: 1920 to Present This most recent period of American English began as the United States achieved the prestige of being a military power after World War I. In addition, more than twice as many people worldwide spoke American English than British English. As America became more of a player in the global economy, the use of American English expanded throughout the world. Radio and later television and the Internet rapidly spread American English around the globe.

New words enter dictionaries when they are used extensively in different media, such as newspapers, radio, and television. A new word (or *neologism*) must fill a need and capture a meaning that no other word does. One of my favorite neologisms was coined in 1933. This **portmanteau word** mixes *celebrity* and *debutante* to form *celebutante* (a celebrity with fashion sense). Two world wars introduced military slang, such as *nose dive, camouflage, radar, roadblock,* and *spearhead*.

American English continues to expand as a result of new immigrants and innovations. Think of the terms that radio, television, computers, and space exploration have added to English! Many of these new words, such as *bandwidth, video-*

cassette, microbits, astronaut, and *television,* are made up of existing word parts that are used to mean something different.

The 1980s and 1990s brought numerous new words and phrases to the language, many from the Internet culture. Lederer (1991) acknowledged terms such as *baby boomer, couch potato, awesome, hunk, channeling, airhead, microwave, Jazzercise,* and *proactive.* Soukhanov (1995) discussed the word *pharming,* a genetic engineering technique that the *San Francisco Chronicle* described as "a marriage of high-tech biology and low-tech agriculture" (as cited on p. 97). This word was voted the most interesting new word in 1992 by the Canadian press but has not become part of everyday usage. Ayto (1999) described new terms such as *cybercafe, decluttering, intermercials* (advertisements on the Internet), and *technoplegia* (paralysis brought on by fear of using technical equipment). The 1990s also brought us *infomercial, helihiking, mudwalking,* and *gephyrophobia* (a fear of crossing bridges). Computer standardization also has led to interesting changes, especially in foreign words. For example, some writers may omit the diacritical markings in words, such as the umlaut in German or tilde in Spanish, as many computer programs cannot display them or do not have characters to represent them.

The 21st century found words such as *blog* (from we*b log*, 2003), the verb *to google,* and *agroterrorism* (2006) entered into the online *OED*. Entries for 2009 included *anyhoo* and *clonable.* Other neonyms in the field of technology include *Wi-Fi, streaming video, nanotechnology,* and *Blu-ray.*

Westbrook (2002) described the contributions of the language of hip-hop culture, which he called "slanguage." He noted that this language is based not only on the jive talk of the 1920s but also on the earlier coded language used by African slaves, who were forbidden to read and write. Through hip-hop culture, MTV, and other media, terms such as *cronies* (friends), *cool* (acceptable), *'hood* (neighborhood), and *marinate* (consider) are filtering into traditional American English.

The American Dialect Society and the *Merriam-Webster Dictionary* both select a word of the year. In 2008, both sources awarded the honor to *bailout,* referring to rescue by the government of companies on the brink of failure. In 2009, Merriam-Webster named *admonish* as its word of the year; runners-up included *furlough, rogue,* and *philanderer.* Check their web sites (http://www.americandialect.org/index.php and http://www.merriam-webster.com) for future winners. The *New Oxford American Dictionary* named *unfriend* its word of the year for 2009, as social networks seek to *friend* people who may later decide to *unfriend* their hosts.

Student Activities on the History of English

Students benefit from a variety of activities related to a historical perspective of the English language. The following exercises for students can supplement instruction on word origins and history:

- Make some cave drawings of events and objects of importance.

- Construct a time line of language events.

- Find out more about various early writing systems, such as Sumerian cuneiform; Egyptian hieroglyphics; and the Greek, Etruscan, and Latin alphabets.

- Use the illustration of Egyptian hieroglyphics to write your name in hieroglyphics (see Figure 2.2).

- Write your name in other alphabets you find.

- Visit http://www.navajocodetalkers.org and find out about the fascinating unbroken code of World War II developed by Navajo soldiers.

- Find words from different languages that are related to everyday activities and topics.

- Using the dictionary, find words with Indo-European roots. For example, *wegh* (to go or transport in a vehicle) resulted in words such as *devious, deviate, way, weight, wagon, vogue, vehicle, vector, envoy,* and *trivial* (Garg, 2009).

- Compare dictionaries to see if new words you use are listed.

- Check for possible variations in a word's meaning among dictionaries.

- Make a chart of new words you hear and read. Research the language of origin or when each word was first used.

- Ask students to visit http://www.americandialect.org and http://www .merriam-webster.com for the word of the year selected by the American Dialect Society and the *Merriam-Webster Dictionary.*

- Use two or three neologisms (new words) in a poem or short story.

- Read several pages from a book by Mark Twain. Make a list of interesting words and phrases.

- Look for words in your social studies and science textbooks. See if you can figure out what the origin of the word is.

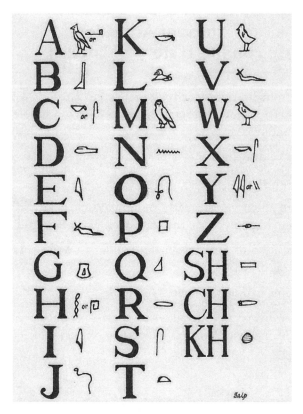

Figure 2.2.   Roman Alphabet with corresponding Egyptian hieroglyphs. (Illustration by Sally Parsons.)

BOOKS ON THE HISTORY OF ENGLISH

Resources for Students

Brook, D., & Zallinger, J.D. (Illus.). (1998). *The journey of English.* New York: Clarion Books.

Klausner, J.C. (1990). *Talk about English: How words travel and change.* New York: Thomas Y. Crowell.

Krensky, S. (1996). *Breaking into print: Before and after the invention of the printing press.* Toronto: Little, Brown.

Samoyault, T. (1996). *Alphabetical order: How the alphabet began.* New York: Penguin.

Resources for Teachers

Ayto, J. (1999). *Twentieth century words.* New York: Oxford University Press.

Balmuth, M. (2009). *The roots of phonics: A historical introduction, revised edition.* Baltimore: Paul H. Brookes Co.

Barnett, L. (1964). *The treasure of our tongue.* New York: Alfred A. Knopf.

Baugh, A.C. (2001). *History of the English language* (5th ed.). New York: Prentice Hall.

Bryson, B. (1990). *The mother tongue: English and how it got that way.* New York: William Morrow.

Claiborne, R. (1983). *Our marvelous native tongue: The life and times of the English language.* New York: Times Books.

Crystal, D. (2006). *The fight for English.* Oxford, England: Oxford University Press.

Lederer, R. (1991). *The miracle of language.* New York: Pocket Books.

Logan, R.K. (1986). *The alphabet effect.* New York: St. Martin's Press.

Manguel, A. (1996). *A history of reading.* New York: Viking.

Martin, H.-J. (1994). *The history and power of writing.* Chicago: University of Chicago Press.

McCrum, R., Cran, S., & MacNeil, R. (1986). *The story of English.* New York: Viking.

Nist, J. (1966). *A structural history of English.* New York: St. Martin's Press.

Pei, M. (1965). *The story of language.* Philadelphia: Lippincott Williams & Wilkins. (Original work published 1949)

Pinker, S. (1994). *The language instinct.* New York: William Morrow.

Soukhanov, A.H. (1995). *Word watch: The story behind the words of our lives.* New York: Henry Holt & Co.

WEB SITES ON THE HISTORY OF ENGLISH

A Brief History of the English Language, http://www.anglik.net/englishlanguagehistory.htm

A Brief History of the English Language, http://www.studyenglishtoday.net/english-language-history.html

History of English: Five Events that Shaped the History of English, http://www.askoxford.com/worldofwords/history

History of the English Language: A Short History of the Origins and Development of English, http://www.englishclub.com/english-language-history.htm

The Origin and History of the English Language, http://www.krysstal.com/English.html

Wordorigins.org, http://www.wordorigins.org

CHAPTER 3

Structure of the English Language

Teachers who comprehend the origins of the English language along with the primary structural patterns within words can improve their assessment skills, enhance their understanding of reading and spelling curricula, communicate clearly about specific features of language, and effectively teach useful strategies to their students. Influences on English orthography (the spelling system) stem from the introduction of letters and words of diverse origins, primarily Anglo-Saxon, Latin, and Greek. When teachers and their students understand the historical basis and structure of written English, they can better understand the regularities as well as the few irregularities in English words.

A blank 3 × 3 matrix representing the word origin/structure framework for instruction was introduced in Chapter 1 (see Figure 1.1). Figure 3.1 illustrates the contents of the matrix. Each of the nine cells is discussed in this chapter.

Most students enjoy learning about the structure and origins of English words. Young students use these strategies to decode and spell short regular words involving letter–sound correspondences, or phonics. These students also learn the common syllable patterns, the Anglo-Saxon compound words, and common prefixes (word beginnings) and suffixes (word endings). Upper-grade students and adult learners receiving instruction in more advanced language structure focus on Latin and Greek morphemes. These prefixes, suffixes, roots, and combining forms

	Letter–sound correspondences	Syllables	Morphemes
Anglo-Saxon	Consonants _bid_, _step_, _that_ Vowels _mad/made_, _barn_, _boat_	Closed: _bat_ Open: _baby_ VCE: _made_ Vowel digraph: _boat_ Consonant-_le_: _tumble_ r-controlled: _barn_	Compounds _hardware_ _shipyard_ Affixes _read, reread,_ _rereading_ _bid, forbid, forbidden_
Latin	Same as Anglo-Saxon but few vowel digraphs Use of schwa /ə/: _direction_ _spatial_ _excellent_	Closed: _spect_ VCE: _scribe_ r-controlled: _port, form_	Affixes _construction_ _erupting_ _conductor_
Greek	_ph_ for /f/ _phonograph_ _ch_ for /k/ _chorus_ _y_ for /ĭ/ _sympathy_	Closed: _graph_ Open: _photo_ Unstable digraph: _create_	Compounds _microscope_ _chloroplast_ _physiology_

Figure 3.1. Word origin and word structure matrix. VCE, vowel-consonant-_e_. (_Source:_ Henry, 1988b.)

provide meaning. With an understanding of morphology, students learning English as a second language find that English is quite regular and is not a language of exceptions after all. Children with or without **specific language disabilities** benefit as they learn effective and efficient strategies to read and spell numerous words (Chall & Popp, 1996; Ehri, 1998; Henry, 1988a, 1988b, 1989).

The reader needs to recognize the sound patterns of speech in the symbols printed on a page. Print, however, does not represent the auditory pattern of heard speech in an exact way (speech is heard as a more or less continuous stream with pauses that do not necessarily correspond to the word or letter boundaries in print). For example, a child is apt to say "Whadjoosay?" (What did you say?) as a single stream. One friend might ask another "Jeetjet?" instead of saying the words separately as "Did you eat yet?" Teachers rarely point out the mismatch between spoken and written language. The problem for the learner is to decode the print to represent for himself or herself a coherent set of sound representations.

English contains approximately 40 phonemes (or discrete sounds). Fromkin and Rodman (1998) estimated that there are 25 consonant sounds and 15 vowel sounds. Some linguists count additional vowel sounds due to dialectical differences. English has many more graphemes (the letters and letter combinations forming patterns found in words) than phonemes.

Paulesu et al. (2001) compared shallow or transparent orthography, which has a more complete one-to-one sound–letter relationship (e.g., Finnish, Italian, Spanish), with deep, opaque, less phonetic, and therefore more complex orthography (e.g., English, French). Paulesu et al. concluded that the orthography of language is especially important in learning to read, particularly for those children with specific reading disability (dyslexia). Unfortunately, because the media have emphasized the researchers' suggestion that there are 1,120 ways to represent 40 phonemes by using different letter combinations, readers might infer that English is an extremely nonphonetic language. Such a conclusion is often made by citing an uncommon spelling that is found in only one or two words in the English lexicon (e.g., *augh* as in *laugh* or *eo* as in *leopard*). Many teachers unfamiliar with the structure of English may conclude that English is an impossible language to teach. However, English has a relatively regular structure, and teachers and their students can readily learn many of the decoding and spelling patterns and rules in English.

Paul Hanna and his colleagues (1971) at Stanford found that in the 17,000 words most commonly used by adult speakers and writers, complete one-to-one letter–symbol correspondence was not uncommon. They estimated that 170 graphemes (letters or letter combinations) spelled a limited set of 42 phonemes that included consonants, vowels, **diphthongs,** and semivowels. Hanna and his group concluded that several almost perfect letter–sound correspondences exist in English. Summarizing the Hanna et al. study, Moats (1995) wrote that at least 20 phonemes have grapheme spellings that are more than 90% predictable and that 10 others are predictable more than 80% of the time. Pinker noted, "Indeed, for about eighty-four percent of English words, spelling is completely predictable from regular rules" (1994, p. 190).

The goal for teachers is to teach the very common letter–sound patterns and to teach the regularities of English orthography. Barnett (1964) explained that English is an extremely flexible system because it transfers meaning with minimal phonetic effort. Thus, with only three sounds, for example /ă/, /k/, and /t/, speakers can create several words with discrete meanings (*act, cat,* and *tack*).

ANGLO-SAXON LAYER OF LANGUAGE

Words of Anglo-Saxon origin are characterized as the common, everyday, down-to-earth words used frequently in ordinary situations. Nist provided a clever inventory of some of the Anglo-Saxon words in English today:

> English remains preeminently Anglo-Saxon at its core: in the suprasegmentals of its stress, pitch and juncture patterns and in its vocabulary. No matter whether a man is American, British, Canadian, Australian, New Zealander or South African, he *still loves his mother, father, brother, sister, wife, son and daughter; lifts his hand to his head, his cup to his mouth, his eye to heaven and his heart to God; hates his foes, likes his friends, kisses his kin and buries his dead; draws his breath, eats*

his bread, drinks his water, stands his watch, wipes his sweat, feels his sorrow, weeps his
tears and sheds his blood; and all these things he thinks about and calls both good and
bad. (1966, p. 9)

As this passage shows, most words of Anglo-Saxon origin consist of one syllable and represent typical, everyday activities and events. Although consonant letters are fairly regular (i.e., each letter corresponds to one sound), vowel spellings are more problematic. Words that are learned early in school are often irregular and may cause difficulty for students with specific reading disabilities. Students must memorize these "outlaw," "red flag," or "weirdo" words, such as *rough, does, only, eye, laugh, blood,* and *said,* because the vowels do not carry the normal short (lax) or long (tense) sounds associated with these spellings.

Letter–Sound Correspondences

Letter–sound correspondences are the relationships between letters and sounds. Consonant letters of the alphabet (e.g., *b, c, d, f, m, p, t*) represent speech sounds produced by a partial or complete obstruction of the air stream. Consonant letters include all those except the vowels (*a, e, i, o,* and *u* and sometimes *y* and *w*). Vowel sounds are created by the relatively free passage of breath through the larynx and oral cavity.

In learning phonics, students must link the phonemes and graphemes (the letter configurations corresponding to each of the phonemes) of English. Teachers generally use dictionary markings (phonic symbols) as guides to pronunciation, whereas linguists and specialists in speech and language disorders tend to use symbols from the International Phonetic Alphabet. Using phonic symbols to represent phonemes, Tables 3.1 and 3.2 show common grapheme–phoneme correspondences and provide examples of words that have these spelling and sound patterns.

Teachers and their students need to be able to link phonemes with their corresponding graphemes. Graphemes are organized into either consonant or vowel patterns. Within these patterns, most of the graphemes fit into one of three categories as illustrated in Figure 3.2. This 2 × 3 matrix showing Anglo-Saxon letter–sound patterns corresponds to the top left-hand cell in the 3 × 3 matrix shown in Figures 1.1 and 3.1. Anglo-Saxon letter–sound correspondences are the first symbol–sound relationships taught to children who are learning to read and write.

Consonants   Single-letter consonant spellings seldom vary; 17 of the 21 consonant letters each stand for a specific sound. Thus, the letter *b* is almost always pronounced /b/, *m* is pronounced /m/, and *p* is pronounced /p/. The consonant graphemes *c* and *g* each have two sounds, but specific spelling patterns guide the reader. For example, *c* almost always has the sound /k/ before *a, o,* and *u* (as in *cat, cope,* and *cub*) but has the sound /s/ before *e, y,* and *i* (as in *cell, city,* and *cycle*). Informally, these are called the hard and soft sounds of *c,* respectively. Likewise, *g* before *a, o,* and *u* (as in *gate, go,* or *gun*) is considered hard, whereas *g* before *e, i,* and

Table 3.1. English consonant spelling–sound correspondences with pronunciation examples

Consonant graphemes	Examples	Phoneme
b	bib	/b/
d	deed	/d/
f, ph; -gh (rare)	fife, phone, laugh	/f/
g	gag	/g/
h	hat	/h/
j, -dge, g	jam, ginger, fudge	/j/
k, -ck, c, ch, -que	kick, cat, chorus, unique	/k/
l, -le	lit, needle	/l/
m	mom	/m/
n	no, sudden	/n/
p	pop	/p/
r	roar	/r/
s, c, sc	sauce, science	/s/
t	tot	/t/
v	valve	/v/
w	with	/w/
y	yes	/y/
z, -s	zebra, dogs	/z/
ch, -tch	church, pitch	/ch/
sh	ship	/sh/
th	thin	/th/
th	that	/<u>th</u>/
wh	when	/hw/
si, su, -ge	vision, treasure, garage	/zh/

From Henry, M.K. (1999). A short history of the English language. In J.R. Birsh (Ed.), Multisensory teaching of basic language skills (pp. 125–126). Baltimore: Paul H. Brookes Publishing Co.; adapted by permission.

y (as in *gem, ginger,* and *gypsy*) is soft. The letter *s* usually sounds like /s/ (as in *snake*) but often carries the /z/ sound in the final consonant position (as in *rose*) or as a plural (as in *dogs*). The letter *y* usually is a consonant at the beginning of words and syllables (as in *yard*) but is a vowel in the middle or end of syllables (as in *gymnasium, by,* and *baby*). Note that *x* is omitted from Table 3.1 because it represents two sounds: /k/ and /s/. In the final position, *x* makes the sound of /ks/ (as in *box*), but at the beginning of some words it makes the sound of /z/ (as in *Xerox* and *xylophone*).

Consonant blends (sometimes called consonant clusters) are made up of two or three adjacent consonant sounds in a syllable; they retain their individual sounds and are common (e.g., *bl* and *mp* in *blimp; spl* and *nt* in *splint*).

It is interesting that few English words begin with *kl* or *kr*. Instead, English words begin with the blends *cl* and *cr* unless they are proper names or Germanic terms (e.g., *Kleenex, Klamath, Paul Klee, Otto Klemperer, Klondike, Kris Kringle*).

Table 3.2.   English vowel spelling–sound correspondences with pronunciation examples

Vowel graphemes[a]	Examples	Phoneme
a	pat	/ă/
a, a-e, ai, ay, ei, eigh, ey	baby, made, pail, pay, veil, eight, they	/ā/
e	pet	/ě/
e, e-e, ee, ea, ie, y, ey, ei	me, scheme, greet, seat, thief, lady, alley, ceiling	/ē/
i	bit	/ĭ/
i, i-e, igh, ie, y, y-e	hi, kite, fight, pie, sky, type	/ī/
o	hot	/ŏ/
o, o-e, oa, ow, oe	go, vote, boat, grow, toe	/ō/
u	cut	/ŭ/
a	father	irregular /ŏ/
(schwa)	alone, item, credible, gallop, circus	/ə/
au, aw	fault, claw	/ô/
oo	book	/o͝o/
ew, oo, ue, u	chew, room, blue, lute	/o͞o/
oi, oy	coin, toy	/oi/
ou, ow	cloud, clown	/ou/
ar	car	/ar/
are	care	/ār/
er, ir, ur, or, ear	fern, bird, burn, corn, heard	/ûr/
er	butter	/ər/
ier, eer	pier, deer	/ēr/

From Henry, M.K. (1999). A short history of the English language. In J.R. Birsh (Ed.), Multisensory teaching of basic language skills(p. 126). Baltimore: Paul H. Brookes Publishing Co.; adapted by permission.

[a]A vowel letter followed by -e represents the vowel-consonant-e spelling pattern.

Consonant digraphs, in contrast, also have two consonant letters adjacent in a syllable but form only one speech sound. **Digraphs** often consist of a consonant letter followed by *h* and usually represent a new sound that is unlike the sound of either of the consonants in the digraph (e.g., *sh* as in *ship*, *ch* as in *chump*, *th* as in *this* or *thin*, *wh* as in *which*). Of interest, the voiced *th* is generally found in function words such as *this, the, those,* and *them,* and the unvoiced *th* is found in content words such as *thick, thin, think,* and *third.* Many students have difficulty discriminating between the voiced /w/ (as in *wail*) and the unvoiced /hw/ (as in *whale*), and not all English speakers use the unvoiced /hw/ sound. The letter combinations *kn-, gn-, wr-, -ck,* and *-ng* are considered digraphs in some systems (*-tch* and *-dge* are *trigraphs,* or three letters that represent one speech sound).

Phonesthemes show the systematic pairing of form and meaning in a language. For example, the English phonestheme *wr* is related to the sense of twisting, as in *wrest, wrestle, wrist, wrench, wring, wrung, wrap, wriggle, wrinkle, writhe,* and *wrack. Sw* conveys a sense of a wide arching movement, as in *swish, swing, swung, sway, swipe, swab, swathe, switch, swim, swallow,* and *swap.*

Consonants		
Single	**Blends**	**Digraphs**
b c d f g h k j l m n p q r s t v w x y z	Initial: *bl-, cl-, fl-, gl-, pl-, sl-;* *br-, cr-, dr-, fr-, gr-, pr-, tr-;* *sc-, sl-, sm-, sn-, sp-, st-; tw-;* *scr-, str-; spl-; spr-...* Final: *-lf, -lk, -lp, -mp, -nd, -st...*	Initial: *wh-, gn-, kn-, wr-...* Initial or final: *ch, sh, th* *(thin), th (that)...* Final: *-ck, -tch...*

Vowels		
Short/long	**r- and l-controlled**	**Digraphs**
a mad/made *e* pet/Pete *i* pin/pine *o* rob/robe *u* cut/cute *y* my/baby ·	*ar* *or* *er, ir, ur* *al, all...*	One sound: *ai, ay, ee, oa,* *aw, au, ou, ue, ew, igh,* *eigh...* Two sounds: *ea, ie, ei, oo,* *ow, ey...*

Figure 3.2.   Anglo-Saxon letter–sound correspondence matrix. (From Calfee, R.C., et al. [1981–1984]. *The book: Components of reading instruction.* Unpublished manuscript, Stanford University, California; adapted by permission.)

Vowels   Vowel sounds tend to be more difficult to learn than consonant sounds, but even they have some consistency. Vowel sounds represented by single letters are generally either short or long. The short /ă/ is spelled with *a* (as in *hat, man,* and *staff*) nearly 100% of the time, and the short /ŏ/ is spelled with *o* (as in *hot, mob,* and *lock*) more than 95% of the time (Smelt, 1976). Perfetti (1986) observed that alphabets fail to provide a unique letter symbol for each vowel sound; thus, we look at certain markers within the spelling of a word. These markers serve as clues to indicate whether the short or long sound should be used. A vowel with a syllable-final consonant after it in the same syllable carries the short sound (e.g., *a* as in *cat, e* as in *let, i* as in *fit, o* as in *fox,* and *u* as in *fun*). In contrast, a vowel at the end of a syllable has the long sound, or "says its own name" (as in *go, baby,* and *pilot*). The silent *e* at the end of a word after a consonant (as in *shape* and *vote*) also signals that the vowel within the word has a long sound. The doubled consonant, as in *pinning* and *cutter,* is there to mark the sound of the vowel before the doubled consonant as short. The doubled consonant cancels the long vowel signal that would otherwise be given by the *i* in *-ing* and the *e* in *-er.* The letter *y* serves as a vowel following a consonant at the end of a word or syllable (as in *my* and *baby*) or following another vowel (as in *day* or *toy*). The letter *w,* when it follows a vowel, also serves as a vowel (as in *few* and *claw*). In this case, the vowel plus *w* or *y* is considered a vowel digraph.

Students will also read words with a vowel plus *r* or *l.* In syllables containing *r,* vowel sounds often change because of the *r.* These patterns are best presented as combinations, such as *ar* (as in *star*), *or* (as in *corn*), *er* (as in *fern*), *ir* (as in *bird*), *ur* (as in *church*), and *al* (as in *falter*).

Vowel digraphs are two adjacent vowels (e.g., *oa, ee, oi, ou, au*) that occur primarily in words of Anglo-Saxon origin. These digraphs usually occur in the middle of words. Vowel digraphs can be divided into two sets—those that are fairly consistently linked to a single sound (e.g., *ee, oa, oi, oy*) and those that may have two pronunciations (e.g., *ea* as in *bead* or *bread, ow* as in *show* or *cow*). Balmuth discussed the historical origins of vowel digraphs and diphthongs and noted that during Middle English times, diphthongs were "especially varied in spelling because of the confusions that resulted from the separation of the written *i* and *y* and the introduction of the *w* and other French spelling conventions" (1982, p. 102).[1] It is often difficult for students to acquire vowel digraphs in Anglo-Saxon words because of their variability and occasional irregularity and because of interference from previously learned associations.

The Schwa   My colleague Gina Cooke wrote an important "Treatise on the Schwa" (2008a, 2008b, 2008c) in three parts, in which she provided the background of the schwa. Although the schwa is actually a phoneme in some languages, as "the unstressed, toneless, neutral vowel sound that is the most common sound in all of English" (2008a, p. 7) it is often the reading teacher's nemesis. In the Part 2 of her treatise, Cooke discussed the necessity of teaching the "-ologies"— phonology, orthography, morphology, and **etymology**—and the role of the schwa in each of these components of reading instruction. Finally, in Part 3, Cooke provided several dos and don'ts for teaching the schwa. Dos include the following: Do become accent conscious, do illustrate the importance of correct accent placement, do develop syllable and accent concepts early and often, and do use multisensory strategies to support schwa and accent instruction. Don'ts include the following: Don't over-enunciate, don't say that you can't "hear" accent, don't teach the schwa as a phoneme, don't insist that you actually do say a pure vowel where there is a schwa, don't give the child excuses about the schwa, and don't hold dyslexic children too accountable for spelling.

By the end of second grade, children should have mastered all the common letter–sound correspondences and **spelling rules** relating to these patterns. For example, at the end of a one-syllable word, the consonants *f, l,* and *s* are usually doubled when they come directly after a **short vowel sound** (e.g., *staff, chill, grass*). Students should recognize that in English words with a short vowel sound immediately followed by a final /k/ sound, *-ck* represents the final sound (as in *sick, stack, deck, clock, stuck*); *k* is used only after two vowel letters (as in *peak*) and directly after consonants (as in *milk*). The same is true for /ch/ spelled as *tch* and /j/

---

[1]Linguists differentiate between the terms *vowel digraph* and *diphthong*. Both constructions contain two adjacent vowels in the same syllable. A diphthong glides from one sound to another. Diphthongs include *oi, oy; au, aw; ou, ow;* and *ue, ew*. Some linguists disagree about the number of diphthongs in English; Venezky (1999) suggested that this disagreement reflects dialectical differences. (In this book, all vowel pairs are called digraphs.)

spelled as *dge* at the end of one-syllable words following a short vowel sound (as in *pitch* and *bridge*). Chapter 6 presents the spelling rules affecting words of Anglo-Saxon origin.

Irregular Words   In addition to learning the common letter–sound correspondences, students must also know how to read and spell the 100–200 common **irregular words** found in primers and primary-grade text. Knowledge of letter–sound correspondences is not much help in either reading or spelling these non-phonetic words, such as *said, blood, love,* and *cough.* Although consonant sounds may be orthographically regular, vowels are not. These troublesome words are often called *red flag words, spelling demons,* or *maverick words.* Our Stanford Reading Project called them *weirdo words.* Adams (1990) noted that only 35 of the 150 most frequent words in printed school English are phonetic. The other 115 must be memorized. (See Chapter 6 for instructional strategies for reading nonphonetic words, and see Appendix B for lists of the most common nonphonetic words.)

Syllable Patterns

Syllables are units of spoken language consisting of an uninterrupted sound formed by a vowel sound alone or a vowel sound with one or more consonants. Words with an Anglo-Saxon origin have a variety of syllable patterns. Students first learn that each syllable must have a vowel. Children generally have less difficulty hearing syllables in words than in recognizing written syllables (Balmuth, 2009; Groff, 1971). Therefore, teachers often begin by having children say their own names and counting the number of syllables. Later, students listen for accent or stress in words of more than one syllable. Anglo-Saxon base words, such as *sleep, like,* and *time,* tend to retain the accent when affixes are added (e.g., *asleep, likely, timeless*).

 Many words that are spelled alike have different stress for different parts of speech. For example, *re'-search* is a noun, whereas *re-search'* is a verb; *rec'-ord* is a noun, and *re-cord'* is a verb.

Groff (1971) emphasized that syllables are not units of writing, grammar, or structure, but rather units of speech. He noted that it is the boundaries of syllables rather than the number of syllables in a word that make their analysis difficult. He made the distinction between how linguists may divide words based on morphemic boundaries and how dictionaries divide syllables based on sounds. For example, some linguists prefer to divide the word *disruptive* as dis/rupt/ive (prefix, root, and suffix), whereas the dictionary usually divides the word as dis/rup/tive. Groff questioned whether teaching syllable division (or **syllabication**) is an important part of teaching reading. Although this argument continues, knowing the alternatives to dividing words into syllables provides students with another strategy for word analysis.

Teachers who know the following six major syllable types and the predominant patterns for syllable division can help children read multisyllabic words; teachers and students will also find syllable division useful in writing hyphenated words. The major types of syllables are 1) **closed,** 2) **open,** 3) **vowel-consonant-*e* (VCE),** 4) **vowel digraph,** 5) **consonant-*le*,** and 6) *r*-**controlled** (Moats, 1995, 2000; Steere, Peck, & Kahn, 1971).

Teachers introduce closed syllables first. In these syllables, the single vowel has a consonant after it, making the vowel sound short (e.g., *map, sit, cub, stop, bed*). An open syllable contains a vowel at the end of the syllable, and the vowel usually makes its long sound (e.g., *go, me, Hi, ho/bo*). Stanback (1992) found that closed syllables alone make up 43% of syllables in English words. Open syllables and closed syllables together account for almost 75% of English syllables. The final *e* in a VCE syllable makes the vowel long or makes it "say its own name" (e.g., *made, time, cute, vote, Pete*). A vowel digraph (or vowel team or vowel pair) syllable contains two adjacent vowels (as in *rain, green, coil,* and *pause*). Children learn the long, short, or diphthong sound of each pattern. A consonant-*le* syllable usually starts with a consonant that is part of that syllable. For example, *bugle* has a long *u* because *gle* stays together, making the first syllable in the word, *bu,* an open syllable. In contrast, *tumble* contains *tum* and *ble,* with *tum* being a closed syllable. *Little* requires two *t*'s to keep the *i* in *lit* short. As discussed previously, vowel sounds in *r*-controlled syllables often lose their identity as long or short and are co-articulated with /r/ (as in *star, corn, fern, church,* and *firm*).

Students also need to learn some common rules for syllable division in order to make multisyllabic words easier to read and spell. By first understanding and practicing how to identify the various syllable types in monosyllables, readers will recognize these common syllable types as they learn to divide words into syllables. Understanding how to spell the vowel sounds in syllables gives readers an advantage and a more productive understanding of syllable division rules. Readers may recognize syllable division patterns such as VC/CV (as in *nap/kin*), V/CV (as in *ho/bo*), VC/V (as in *plan/et*), VC/CCV (as in *hun/dred*), and CV/VC (as in *cre/ate*). These are useful separations to know when analyzing unfamiliar words.

Morpheme Patterns

A morpheme is the smallest meaningful linguistic unit. Compound words, prefixes, suffixes, and roots are the morphemes that help students learn to read and write because they are used in hundreds of thousands of words (Brown, 1947). By knowing the common morphemes, students enhance not only their decoding and spelling skills but also their vocabulary skills.

Linguists use several terms to reflect the main part in a word. The term *base word* or *base element* refers to the morphological base of a word stripped of its affixes, such as *jump* or *read*. The term *base word* can also refer to a complete English word, such as *transmit*, that in turn contains a root (*mit*). The term *root* refers to a word part from an origin language such as Latin or Greek; roots are usually bound in English. Although linguists sometimes use the term *stem*, it is not used in this book, as it has a variety of meanings.

Anglo-Saxon morphemes are found in both compound and affixed words. Decoding and spelling these words tends to be simple because they contain regular orthographic features. A compound word is generally composed of two short words joined together to form a new, meaning-based word. That is, a compound word has a meaning that is based on the meanings of its constituent words. Children enjoy generating compound words, such as *cowboy, blackboard, baseball,* and *campground.* Computer technology has been the impetus for many new compound words, such as *software, firmware,* and *hardware* (with a meaning related to computers, not tools).

Anglo-Saxon base words are generally **free morphemes.** That is, each can stand alone as a word in English (e.g., *spell, hope*). Anglo-Saxon base words may be combined as compounds (e.g., *football, blackboard*) and may also become affixed with the addition of prefixes and suffixes (e.g., *spell, misspell, misspelled; hope, hopeless, hopelessness*).

Morpheme affixes have two forms. Inflectional morphemes indicate grammatical features such as number, person, tense, or comparative forms (e.g., *dog, dogs; wait, waits; walk, walked; small, smaller*). Derivational morphemes, in contrast, are added to existing words to create new words that are often different parts of speech than the base words (e.g., *hope* is a noun and a verb, *hopeless* is an adjective, *hopelessly* is an adverb).

Students in first and second grades begin by adding suffixes to words requiring no change in the base form (e.g., *help, helpless; time, untimely*). By the middle of second grade and in third grade, students must learn rules for adding suffixes that affect some base words, such as when to double a final consonant (as in *big, bigger*), drop the final *e* (as in *blame, blaming*), or change *y* to *i* (as in *copy, copied*).

The term *morphophonemics* refers to the condition whereby certain morphemes keep their written spelling even though their phonemic forms change (Venezky, 1999). This concept provides students with a logical reason for many English spellings. For example, in *knowledge,* the morpheme *know* is pronounced differently from the base word *know.* The meaning of *knowledge* is based on the base word *know,* however. Balmuth noted that

> It can be helpful to readers when the same spelling is kept for the same morpheme, despite variations in pronunciation. Such spellings supply clues to the meanings of words, clues that would be lost if the words were spelled phonemically, as, for example, if know and knowledge were spelled noe and nollij in a hypothetical phonemic system. (2009, p. 199)

LATIN LAYER OF LANGUAGE

The Latin layer of language consists of words used in more formal settings. Latin is the basis for the Romance languages. Romance languages include French, Italian, Portuguese, Romanian, and Spanish. Latin-based words are often found in literature or social studies texts in the upper elementary and later grades. Because Latin-based words are longer, many students expect them to be more complex. Yet in most cases, the words follow simple letter–sound correspondences.

Letter–Sound Correspondences

Most Latin roots contain short vowels, as in *rupt, script, cred, vent, tens, pend,* and *vis.* The syllable-final consonant combination *-ct* is a signpost for words of Latin origin, as in *dict, duct, tract, struct,* and *ject.* Words such as *disruptive, reconstructed,* and *extracting* are examples of multisyllabic Latin-based words that are easy for children to read and spell once they learn the constituent patterns.

Vowel digraphs appear only rarely in Latin-based words. As mentioned previously, Anglo-Saxon vowel digraphs are often difficult for students to acquire. Similarly, in words of Latin origin, spellings for vowel digraphs are also difficult for students to acquire. These digraphs generally appear in suffixes such as *-ion, -ian, -ient,* and *-ial,* which are taught as units. However, students can learn some spelling patterns for these digraphs: The suffix *-ion* is usually preceded by *t* or *s* (as in *tion* and *sion*), the suffix *-ian* usually comes after *c* (as in *cian*), and the suffixes *-ient* and *-ial* usually come after *t* (as in *tient* and *tial*).

In addition, students may have trouble acquiring Latin-based words with a vowel digraph because the consonant before the digraph suffix is typically variable. When a vowel digraph comes after the letters *c, s,* and *t,* it combines with those letters to create the /sh/ sound, as in *nation, partial, social,* and *admission.* (The suffix *-sion* is sometimes pronounced as /zhən/, as in *erosion* and *invasion.*)

Syllable Patterns

The main syllable types found in Latin roots are closed (e.g., *spect, rupt, script*), VCE (e.g., *scribe, -voke*), and *r*-controlled (e.g., *port, form*). Patterns of syllable division are similar to those found in words of Anglo-Saxon origin. For example, *disruption* has two VC/CV separations: *dis/rup/tion.* The V/CV syllable division pattern can be found in the words *re/port* and *pro/trac/tor.*

Although the stress usually occurs on the Latin root, the stress patterns in Latin-based words can be fairly complex. The schwa, or neutral vowel in an unstressed syllable, is often found in words of Latin origin (e.g., *excellent, direction*). When one pronounces *excellent,* for example, the stress occurs on the first syllable, so the initial *e* receives the regular short sound. The following two *e*'s, which appear in unstressed syllables, have the schwa sound (/ə/). Listening for the unstressed vowels in open and closed syllables is an advanced skill that students with reading difficulties need to learn. Students who can discover the base word (e.g., *excel*) often are able to spell the longer word. The schwa is often found in unaccented prefixes and/or suffixes. Any vowel may be pronounced as schwa when it appears in an unstressed syllable. The schwa is discussed more fully in later chapters.

Morpheme Patterns

Although Anglo-Saxon base words can make up compound words (e.g., *sleepwalk*) and can have affixes added to them (e.g., *nightly*), Latin root words can only be affixed. Nist provided another key example: "So great, in fact, was the penetra*tion* of Latin *affixing* during the *Renaissance* that it quite *un*did the Anglo-Saxon habit of *com*pounding as the leading means of word form*ation* in English" (1966, p. 11). Words of Latin origin become affixed by the addition of a prefix or a suffix to the root, which rarely stands alone (e.g., *rupt, interrupted; mit, transmitting; vent, prevention*). Latin-based roots are nearly always considered **bound morphemes** because the root does not stand alone; a prefix and/or a suffix is added. For example, the prefix *in-* can be added to the bound morpheme *spect* to get *inspect,* and the suffix *-ion* can be added to get *inspection.*

The final consonant of a Latin prefix often changes based on the beginning letter of the root. For example, the prefix *in-,* meaning "in" or "not," changes to *il-* before roots beginning with *l* (e.g., *illegal*); to *ir-* before roots beginning with *r* (e.g., *irregular*); and to *im-* before roots beginning with *m, b,* and *p* (e.g., *immobile, imbalance, important*). These changes are due to euphony (from Greek: *eu* meaning "well" and *phon* meaning "sound"). Thus, the words with the changed prefixes sound better and are easier to say than, for instance, *inlegal* or *conmunicate.* These "**chameleon,**" or **assimilated,** prefixes have several forms and are explained in Chapter 7.

Numerous suffixes can be added to Latin roots. Students need to learn the rule for doubling final consonants in polysyllabic base words. If a word ends in one consonant and is preceded by a short vowel, and if the accent is on the final syllable of the base word, the final consonant is doubled when the suffix begins with a vowel. For example, *transmit* + *-ed* becomes *transmitted* because the accent of the base word is on the final syllable, *mit.*

Special note must be made about the suffix *-ion* (*-tion, -sion, -cian*). Some sources, such as Barnhart (1988), Gillingham and Stillman (1956, 1997), and *Webster's New Universal Unabridged Dictionary, Second Edition* (1983), consider *-tion* and *-cian* to be noun suffixes. Others teach *-ion* and *-ian* as suffixes added to roots, such as *invent, invention* and *music, musician.* Students can be taught that *-ion* and *-ian* are suffixes but that pronunciation dictates that the syllable be *-tion, -sion,* or *-cian.* The same is true for *-al* suffixes preceded by *ti* and *ci* (as in *substantial* and *judicial*): *-al* is the suffix, and the syllables are *-tial* and *-cial.*

Latin word roots form the basis of hundreds of thousands of words (Brown, 1947; Henry, 1993). Longer words of Latin or Greek origin (the majority of words in the English language) are often easier to spell than short words because the longer words contain recognizable word parts that are used in thousands of words. Students can readily observe the prefixes, roots, and suffixes in words such as *prediction, incredible, extracting,* and *reconstructionist* and see that these common word parts assist in decoding, spelling, and enlarging vocabulary. Learning word roots is useful for all students, including those with reading disabilities, those studying for the SATs, and those who are English language learners (Henry, Calfee, &

Avelar-LaSalle, 1989). In fact, the Latin roots in English words are often the very same roots that prevail in Spanish words, such as *descripción* (*description*), *prosperidad* (*prosperity*), and *habitante* (*inhabitant*). Note that the affixes, not the roots, are usually what differ between the Spanish and English spellings.

A study by the National Committee for Latin and Greek found that taking Latin helps increase SAT scores. In 2002, the mean Verbal SAT score for all students was 504, whereas the mean score for students who took Latin was 666 (National Committee for Latin and Greek, 2009). In addition, studying Latin enriches English vocabulary and sharpens grammar skills. Knowledge of Latin and Greek also equips students with a solid foundation for learning other languages.

Understanding **morphophonemic relations** is especially important for learning Latin roots. When prefixes and suffixes are added, the stress often changes, and therefore the entire pronunciation of the word changes. Think about words such as *excel, excellent; ridicule, ridiculous; prepare, preparation;* and *solid, solidify.* Vowel sounds can be heard in the accented syllables but not in the unaccented syllables. Not being able to hear the vowel sounds in the unaccented syllables makes spelling difficult, and students must try to find the base word before spelling the affixed word.

Latin word roots are probably among the most productive elements for students to learn in the sense that they are important for vocabulary enhancement, for decoding, and for spelling. A relatively small number of Latin roots and affixes and Greek combining forms appear in hundreds of thousands of words.

GREEK LAYER OF LANGUAGE

During the Renaissance, Greek words entered English by the thousands to meet the needs of scholars and scientists. Bodmer noted that "the terminology of modern science, especially in aeronautics, biochemistry, chemotherapy, and genetics" (1944, p. 246) is formed from Greek. Greek word parts tend to be compounded and to appear largely in scientific texts (e.g., *microscope, hemisphere, physiology*). The roots are often termed *combining forms* in modern dictionaries, although many teachers use the terms *Greek combining forms* and *Greek roots* interchangeably.

The following passage from a middle school science text shows not only how short words of Anglo-Saxon origin mix with longer Romance words but also how the scientific terminology is couched in words of Greek origin (italicized here):

> Suppose you could examine a green part of a plant under the *microscope*. What would you see? Here are some cells from the green part of a plant. The cells have small green bodies shaped like footballs. They give the plant its green color. They are call *chloroplasts*. A single green plant cell looks like this. *Chloroplasts* are very important to a plant. As you know, plants make their own food. This food-making process is called *photosynthesis*. It is in these *chloroplasts* that *photosynthesis* takes place. (Cooper, Blackwood, Boeschen, Giddings, & Carin, 1985, p. 20, emphasis added)

Letter–Sound Correspondences

Letter–sound correspondences in words of Greek origin are similar to those found in words of Anglo-Saxon origin, but words of Greek origin also often incorporate new letter–sound correspondences. Thus, students need to know that *ch, ph*, and *y* in the word *chlorophyll* correspond to the sounds of /k/, /f/, and /ĭ/, respectively. These peculiar consonant combinations were introduced by Latin scribes and make words of Greek origin easily recognizable (Bodmer, 1944). Less common Greek letter–sound correspondences, found in only a handful of words, include *mn* as in *mnemonic, rh* as in *rhododendron, pt* as in *pterodactyl, pn* as in *pneumonia*, and the more well-known *ps* as in *psychology* and *psychiatry*.

Syllable Patterns

As words of Greek origin are often made up of two Greek combining forms, students need to know that syllables in each combining form usually retain their stress (e.g., *pho'/no/graph'* and *mi'/cro/scope'*). This occurs even in words containing three combining forms, such as *pho'/to/he'/li/o/graph'*.

The syllable types most prevalent in Greek-based words are closed (CVC, as in *graph*) and open (CV, as in each syllable of *pho/to*). In addition, a unique syllable pattern, that of adjacent vowels in separate syllables (as in *the/a/ter, cre/ate, cha/os*, and *the/o/ry*) can be found. Note that although *ea* is often a vowel digraph (as in *read* and *teach*), in *theatre* and *create* the vowels represented by the letters *ea* are in separate syllables. In addition, *ao* and *eo* are never vowel digraphs. These "unstable" digraphs appear in distinct syllables and therefore have distinct sounds.

Syllable division in words of Greek origin generally follows the rules given here for Anglo-Saxon words, especially for open syllables (e.g., *phono, photo, meter, polis*). The letter *y* sounds as short /ĭ/ in closed syllables (e.g., *sym/pho/ny, gym/na/si/um*), and these syllables divide after the consonant. The letter *y* sounds as long /ī/ in open syllables (e.g., *cy/clone, gy/ro/scope, hy/per/bo/le*), and these syllables divide directly after the *y*. In words containing unstable digraphs, syllable division occurs between the vowels, as in *zo/ol/o/gy* and *char/i/ot*.

Combining forms such as *semi* (VC/V), *hemi* (VC/V), and *micro* (V/CCV) do not follow V/CV or VC/CV division. Students rarely need to depend on strategies for syllable division in Greek-based words because they learn the orthographic patterns as wholes.

Morpheme Patterns

Greek combining forms can make up compound words just as Anglo-Saxon roots do. Students can learn to read and spell many thousands of words by recognizing relatively few Greek combining forms. By learning the common Greek combining forms that hold specific meaning, such as *micro, scope, bio, graph, helio, meter, phono, photo, auto*, and *tele*, students begin to read, spell, and understand the meanings of many words, such as *microscope, telescope, phonoreception, telephoto, telescopic, photo-heliograph, heliometer, biography,* and *autobiography.* Many Greek combining forms are often called prefixes because they appear at the beginning of words (e.g., *auto* in *autograph, hyper* in *hyperbole, hemi* in *hemisphere*). Numeral prefixes such as *mono-* (1), *di-* (2), *tri-* (3), *tetra-* (4), *penta-* (5), *hexa-* (6), *hepta-* (7), *octo-* (8), *nona-* (9), *deca-* (10), and *kilo-* (1,000) are useful in the study of mathematics and geometry. (See Appendix D for Latin and Greek number prefixes.)

SUMMARY

Treiman (1993) concluded that although children may pick up spelling patterns on their own, most children might learn the patterns more rapidly if regularities are spelled out for them. For example, teachers can point out that *-ck* and *-tch* never appear at the beginning of words and that consonant blends containing *r,* such as *cr, pr,* and *tr,* do not come at the end of words.

By learning the origin and structural framework of words, students gain strategies for decoding and spelling unfamiliar words. Students learn that words are made up of letters that have sounds and that words are also made up of syllables and morphemes and so can be broken down in several ways. Thus, children need to learn the following:

- A number of letter–sound correspondences within categories such as consonants, vowels, consonant blends, consonant digraphs, and vowel digraphs

- **High-frequency,** nonphonetic words

- The most common ways to divide words into syllables

- Common morpheme patterns—compound words, prefixes, suffixes, and roots

- The productive rules of the written form of the language

- An understanding of the history of written English

Activities

- Ask students to find words for the phonestheme *fl* (conveys the sense of sudden movement, such as in *flee, fled, flash*).

- Ask students to find words for the phonestheme *gl* (conveys brightness and light, such as in *glisten, glitter*)

- Make lists of one-syllable words. Ask students how many phonemes each word has, and have students circle consonant blends or consonant digraphs. Have students underline short vowels, vowel digraphs, and so forth.

- Write numerous words on 3 × 5 cards. Have students sort the cards by word structure (e.g., by putting all words containing consonant blends in one pile, those containing vowel digraphs in another).

- Make lists of polysyllabic words. Ask students how many phonemes, syllables, and/or morphemes each word has.

Instruction

CHAPTER 4

Lesson Fundamentals

New forms of service delivery have been introduced since the first edition of *Unlocking Literacy* was published in 2003. Response to Intervention (RTI) and differentiated instruction seek to identify struggling readers early on and provide appropriate intervention as soon as possible (Berninger & Wolf, 2009; Connor, 2009). Vaughn, Wanzek, Woodruff, and Linan-Thompson reported on the RTI model, concluding, "The use of the Three-Tier Model can provide a framework for assisting educators in providing effective instruction, identifying struggling readers early, providing appropriate interventions, and making instruction decisions throughout the school year" (2007, p. 25). I reiterate the importance of starting instruction as early as possible, as students who do not get help early are likely to continue to struggle with reading. Torgesen (2004) called for preventive rather than remedial models of intervention. RTI provides that preventive instruction.

The lesson fundamentals presented in *Unlocking Literacy* can be used as Tier 1, 2, or 3 interventions. The lesson format and procedures presented in this chapter and used throughout later chapters feature elements related to **metacognition, multisensory instruction,** and presentations in a discussion format. Teachers act as facilitators during these lessons.

METACOGNITIVE ASPECTS OF READING AND SPELLING

Although decoding has long been considered a cognitive activity, the related areas of metacognition, **metalinguistic awareness,** and **metalanguage** are also important. All three deal with knowing about knowing. *Metacognition* is the ability to reflect upon and monitor cognitive activity (Flavell, 1985). *Metalinguistic awareness* is the ability to think about and reflect upon the nature and function of language (Pratt & Grieve, 1984). *Metalanguage* is the language used to describe language—terms such as *phoneme, word,* and *phrase* (Tunmer & Herriman, 1984). The Decoding–Spelling Instruction Register, a set of terms necessary for thinking about and discussing decoding and spelling concepts, is described in the section on metalanguage. The ability to monitor whether what has been decoded is correct or incorrect and the capacity to reflect on alternative strategies for decoding unfamiliar words fit into the domain of metaknowledge.

Metacognition

Forrest-Pressley and Waller (1984) suggested that with regard to decoding, metacognition is knowledge about decoding and the ability to control decoding activities through monitoring, predicting accuracy, and deliberately changing decoding strategies. Strategies of interest to Forrest-Pressley and Waller were 1) recognizing whole words, 2) sounding out a word, 3) "guessing" from context, and 4) asking the teacher for the pronunciation of the word. They noted that in order for a teacher to assess a child's knowledge of cognitive processes, it is necessary for the child to have a conscious awareness of these processes and to be able to talk about them. Forrest-Pressley and Waller measured metacognitive aspects of decoding by assessing children's use of decoding strategies and assessing their ability to verbalize the different strategies and predict their efficiency. They concluded that many readers, especially poor readers, have learned to cope instead of learning "why or how a particular strategy is useful" (p. 30).

With respect to decoding, being metacognitively aware means simply that the reader is able to monitor his or her reading in order to identify errors in decoding individual words and is able to select alternative strategies for word identification. Yet unless the student actually knows that he or she has read the word incorrectly and knows how to correct it, the word will remain incorrectly read.

Metalinguistic Awareness

Metacognition involves reflecting on and monitoring any cognitive activity, whereas metalinguistic awareness and metalanguage focus on knowing about language function and structure. The earliest studies in metalinguistic awareness emphasized children's concepts of *reading* and *word* (Reid, 1966). More recent investigations have described the use of language to analyze and discuss language.

Most researchers dealing with metalinguistic awareness—or linguistic aware-ness, as it is often called (Liberman, 1973)—refer primarily to spoken language. Holdaway (1986) viewed metalinguistic awareness as the ability to reflect upon linguistic processes, not simply to use them. For example, to understand phonics is to be explicitly aware of a very sophisticated stratagem. Liberman and Mann re-viewed findings from a number of studies and concluded that the difficulty for most "children who have problems in learning to read is basically linguistic in nature—not visual, or auditory, or motor, or whatever—but rather in the ineffec-tive use of phonologic strategies" (1981, p. 151). Liberman and Mann found that the ability to segment words by phonemes or by syllables was highly correlated with ease of reading acquisition and concluded that "linguistic awareness may be necessary for the acquisition of reading" (p. 154).

Templeton broadened the scope of metalinguistic awareness by referring to it as "the ability to reflect upon and analyze the structures of both spoken and writ-ten language" (1986, p. 295). Thus, metalinguistic awareness provides the student with ways to talk about language.

The introduction to formal schooling and the act of learning to read bring about an increase in metalinguistic awareness. This awareness can be explicitly taught by guiding students to reflect on the patterns they are using and to become more analytical.

Metalanguage

Closely related to metalinguistic awareness is metalanguage, or the language used to talk about both spoken and written language. Reid (1966) discussed the role of language as a mediating process in learning and concept formation. He described the "technical vocabulary" of 5-year-olds as they referred to *pictures, letters, writ-ing,* and *names.*

Several researchers have noted that the learner needs to develop concepts for thinking about reading (Adams, 1990; DeStefano, 1972; Downing, 1979; Yaden & Templeton, 1986) and that a specialized language is useful in this respect. The terms we use provide labels for the concepts we discuss. Few beginning readers (and even their teachers) have adequate vocabularies to discuss reading concepts. To enhance reading and writing instruction, teachers can explicitly teach terms re-lated to language learning.

DeStefano (1972) coined the phrase *Language Instruction Register* for the tech-nical terms used in discussing reading and writing. The terms useful for establish-ing an instruction register for discussing decoding are shown in Table 4.1. Having a shared vocabulary facilitates discussion between teachers and students. When teachers in all grades in a school use the same terms, continuity for talking about decoding and spelling concepts develops throughout the grades.

Table 4.1. Decoding–Spelling Instruction Register

Linguistic terms	Letter–sound correspondences	Morphemes
grapheme	consonant	compound word
phoneme	vowel	prefix
morpheme	short vowel	root
word	long vowel	suffix
syllable	blend	combining form
phonics	consonant digraph	
schwa	vowel digraph	
segmentation	blending	

Source: Henry, 1988b.

MULTISENSORY INSTRUCTION

Multisensory instruction is the linkage of visual, auditory, and kinesthetic–tactile modalities. Students simultaneously link the visual symbol (what they see) with its corresponding sound (what they hear) and kinesthetic–tactile input (what they feel) when they write the pattern accurately and when they say the corresponding sound(s). Teachers are encouraged to use a multisensory approach in these lessons. Even the Sumerians 5000 years ago provided guidelines for multisensory instruction when they encouraged teachers to "make sure that encoding (spelling) and decoding (reading) are connected at every level of instruction via looking (visual memory), listening (auditory memory), and writing (kinesthetic memory)" (McGuinness, 2004, p. 38).

Children do not learn only by considering phonics or by memorizing words by sight. In fact, the visual, auditory, and kinesthetic–tactile modalities are all linked as new spelling patterns and rules are presented. This approach to learning is not new—it was applied to reading in the 1930s by Anna Gillingham and her colleague, Bessie Stillman. Gillingham and Stillman were influenced by the theories of Samuel T. Orton, a physician who also studied reading and reading disorders. Orton proposed a multisensory approach for teaching children with reading problems. For the kinesthetic–tactile modality, he relied on the ideas conveyed by Grace Fernald and Helen Keller in 1921, when they wrote about several cases they had studied:

> Lip and hand kinaesthetic elements seem to be the essential link between the visual cue and the various associations which give it word meaning. In other words, it seems to be necessary for the child to develop a certain kinaesthetic background before he can apperceive the visual sensations for which the printed words form the stimulus. Even the associations between the spoken and the printed word seem not to be fixed without the kinaesthetic links. (p. 376)

This instruction is known today as the Orton–Gillingham approach (Orton, 1966). Gillingham and Stillman insisted that children with specific reading difficulties could not learn to read by sight-word methods, even when these are later rein-

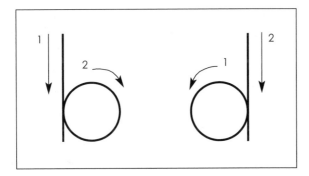

Figure 4.1.   Print letter formation for b and d.

forced by functional, incidental, intrinsic, or **analytic phonics.** Gillingham and Stillman noted that their technique "is based upon the constant use of associations of all of the following: how a letter or word looks, how it sounds and how the speech organs or the hand in writing feels when producing it" (1956, p. 17).

In their manuals, Gillingham and Stillman (1956, 1997) directed teachers to assist children in making numerous linkages. For example, as a child sees a letter, he or she may trace it and say the letter name and/or sound. Or, the teacher may make the sound and the student give it its name.

Correct letter formation is emphasized while children are learning the letters and their corresponding sounds. Because children with dyslexia often persist in reversing letters or transposing letters within words, knowing how to form the letters helps in correcting these reversals. To assist children in correcting reversals, teachers point out the different order of strokes for letter formation. For example, to form *b*, one first draws the vertical line, followed by the circle. In contrast, *d* is formed with the circle (or a partial circle in the shape of *c*) first, followed by the vertical line (see Figure 4.1).

Slingerland (1996) guided students by having them talk through the process for both **manuscript writing** (often called **printing**) and **cursive writing.** For example, as students form *b*, the teacher guides their thinking by saying the following:

> We start at the top and make the tall stem go all the way down. Now go up over the same line without lifting your arm, but stop and think which way the arm is going to go before making the round part. (p. 62)

In contrast, as they write *d*, students learn to say "Round like an *a*, tall stem, straight down to the line" (p. 63). Slightly different directions are given to left-handers. Berninger and Wolf (2009) noted the importance of explicit instruction in handwriting in the first two grades in order to prevent later problems with spelling and written composition.

Margaret Rawson's thoughtful description of multisensory instruction is useful to consider:

> Dyslexic students need a different approach to learning language from that employed in most classrooms. They need to be taught, slowly and thoroughly, the

basic elements of their language—the sounds and the letters which represent them—and how to put these together and take them apart. They have to have their writing hands, eyes, ears, and voices working together in conscious organization and retention of their learning. (as cited in Henry, 1998, p. 1)

Berninger and Wolf concluded that "a multimodal brain system with two sensory input systems (auditory listening and visual reading) and two motor output systems (oral motor productions through the mouth and graphomotor productions through the hand) support literacy learning" (2009, p. 110). This form of instruction is beneficial for all children and is a real necessity for children with specific reading disabilities. (See also Moats & Farrell, 2005.)

LESSON PROCEDURES IN A DISCUSSION FORMAT

Project READ (Calfee & Henry, 1986; Calfee, Henry, & Funderburg, 1988) was developed by a Stanford University research team in collaboration with several elementary schools in the San Francisco Bay area. It provides a discussion-based format for instruction. (Project READ has since been renamed Project READ Plus to avoid confusion with Enfield and Greene's Project Read in Minnesota.) Lessons focus on specific spelling patterns within the historical and structural categories of the language (e.g., consonant blends, spellings of Latin affixes and Greek combining forms) and are designed to be presented sequentially in 30- to 50-min sessions. Each lesson consists of a discussion related to language and reading/spelling concepts. Metalearning comes about not from isolated study but from social exchange. Students and teachers actively think about new patterns and rules. Teachers follow a procedure containing opening, middle, closing, and follow-up activities (see Figure 4.2).

In the opening, the teacher describes the purpose and content of the lesson and explains the lesson procedures. Following the opening, the teacher provides several middle activities. Patterns presented in previous lessons may be reviewed, and new patterns may be introduced. Students generate words fitting the targeted pattern or patterns. Students have the opportunity to read, spell, and discuss the patterns and concepts presented. Students also practice reading and writing common irregular words (e.g., *the, said, love*), often in the context of phrases or sentences. Lessons can be adapted for individual tutorial instruction.

Although this discussion-based procedure may seem scripted, it is not, nor is it based on specific commercial materials. Teachers can bring their own teaching styles and choice of materials to enhance each lesson. For example, teachers may choose to use graphic organizers as they discuss word relationships or use magnetic letters or flipcharts in a variety of activities to reinforce concepts.

A necessary part of these discussion-based lessons is having students fully discuss new patterns and concepts in a small-group format. The teacher facilitates the discussion, carefully introducing new terminology and concepts. The teacher may begin with visual and auditory drills to practice automaticity for letter–sound

```
┌─────────────────────────────────────────────────────┐
│                                                       │
│   Opening                                             │
│                                                       │
│   Middle                                              │
│   Conduct visual, auditory, and blending drills as    │
│   needed.                                             │
│   Review taught pattern(s) and/or rule(s).            │
│   Teach new pattern(s) and/or rule(s).                │
│       Students generate words, if appropriate.        │
│       Discuss new pattern(s), rules(s) and related    │
│          concepts.                                    │
│       Students read numerous words.                   │
│       Students spell numerous words from dictation.   │
│                                                       │
│   Closing                                             │
│   Summarize and reflect on material covered.          │
│   Have final discussion.                              │
│                                                       │
│   Follow-up                                           │
│   Have students practice in groups or alone.          │
│   Give after-school assignments.                      │
│                                                       │
└─────────────────────────────────────────────────────┘
```

Figure 4.2. Project READ lesson format. (*Sources:* Calfee & Henry, 1986; Calfee, Henry, & Funderburg, 1988.)

and sound–letter relationships. Students practice using strategies for decoding and spelling unknown words as they read and spell single words, phrases, and sentences. Older students practice analyzing long, unfamiliar words. While reading multisyllabic words, students follow the sequence that most fluent readers use when they try to decode a word. Students first check for recognizable morphemes (affixes and roots) and, if necessary, divide words into syllables. Only if these two strategies fail do students sound out individual letters (using letter–sound correspondences). In spelling, students are taught to repeat the word, to listen and count the number of syllables, and to identify common affixes and roots. As with decoding, students use letter–sound correspondences to spell only after attempting to use the morpheme and syllable strategies. Students learn productive spelling rules (e.g., rules for adding suffixes) to assist in spelling words from dictation.

Numerous opportunities for practice in both reading and spelling are provided for each pattern presented. Students read words, phrases, and sentences containing targeted patterns. Students also spell words, phrases, and sentences from dictation. Teachers should be aware that frequent review is necessary for many students and beneficial for all. (Sample lessons are provided at the end of this chapter and in the final four chapters of this book.)

At the end of each session, the teacher and students review and summarize the concepts and patterns learned that day. This closing is an important facet of any lesson. During the closing, students and the teacher summarize and reflect on the lesson content, structural patterns, and procedures. The teacher assigns follow-up activities for many of the lessons in order to reinforce new concepts and strategies. Some of these activities take place directly after the lesson, and others are to be completed as homework. For example, students might be asked to underline vowel digraphs in a passage or find words containing Latin word roots in a newspaper article. Students might look for as many Greek words as possible in a chapter of their science text. Or students may write a paragraph using specific patterns (e.g., consonant blends, prefixes, suffixes).

As each pattern and its corresponding sound are taught, the teacher should use the following sequence: Show a card with the new pattern printed on it. Give the sound and a key word (a common noun beginning with the new sound). Have the students repeat the sound and then write the target letter or letters. Models of the pattern should be provided on paper for each student. He or she traces the letter(s) several times while giving the sound. The student then copies the pattern and finally writes it from memory, always saying the corresponding sound.

Letter formation is of utmost importance. Teachers need to monitor letter formation as students begin to write new patterns. This kinesthetic–tactile reinforcement is necessary to promote learning of the pattern. Careful attention should be paid to pencil grasp, writing posture, and actual letter formation. Teachers should schedule writing practice for students who have difficulty with either manuscript or cursive letter formation. Handwriting drills may include tracing and copying a model, working at the chalkboard, writing in rice or in sand, or drawing large letters on newsprint. Connections between cursive letters need to be specifically taught. Difficult connections include cursive *br, be, on, own, ou, os, wh, wr, re, ro, ry, eri, ory* and *of*.

As each new consonant and vowel spelling pattern is presented, students can place the pattern in the appropriate cell in the blank 2 × 3 matrix (see Figure 4.3). Once students have mastered several consonant and vowel sounds, visual and auditory drills, along with **blending** drills, should be incorporated into each lesson. The following drills, modeled after Gillingham–Stillman (1956, 1997) drills, foster automaticity and fluency.

Visual Drills

The teacher should make or purchase 4 × 6 cards for each common grapheme (listed in Tables 3.1 and 3.2). For visual drills, the teacher shows students the patterns already taught, one pattern at a time. Students can respond individually or as a group with the appropriate sound(s). If the sound given is incorrect, students should trace the letter on paper or on their desk with the index finger of their writing hand. This kinesthetic–tactile reinforcement may provide a stimulus for the correct response. If not, the teacher should give the sound and have students write the pattern and simultaneously say the correct sound.

Auditory Drills

During auditory drills, the teacher says the sound, and students can respond individually or as a group with the letter name(s). Students should repeat the sound for kinesthetic and auditory reinforcement. Students should not guess the sound. When the students do not know the correct response, they should be shown the appropriate card; they then write the letter(s) while saying the sound aloud.

Consonants		
Single	Blends	Digraphs
Vowels		
Short/long	r- and l-controlled	Digraphs

Figure 4.3. Blank 2 × 3 letter–sound correspondence matrix. (From Calfee, R.C., et al. [1981–1984]. *The book: Components of reading instruction.* Unpublished manuscript, Stanford University, California; adapted by permission.)

Blending Drills

Blending sounds together is an extremely important linguistic task as students begin to read words. Card blending drills help students identify changes in syllable patterns as the teacher changes the letters that are displayed. Initial consonant graphemes, including blends and digraphs, are laid face up on the table, followed by medial vowels, and then by final consonants to make one-syllable words or nonwords. For groups, the teacher can set the cards on the ledge of the chalkboard or use a flipchart with three columns. The teacher exchanges one or more of the displayed cards with new cards to make new words, real or nonsense, and the students sound out each grapheme before saying the complete syllable. Cards should be placed in a logical order following correct orthographic sequence. For example, *x* should not come in an initial position, and *-ck* should not follow a vowel digraph. The letters *l, f,* or *s* should not be placed singly at the end of the word, because each is usually doubled following a short vowel sound. Beginning readers need a great deal of exposure to card drills. Teachers are reminded to change the cards infrequently at first, giving students the opportunity to practice each new letter and sound. Figure 4.4 illustrates a drill for students with several learned consonant and vowel patterns.

In the setup shown in Figure 4.4, the teacher first lays cards on the table to spell the word *mad.* Students sound out and blend the word /măd/. Then the

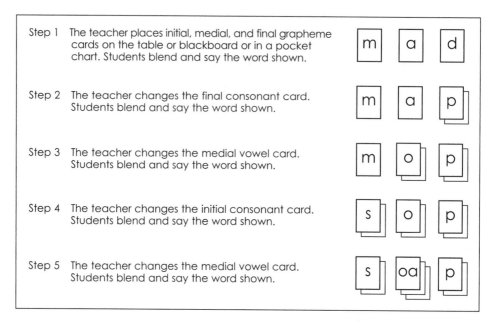

Step 1	The teacher places initial, medial, and final grapheme cards on the table or blackboard or in a pocket chart. Students blend and say the word shown.	m a d
Step 2	The teacher changes the final consonant card. Students blend and say the word shown.	m a p
Step 3	The teacher changes the medial vowel card. Students blend and say the word shown.	m o p
Step 4	The teacher changes the initial consonant card. Students blend and say the word shown.	s o p
Step 5	The teacher changes the medial vowel card. Students blend and say the word shown.	s oa p

Figure 4.4. Card blending drills.

teacher takes away the *d* card and replaces it with *p*. Students then read /măp/. Then the teacher changes the vowel to *o*, and students read /mŏp/. They then read /sŏp/ when the teacher changes the initial consonant to *s*. When the teacher replaces the *o* card with the vowel digraph *oa*, students read /sōp/, and so forth as the teacher exchanges the cards. The teacher decides which graphemes to use based on the patterns that the students need to practice the most.

While blending the sounds on the cards, students should connect the vowel sound to the initial consonant sound (e.g., /mă/, /măd/; /mă/, /măp/; /mŏ/, /mŏp/) to prevent choppy blending. (Choppy blending produces a schwa after an initial consonant that does not actually exist in the syllable.) The teacher should be sure that students say each word as a whole after saying its separate sounds. Once students blend easily and fluently, the blending drills may be given less often, and word lists can be substituted to enhance automaticity and fluency. Students read the words in the lists, blending when necessary. Word lists are more effective for the learning of words and nonwords with four, five, and six sound units and for the learning of multisyllabic words (e.g., *stick, blimp, splint, basket*).

Following the card blending drills, teachers generally review a previously taught pattern or rule with students, introduce a new pattern or rule, and provide numerous opportunities for practice. Students read words, phrases, and sentences containing the target patterns and spell words from dictation.

─────────────── | **Sample Lessons** | ───────────────

Two sample lessons, one for primary grade students and one for upper elementary or middle school students, may be useful to review. Although the format for discussion-based instruction is similar for lower and upper level lessons, the content differs between the levels, as shown in the second lesson, which focuses on Greek combining forms. Teachers are urged to overplan for discussion-based lessons. Teachers should try never to run out of things to teach. In addition, teachers should have a new nonphonetic word or a new spelling pattern ready to teach, a couple of sentences to dictate, or some phonemic awareness activities for review in case the lesson moves faster than planned.

 In all of the lesson plans in this book, answers are presented as [*bracketed, italicized text*].

| LESSON | **Consonant Blends**

Grade 1 or 2 Prerequisites: Knowledge of consonant and short vowel sounds

Opening

"Today we will continue to study consonant blends. You may remember that when two or three consonants are adjacent in the same syllable and keep their individual sounds they are called consonant blends. We will read and spell numerous words that contain consonant blends."

Middle

"Who can name some common blends?" Write the examples given by the students on the board. If students name a consonant digraph, remind students that in a consonant blend each sound has to be heard and then blended together.

Write the following words on the board one column at a time, or have them on a flipchart:

spot	drab	silk
clap	stab	best
blot	swim	rust
flat	twin	risk
slot	split	bend
plant	frill	melt
crib	left	lump

next	blend	spend
hint	drift	plump
sift	twist	stamp
bulk	blimp	crust
help	swift	print

"Let's read the first list aloud. Where are the blends?" [*at the beginnings of the words*] Circle the blends as students name them.

"Let's read the second list. Where are the blends?" [*at the ends of the words*] Circle the blends as before.

"Let's read the third list. Where are the blends?" [*at the beginnings and ends of the words*] Circle the blends as before.

Ask students to spell 10–20 words containing blends. Dictate each word twice before moving on to the next word. Alone or in groups, students should repeat each word, isolate the blend(s), then write the word while sounding it aloud.

Closing

"What kind of patterns did we work on today? Who can define a consonant blend? Where do they come in words? What did we do with consonant blends?"

Follow-Up

Have students look for consonant blends in their literature book or in a content area textbook.

After reviewing the concept of blends, present some patterns individually. Begin with *s* blends (i.e., *st, sl, sm, sn, sp, sk, sc, sw*) and go on to blends ending in *r* or *l*. Then add other initial and final blends. Have students trace, copy, write, and say sounds. Place new patterns in the consonant blends cell on the 2 × 3 matrix (see Figure 4.3). See if students can generate words beginning with each new blend before reading and spelling numerous words, phrases, and sentences.

From Henry, M.K. (2010). *WORDS: Integrated decoding and spelling instruction based on word origin and word structure* (2nd ed., pp. 13–15). Austin, TX: PRO-ED; adapted by permission.

 Introducing Greek Combining Forms

Grade 5 Prerequisites: Knowledge of most letter–sound correspondences

Opening

"You'll remember that many of the Latin word roots studied previously were actually borrowed from the Greeks. The Greek word parts are often called combining forms because the two roots are of equal stress and importance and combine to form a word, as in many Anglo-Saxon compound words. Some of the forms appear only at the beginning of a word (and so may be considered prefixes), others come at the end (and are sometimes thought of as suffixes), and some forms can be used in either position.

"Here are some words of Greek origin. Do any of you know what is 'Greek' about the letter–sound correspondences in these words?" Show students that although Greek-based words contain many of the same letter–sound correspondences found in Anglo-Saxon and Latin-based words, Greek-based words also have unique letter–sound relationships (e.g., *ph* says /f/ as in *photograph; ch* says /k/ as in *chemist; y* is either a short or long /i/ sound as in *physician* or *typhoon*, respectively). Write words such as *photograph, phonology, physician, orchestra, chemical, chlorophyll,* and *hydrometer* on the board.

Middle

"Today we will be introduced to six new combining forms and their English meanings." Introduce the new combining forms, and have students carefully write each form, along with its meaning, on their paper.

phon, phono (sound)	*auto* (self)
photo (light)	*tele* (distant)
graph, gram (written/drawn)	*ology* (study), from *logos, logue* (speech, word)

"Can you generate words containing the combining forms? You may add other suffixes or combining forms to make words." Write the students' words on the board or on a transparency. Have the students then read other words you have prepared that contain some of the new forms, such as

phone	phonics	phonogram	phonology
phonological	phoneme	phonemic	photosynthesis
phonograph	graphite	graphics	autograph
photograph	photography	photographer	photocopy
photoflash	photogram	telecast	telegram
telephone	telephoto	telethon	automation
automatic	automobile	photology	telephotography
monologue	prologue	dialogue	epilogue

"Which school subjects might use these Greek-based words?" [*science, literature, social studies, often also math*]

Have students spell words containing the six target combining forms from dictation.

Have students read and spell sentences containing Latin- and Greek-based word parts, such as the following:

He *collected* several *autographs* from the *conductors.*

The *photographer* used her new *telephoto* lens on the *spectators.*

Phonics instruction is useful in *developing* reading and writing skills.

Closing

"What kind of words were we reading and spelling?" [*Greek-based words*] "What is the meaning of *auto, tele, phon/phono*?" [*self, distant, sound*] "How does knowing the meaning of the combining forms enhance your vocabulary?"

Follow-Up

Have students look for Greek-based words in science and mathematics textbooks.

Continue adding additional combining forms in subsequent lessons, including these combining forms: *micro, meter, therm, bio, scope, hydro, helio, biblio, crat/cracy, geo, metro, polis, dem, derm, hypo, chron, cycl, hyper,* and *chrom.*

From Henry, M.K. (2010). *WORDS: Integrated decoding and spelling instruction based on word origin and word structure* (2nd ed., pp. 49–51). Austin, TX: PRO-ED; and Henry, M.K., & Redding, N.C. (2002). *Patterns for success in reading and spelling* (2nd ed., pp. 281–284). Austin, TX: PRO-ED; adapted by permission.

SUMMARY

Students need ample opportunities to read and spell many words containing the patterns targeted in discussion-based instruction. Words should be read and spelled as single words, in phrases, and in sentences. Teachers should follow up with reading of connected text as in textbooks, magazines, or newspapers. More examples of discussion-based lessons are found in the following chapters. In addition, interesting word facts and information for teachers appear in Word Wisdom highlights. Some of this material can be shared with students. Subsequent chapters also include numerous sample activities for reinforcement.

CHAPTER 5

First Steps

Early Instruction for Effective Decoding and Spelling

We know the importance of early oral interactions between young children and their families, friends, and caregivers. As Berninger and Wolf stated, "Oral language is the key to learning at school" (2009, p. 31).

Hart and Risley (1995) discussed the quality interactions they saw in everyday parenting. They noted that both the vocabulary that parents use with their children and the sentences they speak transmit cultural values and expectations. Hart and Risley concluded that experiencing frequent though brief and encouraging interactions in the first 2–3 years of life contributes to "breadth of knowledge, analytic and symbolic competencies, self-confidence, and problem solving, which are among the interlocking attitudes, skills, and knowledge required for entry and success in an increasingly technological world of work" (p. 192).

As toddlers gain more facility with oral language, their interests in "grown-up" activities may grow. They may see their parents reading books and magazines and writing grocery lists or letters either on paper or on the computer. Children become aware of print tasks. Parents often wonder how they can capitalize on these interests in a way that may improve their child's future academic performance.

Scientists have found that literacy development begins long before formal instruction. In 1985, the Center for Reading published *Becoming a Nation of Readers*

(Anderson, Hiebert, Scott, & Wilkinson, 1985). The authors recommended that to promote reading and writing, parents provide books, letters, magazines, and other print matter in the home. Anderson et al. promoted literacy experiences in the home and community. These literacy activities include frequently reading to the child, taking the child to libraries, subscribing to magazines, and linking familiar signs (e.g., McDonald's) with the words on the signs. Children do explore print on their own with active engagement from adults. Exposure to print plays an extremely important role as a predictor of many verbal skills, including reading acquisition (Stanovich, 1996).

Manguel wrote that as early as 1485, the Italian scholar Leon Battista Alberti noted that children should be taught the alphabet at the earliest possible age: "Children learned to read phonetically by repeating letters pointed out by their nurse or mother in a hornbook or alphabet sheet" (1996, p. 72). Manguel remembered, "I myself was taught this way, by my nurse reading out to me the bold-type letters from an old English picture-book; I was made to repeat the sounds again and again" (p. 72).

PRESCHOOL

The preschool years should be a time of exploration and discovery. Cicci stated that "children need the preschool years as a time of exploration and discovery—for general cognitive, language, emotional, and social development that form the undergirdings for the rest of their lives" (1995, p. 1). Parents and caregivers can foster later reading development through informal, everyday activities involving language in meaningful ways. Children benefit from pretend play as they give tea parties or as they "cook" a meal using plastic bowls, utensils, and measuring cups. Children need to learn to categorize and classify objects by following such instructions as "Put all of the yellow objects here" or "Find all of the round objects on the table." Children can begin to match like objects as they find "the four red apples." The richer the oral language base, the better for reading acquisition. Parents can also encourage writing by having finger paints, chalk, felt-tip markers, and other tools available. Parents can play with their child as he or she explores this new domain. Oral and written language relationships between parent and child continue to be important throughout the first years of formal schooling.

Many children attend preschool or child care centers during their early years. Fielding-Barnsley recommended that preschool teachers prepare children for later reading instruction:

> To me, this means that the child arrives at school with five critical building blocks for literacy in place: (1) letter identification, the ability to recognize and label some letters of the alphabet; (2) phonological awareness, an appreciation that spoken words are made up of, and can be broken into, small speech elements; (3) vocabulary knowledge, an age-appropriate ability to produce and understand a wide range of terms; (4) print concepts, an understanding of the

characteristics of books, the purposes for reading and writing, and so forth; and (5) motivation, a positive attitude toward books and reading and a desire to learn more. (1999, p. 6)

A comprehensive book on the importance of rich literacy environments during the preschool years for later literacy acquisition is *Beginning Literacy with Language,* edited by Dickinson and Tabors (2001). The book includes three sections supporting language and literacy development in the home, the preschool classroom, and homes and classrooms together. This accumulation of research findings and implications for future instruction is invaluable for teachers and parents alike. Dickinson (2001) concluded that preschool teachers who use varied vocabulary, challenge students to think, and stimulate their curiosity and imagination support literacy development in kindergarten.

The 5- to 6-year-old child typically speaks in complete sentences, has a vocabulary of about 2,500 words, asks questions using complex verb forms, and answers questions more specifically than a 4-year-old does. Oller, Oller, and Baden stated that the typical 4- to 5-year-old child

- Pays attention to a short story and answers simple questions about it

- Hears and understands most of what is said at home and in school

- [Makes] voice sounds [that are] clear like [those of] other [age-matched peers]

- Uses sentences that give lots of details (e.g., "I like to read my books")

- Tells stories that stick to topic

- Communicates easily with other children and adults

- Says most sounds correctly except a few like *l, s, r, v, z, j, ch, sh,* and *th*

- Uses the same grammar as the rest of the family (2006)

Some educators believe that reading and writing develop simultaneously in natural contexts, and some children do appear to "pick up" the system with little difficulty. Indeed, preschoolers invent their own spelling systems long before they are able to read (Read, 1971). These systems persist well into first grade and may seem implausible to parents and teachers. Although students know a system of phonetic relationships that have not been formally taught, they do not know a set of lexical representations and the system of phonetic rules that account for much of standard spelling. Typical invented spellings include *da* (day), *kam* (came), *tabil* (table), *lade* (lady), *fel* (feel), *lik* (like), and *tigr* (tiger).

Clearly, most children require some formal instruction in order to learn to read, spell, and write. Children need to learn specific conventions of print, such as writing from left to right, top to bottom, and front to back. When these conventions are taught, the following problem does not exist. Josh's preschool teacher told Josh's mother that her son was probably "dyslexic" because he copied three sentences from the board going from right to left and reversed or transposed many letters. Yet Josh was only 4 years old, and no one had taught him the conventions of print, the letters, or even how to hold a crayon for writing.

KINDERGARTEN

Kindergarten marks that magical transition year when children expand the more private, informal language of the home or child care to the more public, formal language of the school. Historically, kindergarten has been a time for developing oral language in the form of listening and speaking activities and a time for developing physical and motor control. Today, however, the kindergarten curriculum moves directly into reading and writing as formal instruction in literacy begins. Still, teachers and parents can encourage listening and speaking activities through poetry and rhyme, songs, and sociodramatic play. Listening activities such as listening for sounds and following directions need to be fostered. More formal speaking is encouraged through show-and-tell times as children bring their toys or pets to share or as they retell stories.

Prior to learning letter–sound correspondences, children benefit from training in phonological and phonemic awareness tasks, such as rhyming, segmentation, and blending. When they lack awareness of the role that sounds play in words, children rarely learn to read easily. Fortunately, training in this area is often successful in teaching children to isolate individual sounds, to segment words into the sounds and syllables necessary for spelling later on, and to blend sounds and syllables to make words (Ball, 1993; Tangel & Blachman, 1995).

The National Reading Panel reported that "teaching two PA [phonological awareness] skills to children has greater long-term benefits for reading than teaching only one PA skill or teaching a global array of skills" (National Institute of Child Health and Human Development, 2000, p. 2-21). The panel noted that learning the two skills of blending and **segmenting** had a larger effect on spelling performance than did a multiple-skill treatment.

Phonological and phonemic awareness are key factors in reading acquisition. Deficits in such awareness are characteristic early markers of dyslexia (Uhry, 2005). Parents and teachers can assess this ability through informal word play and games. Children can be asked to rhyme words and manipulate sounds. For example, the teacher can say the word *sat* and ask for as many rhyming words as possible. The teacher can say the word *meat* and ask the child to say the word without the /m/ sound, or the teacher can say the word *plant* and have the child say the word without the /t/ sound. In order to assess blending ability, the teacher can say three sounds, such as /t/ /ĭ/ /n/, and see if the child can pull the sounds together to say a word (*tin*). Segmentation requires the ability to break words and syllables into their constituent sounds. For example, the teacher can say *butterfly* and find out whether the child can segment the syllables as /bŭt/ /tər/ /flī/. Or the teacher can say the word *map* and see whether the child responds with /m/ /ă/

/p/. These activities can be presented one-to-one, in small groups, or in large groups.

Note that these activities do not require knowledge of alphabet letters. Emphasis is on the sounds at either the phoneme or the syllable level. The teacher must articulate all syllables and sounds very clearly and precisely. The teacher can give children visual cues by asking students to observe his or her lips. Remember that students can also receive direct training in phoneme segmentation, blending, and sound manipulation.

Phonological and Phonemic Awareness Activities

Activities to develop phonological awareness skills include the following:

- *Rhyming:* The teacher says two or three words that rhyme and asks for additional rhyming words. For example, "Here are some rhyming words: *pat, sat, hat.* Can you tell me some other words that rhyme with these three words?" [*fat, mat, cat, flat, slat,* etc.]

- *Syllable awareness:* The teacher says several multisyllabic words that are familiar to students and asks the students to count the syllables. For example, "How many word parts do you hear in *Carlos, Martha, city, rereading, population?*" [2, 2, 2, 3, 4] Or "Clap the word chunks (or syllables) in these words: *Emily, Trevor, Allison, alphabet.*" [3, 2, 3, 3]

- *Sound awareness:* The teacher clearly articulates one-syllable words that each have two to six sounds. For example, "How many sounds do you hear in *cow, sheep, stamp?*" [2, 3, 5]

- *Syllable deletion:* The teacher says compound words or other multisyllabic words and asks students to delete the initial or final syllable. For example, "Say *railroad* without *road.*" [*rail*] "Say *sailboat* without *sail.*" [*boat*]

- *Sound deletion:* The teacher says a one-syllable word and asks students to delete the initial or final consonant sound or to delete a sound within a consonant blend. For example, "Say *pink* without /p/." [*ink*] "Say *belt* without /t/." [*bel*] "Say *blimp* without /m/." [*blip*] "Say *plan* without /l/." [*pan*]

 The deletion of blends, especially in the last two sound deletion examples here, is considerably more difficult than the deletion of single consonants. Teachers should be sure to choose target words carefully. For example, do not say, "Say *wing* without /n/," because *n* in the *-ing* pattern does not say /n/.

- *Syllable blending:* The teacher says two syllables and asks children to put the syllables together to form a word. For example, "Blend these word parts and make a word: *Car/los, va/ca/tion.*" [*Carlos, vacation*]

- *Syllable segmentation:* The teacher says a multisyllabic word and asks students to separate the word into its parts. For example, "Break each word into its parts: *Lisa, cucumber.*" [*Li/sa; cu/cum/ber*]

- *Sound blending:* The teacher says three to six sounds and asks students to put the sounds together to make a real word. For example, "Blend these sounds to make a real word: /m/ /ă/ /p/, /m/ /ĭ/ /s/ /t/." [*map, mist*]

- *Sound segmentation:* The teacher says a one-syllable word and asks students to separate the word into its parts. For example, "Break each word into its parts: *pan, plan, grasp*." [/p/ /ă/ /n/, /p/ /l/ /ă/ /n/, /g/ /r/ /ă/ /s/ /p/]

Blending and segmenting words into syllables are easier tasks than blending and segmenting syllables into sounds. Many 6-year-olds are unable to accurately blend and segment. Also, blending and segmenting words containing consonant blends are especially difficult for many children. (See the end of this chapter for several resources for teaching phonological awareness.)

BEGINNING TO READ AND WRITE

As mentioned previously, once children enter kindergarten, more formal literacy instruction begins. Most children are eager and willing to learn to read and look forward to learning to read and write. Even those with little exposure to print expect to begin to read in kindergarten. Children become acquainted with symbols and what they represent. Informal activities to promote future literacy are useful. While reading a story to children, parents or teachers can ask questions and ask children to predict what comes next. Children may begin to identify specific letters. As they do this, they can look for letters on billboards and street signs while in the car with their parents. Parents can play language games with children and embed literacy experiences naturally into routine events.

Letter naming is an important factor in learning to read. Teachers need to know which letter names their students know. Children learn letter names at varying rates. Students who are at risk for reading disability need significantly more time learning letter names than those who are not at risk for having trouble learning to read and spell.

Teachers must also find out if their students know the relationship between upper- and lowercase letters. Many children do not automatically make these connections. Understanding of this relationship can be assessed by having children play a card game such as Go Fish or by having children try to match upper- and lowercase letters placed in a bowl.

As they begin to learn letter names, children need to know how to form the corresponding symbols. Teachers need to provide a model of the target letter for children to trace, copy, and name several times before students write the letter from memory. As students learn to form letters, the importance of appropriate pencil grasp and correct writing posture cannot be overemphasized. Teachers should monitor pencil grasp, posture, and letter formation carefully.

In some kindergartens, students begin to learn the speech sounds that correspond with the letters. A suggested order of presentation can be found in Chapter 6.

Lessons can follow the format and procedures discussed in Chapter 4. The following lesson provides a possible script for a lesson on rhyming.

| LESSON | **Rhyming** |

Opening

"Today we'll talk about words that rhyme. Who knows what a rhyme is?" [*Students may respond by saying rhyming words, by noting they sound alike at the end, or by actually reciting a poem.*] "Listen to several common rhymes and hear words that rhyme. We'll practice listening for rhyming words together."

Middle

"A rhyme happens when words end in the same sounds. Listen to *at, cat, fat, sat.* How do they end?" [/ăt/] "Can you think of other words that end in /ăt/? [*mat, hat, rat, pat, that, chat, vat,* etc.]

"Here's a favorite poem. I'll read it and you tell me why it's a poem." [*It has rhyming words, and poems often have words that rhyme.*]

Little Boy Blue, come blow your horn.

The sheep's in the meadow, the cow's in the corn.

Where's the boy that looks after the sheep?

He's under the haystack, fast asleep.

"Which words rhyme?" [*horn, corn; sheep, asleep*]

"Let's see if we can make some other rhyming words. Who can say a word that rhymes with *pin* and *thin*?" Write the words on the board, and show that the letter patterns at the end of rhyming words may be similar.

Closing

"What did we learn about today?" [*Rhyming words; they sound alike at the end of the word; words that rhyme may also look alike at the end.*]

Follow-Up

"Get a partner and make up a poem together." Write the poems if students are not yet able to write.

 The following guided question activities can be done with or without the teacher, individually or in groups or "term teams."

Classroom Activities

KINDERGARTEN: PHONOLOGICAL AND PHONEMIC AWARENESS

Numerous phonological awareness activities appear in *Phonemic Awareness in Young Children: A Classroom Curriculum* (Adams, Foorman, Lundberg, & Beeler, 1998) and *Road to the Code: A Phonological Awareness Program for Young Children* (Blachman, Ball, Black, & Tangel, 2000), both published by Paul H. Brookes Publishing Co. Adams et al. included the following types of activities in *Phonemic Awareness in Young Children*.

- *Listening to Sequence of Sounds (p. 17):* Children listen to distinctive sounds that the teacher makes with household objects, such as the sound of a whistle blowing, a bell ringing, scratching, cutting with scissors, or an apple being eaten. Students first identify single sounds and then identify each one of a sequence of sounds.

- *Nonsense (p. 23):* Children close their eyes as the teacher tells a familiar story or poem but reverses or substitutes words, such as "Song a sing of sixpence" or "Baa baa purple sheep." Children are asked to detect such changes whenever they occur.

Adams et al. also described activities for analysis and synthesis (segmentation and blending) of words and for listening for two to four phonemes in a word (e.g., *pie,* two sounds; *spy,* three sounds; *spice,* four sounds).

In *Road to the Code,* Blachman et al. (2000) showed teachers how to extend phonological awareness while introducing letters that correspond with their phonemes. Students repeat alliterative sentences spoken by the teacher. For example, as children learn the letter *s,* they practice saying "Six silly, slimy, slithering snakes." Students then trace the letter in the air.

ACTIVITY **Beginning Reading**

The following activities can supplement formal instruction as children learn to read.

- Have numerous alphabet books in the classroom. Read to the children. Ask them to find pictures of objects beginning with target letters. (Several excellent alphabet books are listed at the end of this chapter.)

- Purchase or make wooden or cardboard puzzles that allow children to put the letters of the alphabet in sequential order.

- Have children play Go Fish to match upper- and lowercase letters with a partner.

- Use plastic letters on the overhead projector. Ask children, "Give me words that begin with *m* /m/," as you show the letter *m* on the projector.

- See if children can recognize different forms of a letter (e.g., A, a, /a/).

- Match visual to visual. Show the word *man*. Have the students circle the correct word out of four that are printed on the paper (e.g., map fan (man) sat).

- Match auditory to visual. Say the word *map*. Have the students circle the correct word out of four that are printed on the paper (e.g., man fit fat (map)).

- When children know several consonants and at least one vowel, make words with plastic letters on the overhead projector. Manipulate the letters to form new words. With only *s, f, t, n, g, p,* and *i*, one can make more than 30 words, such as *it, sit, fit, pit, in, fin, pin, sin, pig, fig, nip, sip,* and *tip*. Nonwords can also be made using these letters.

- Pick a topic, such as vegetables, colors, famous people, or fruits. Have each child, one after the other, say an appropriate item in alphabetical order. For example, vegetables could be *asparagus, broccoli, corn, dandelion greens, eggplant,* and so forth. (This is a favorite activity of my young granddaughters while riding in the car. They now find their own categories. My favorite is celebrities with double letters, such as Ansel Adams, Donald Duck, Marilyn Monroe, etc.)

- Give each child (or small group of children) a set of letters. Ask the children to find target letters. Point to one of the letters in the set and ask children if that letter comes near the beginning or near the end of the alphabet. See if the children can put the set of letters in alphabetical order.

- As children begin to learn words, have them look for specific words in a story. For example, while reading "Goldilocks and the Three Bears" out loud, have children raise their hands when they hear the words *bear* and *bears.*

- Play games such as letter or word bingo. Or play "Spin the Wheel," in which players must read the letter(s) or word(s) the dial points to.

- Read enjoyable stories such as *Horton Hears a Who* by Dr. Seuss. Ask the children to listen for the different kinds of animals that try to stop Horton from saving his friends. When done reading, ask the children to recall the animals' names and the ways they tried to stop Horton.

ACTIVITY | Beginning Writing

Kindergartners can also be given formal writing activities.

- Provide a model for tracing and copying letters as they are introduced. Display an alphabet strip showing upper- and lowercase letters on the wall for children to refer to.

- Provide opportunities to draw and print using markers, crayons, and pencils at a writing area that is separate from the book area or classroom library. This writing area should be stocked with paper, writing utensils, letter stencils, and letter shapes (e.g., large plastic or cardboard letters).

- Encourage students to spell words that they know how to read.

- Use computer programs, such as Kidspiration (Inspiration Software; see http://www.inspiration.com/productinfo/kidspiration/index.cfm), to give young children opportunities to match pictures and words and to create stories.

Kindergarten

The word *kindergarten* comes from the German *kinder,* meaning "children," and *garten,* meaning "garden." Kindergarten was originally a place for children to prepare for formal schooling. Lessons and activities centered around play, games, music, drama, and conversation. Now, however, kindergarten is much less playful, and more and more instruction is taking place.

Alphabet

Firmage explained that the French introduced the word *alphabet* into England and that the word was in common use by the 16th century: "The Old English term was 'abecede,' which by the mid-fourteenth century had shortened in Middle English to 'abece,' 'abse,' or 'ABC'" (1993, pp. 58–59). Long before the term came to Great Britain, *alpha* became the first letter of the Greek alphabet and *beta* the second letter.

RESOURCES FOR TEACHERS

Phonological and Phonemic Awareness

Adams, M.J., Foorman, B.R., Lundberg, I., & Beeler, T. (1998). *Phonemic awareness in young children: A classroom curriculum.* Baltimore: Paul H. Brookes Publishing Co.

Blachman, B.A., Ball, E.W., Black, R., & Tangel, D.M. (2000). *Road to the code: A phonological awareness program for young children.* Baltimore: Paul H. Brookes Publishing Co.

Catts, H., & Olsen, T. (1993a). *Sounds abound: Listening, rhyming, and reading.* East Moline, IL: LinguiSystems.

Catts, H., & Olsen, T. (1993b). *Sounds abound game* [Board game]. East Moline, IL: LinguiSystems.

Goldsworthy, C. (1998). *Sourcebook of phonological awareness activities: Children's classic literature.* San Diego: Singular Publishing Group.

National Institute of Child Health and Human Development. (2000). *Teaching children to read: An evidence-based assessment of the scientific research literature on reading and its implications for reading instruction* (National Institutes of Health Publication No. 00-4754). Washington, DC: U.S. Government Printing Office. (See Chapter 2 in particular.)

Torgesen, J., & Bryant, B. (1997). *Phonological awareness training for reading.* Austin, TX: PRO-ED.

Alphabet Books: A Few Favorites

Anno, M. (1974). *Anno's alphabet.* New York: Thomas Y. Crowell (hardcover), HarperCollins (softcover).

Base, G. (1986). *Animalia.* New York: Harry N. Abrams.

Bowen, B. (1991). *Antler, bear, canoe: A Northwoods alphabet year.* Boston: Little, Brown.

Cassie, B., & Pallotta, J. (1995). *The butterfly alphabet book.* Watertown, MA: Charlsbridge.

Gorey, E. (1997). *The Gashlycrumb tinies* (Reprint ed.). Orlando, FL: Harcourt.

Gustafson, S. (1990). *Alphabet soup: A feast of letters.* Chicago: Calico Books.

Henry, M.K. (2007). *The Madeline Island ABC book.* LaPointe, WI: Loon Coommons Press.

Jonas, A. (1990). *Aardvarks, disembark.* New York: Greenwillow Books.

Kellogg, S. (1987). *Aster Aardvark's alphabet adventures.* New York: Morrow Junior Books.

Manuelian, P.D. (1991). *Hieroglyphs from A to Z* [Book with punch-out stencils]. Boston: Museum of Fine Arts.

Musgrove, M. (1977). *Ashanti to Zulu.* New York: Dial Books.

Napier, M. (2002). *Z is for Zamboni: A hockey alphabet.* Chelsea, MI: Sleeping Bear Press.

Pallotta, J. (1995). *The flower alphabet book.* Watertown, MA: Charlsbridge. (Many other themed alphabet books by this author are available from Charlsbridge.)

Smith, L., & Kalscheur, J.F. (2003). *ABC's naturally: A child's guide to the alphabet through nature.* Black Earth, WI: Trails Books.

Wargin, K. (2002). *V is for Viking: A Minnesota alphabet.* Chelsea, MI: Sleeping Bear Press. (ABC books for numerous states are available from Sleeping Bear Press.)

Wegman, W. (1994). *ABC.* New York: Hyperion.

Wilks, M. (1986). *The ultimate alphabet.* New York: Henry Holt.

Yolen, J. (1990). *Elphabet: An ABC of elves.* Boston: Little, Brown.

WEB SITES OF INTEREST TO TEACHERS AND PARENTS

American Speech-Language-Hearing Association, http://www.asha.org

Get Ready to Read (National Center for Learning Disabilities), http://www.get readytoread.org

International Dyslexia Association, http://www.interdys.org

Kidspiration (Inspiration Software), http://www.inspiration.com/productinfo/ kidspiration/index.cfm

Reading Rockets, http://www.readingrockets.org

ReadWriteThink (International Reading Association), http://www.readwritethink .org

CHAPTER 6

Beginning Readers

Time for the Anglo-Saxon Layer of Language

Most children entering first grade eagerly await the introduction to formal reading and writing instruction. During first grade, children need to master most of the alphabetic code. Instruction on the alphabetic code focuses on pairing the sounds of the language (or phonemes) with letters or combinations of letters of the alphabet (or graphemes). In addition, students need to identify common sight words, many of them nonphonetic. When formal instruction in reading and spelling begins, teachers need to be familiar with common Anglo-Saxon letter–sound correspondences, important irregular words, common syllable patterns, and Anglo-Saxon morphemes (base words, compound words, prefixes, and suffixes).

Teachers must first find out what each child knows about the alphabet, common patterns, and related sounds. Purchase or make cards with the major orthographic patterns (i.e., consonants, vowels, consonant blends, consonant digraphs, vowel digraphs, *r*-controlled vowels). Begin with single letters. See if the child can give the letter name and the corresponding sound. Keep a checklist of what the child already knows. Many children will have picked up the letter names and even corresponding sounds for most consonants in kindergarten. If students know the sounds of most of the consonants and vowels, go on to letter combinations such as *ar, oo, oy, bl,* and *sh.*

Then begin adding to what the child already knows. This is easily accomplished while working with a child on a one-to-one basis. Follow a more specific sequence when working with groups of children. Begin with consonants; choose five or six used frequently in primers, such as *p, t, b, s, m,* and *g.* Immediately present a short vowel and beginning words for blending. Usually short /ă/ or short /ĭ/ come first. The following real words (and many others) can be read and spelled with *p, t, b, s, m,* and *a:*

am	Pam	taps
at	tam	mast
bat	bat	mats
pat	tap	maps
sat	sap	bats
mat	map	past
Sam	tab	

In addition, many nonsense words, such as *pab* or *bap,* can be created. Always begin with the shortest and easiest words to read and spell, and then move to the longer and harder words.

One logical sequence for introducing orthographic patterns, provided in *Patterns for Success in Reading and Spelling, Second Edition* (Henry & Redding, 2002), is as follows:

1.   The letters *m, l, s, t, a, p, f, c, n, b, r, j, k, i, v, g, w, d, h, u, y, z, x, o,* and *e* are introduced.

2.   Initial blends, spelling rules, consonant digraphs, consonant blends, and other common patterns are introduced as follows: *st-, sm-, sn-, qu-,* VCE rule, *sl-, sp-, ay, sc-, sk-, -ff, -ll, -ss, -ck, sh, ee, bl-, cl-, ea, fl-, gl-, pl-, y* as long /ī/, *ch,* plural *-s, ing, ar, th* (unvoiced /th/ sound), *oy, all, th* (voiced /th/ sound), *br-, cr-, ow, dr-, fr-, gr-, pr-, tr-, er, oo, -ed, -ang, -ong, -ung, or, ow, wh-,* plural *-es, -ink, -ank, -onk, -unk, aw, sw-, tw-,* final blends (e.g., *-mp, -nd, -sk, -ft, -lk, -ld*), *oo, ai,* and *oa.*

3.   Lessons continue with the following: three-letter blends (*spr, str, scr, spl*), *s* as /z/, *ie, ou, -tch, ea, oi, au, -dge,* soft *c* and *g, kn-, wr-, ph-, -igh, ue, ew, ear, -augh, -ough, -eigh, wor, war, ui, ey, -ind, -ild, -old, -ost, ei, gn,* and *-mb.*

4.   Common syllable patterns, common prefixes, common suffixes and corresponding rules, compound words, possessives, and other plural spellings are introduced.

CONSONANTS

Most children learn consonant graphemes and phonemes rather easily. Certain pairs of sounds, however, may be difficult for some children to discriminate. Although the sounds in each are similar, one sound is **voiced;** that is, the vocal cords vibrate when making the sound. The vocal cords do not vibrate when making the related but **voiceless** (or **unvoiced**) sound.

Voiced		Unvoiced	
/b/	[*bat*]	/p/	[*pat*]
/d/	[*dug*]	/t/	[*tug*]
/g/	[*goat*]	/k/	[*coat*]
/j/	[*jug*]	/ch/	[*chug*]
/v/	[*vine*]	/f/	[*fine*]
/z/	[*zip*]	/s/	[*sip*]
/<u>th</u>/	[*that*]	/th/	[*thin*]
/w/	[*wail*]	/hw/	[*whale*]

Auditory discrimination drills should be performed with children who have difficulty differentiating these sounds. For example, columns on paper can be headed with the target pair of sounds, such as /d/ and /t/. The teacher says a word containing one of the target sounds, and students repeat the word and check the appropriate column or, if able, write the word in the correct column.

VOWELS

Vowel sounds and spellings are the most difficult patterns for many students to learn. Most short vowels are rather close on the sound spectrum. For example, the short vowel sounds /ă/, /ĕ/, and /ĭ/ are especially difficult to discriminate. Therefore, it is suggested that vowel sounds not be taught in alphabetical order. Even more difficult for many than spellings for single-letter vowels are spellings for vowel digraphs such as *ee, ea, oi,* and *ou.*

Elsie Smelt (1976), an Australian educator, summarized the Hanna et al. (1971) study of spelling patterns in English (see Table 6.1) and found that 95% of the target words that contained a long /ā/ sound were spelled one of four ways: 80% were open syllable *a* (as in *baby*) or *a*-consonant-*e* (as in *made*); 9% used *ai,* usually in the middle of words (as in *pail* and *pain*); and 6% used *ay,* usually at the end. All of the words containing a short /ă/ were spelled with the letter *a.*

In these early stages, teachers should concentrate on the most productive spellings in English, not those that are used in only a handful of words. Remember, also, that word construction is cumulative. It is useful to move from two- and

Table 6.1.   Proportion of alternative spellings of vowel sounds

Although the most common way of writing each vowel sound is with one letter, in a comparatively small proportion of words, the vowel sound is written with two letters. Children often have difficulty knowing which vowels to use. The following calculations, compiled by Elsie Smelt (1976), were based on the Stanford Spelling Study (Hanna et al., 1971). The study used more than "17,000 words (from a core vocabulary containing most of the words used by educated speakers and writers)" (Hanna et al., 1971,p. 80). Teach children to rely on the most commonly used letter–sound correspondences.

The sound . . .	Is written as . . .	In X% of words	Examples
/ā/	a	80	mate, vacation
	ai	9	nail
	ay	6	day
/ē/*	e	72	me, zero
	ee	10	deep
	ea	10	heat
/ī/	i	74	hide, pilot
	y	14	try
	igh	6	sigh
/ō/	o	87	hope, hobo
	oa	5	boat
	ow	5	low
/o͞o/	u	90	tune, mute, cupid
	ew	3	new
	eu	2	feud
	ue	2	due
/ă/	a	100	hat
/ě/	e	93	bet
	ea	4	head
/ĭ/	i	73	hid
	y	23	funny, symphony*
/ŏ/	o	95	hot
/ŭ/**	u	88	hut

From Smelt, E. (1976). *Speak, spell and read English* (p. 102). Melbourne: Longman Australia; adapted by permission.

*Many dictionaries that were published before the 1980s gave the final letter y as in *funny* or *muddy* the short /ĭ/ sound. This grapheme is now pronounced more frequently as long /ē/, especially in the Midwest and western United States.

**Smelt noted that many short words that contain the sound of ŭ contain an o. I prefer to teach these words, such as *son*, *love*, *mother*, and *done*, as nonphonetic memory words.

three-letter VC and VCV words, such as *at* and *pat*, to those with consonant blends and consonant and vowel digraphs, to two-syllable words, to affixed base words.

SPELLING RULES

Students also need to learn six categories of spelling rules. Most apply to Anglo-Saxon words and occur because of the short vowel sounds. Many teachers talk about "rules" that are actually not orthographic rules. Melvyn Ramsden cautioned teachers that "if you find an 'exception' don't blame the system—you might have got [*sic*] your 'rule' wrong" (2000, p. 11). For example, teachers often say, "When two vowels go walking, the first does the talking." Smelt (1976) found that this statement is only true 37% of the time; it works for *ai, oa, ay,* and *ee* but not for *oo, oy, ew, au,* and *aw.*

Teach the following rules when students are ready for them:

1. Silent *e* rule (VCE rule)

    a. Silent *e* on the end of a word signals that the single vowel immediately preceding a single consonant is long, as in *cube* and *vote* (i.e., the silent *e* makes the vowel sound like [or "say"] its name; sometimes this rule is called the "magic *e* rule").

    b. Silent *e* makes *y* sound like /ī/ as in *type* and *style.*

A preceding single vowel may or may not be long before -*ve.* The vowels in *gave, five,* and *drove* are long; the vowels in *have, give,* and *love* are not long.

2. Doubling rule (-*ff, -ll, -ss, -zz*)

Double final *f, l, s,* and sometimes *z* immediately following a single vowel in a one-syllable word, as in *staff, bluff, tell, still, grass, bliss, buzz,* and *jazz.* (Common exceptions are *pal, gal, if, clef, gas, this, us, thus, yes, bus, plus,* and *quiz.* Although *quiz* contains two vowel letters, *q* is always followed by *u* in English words, so only *i* is considered a vowel in *quiz.*)

3. Soft *c* and *g* rule

The letters *c* and *g* have a "soft" sound when they appear directly before *e, i,* and *y.*

    a. The letter *c* has the /s/ sound before *e, i,* and *y,* as in *cent, city,* and *cycle.*

    b. The letter *g* has the /j/ sound before *e, i,* and *y,* as in *gentle, ginger,* and *gym.* (Exceptions to the soft *g* rule do not present spelling problems because in such exceptions, *g* has its "hard" sound, as in *get, give, buggy,* and *bigger.*)

The hard sounds of c (as in *cat, coat,* and *cub*) and g (as in *gas, got,* and *gum*) are taught first. Only after these are well established are the soft sounds and the corresponding rule introduced.

4. The -*ck, -tch, -dge* rule

    a. Use -*ck* to spell the /k/ sound immediately after one short vowel at the end of a one-syllable word, as in *back, clock, duck, stick,* and *deck.*

    b. Use -*tch* to spell the /ch/ sound immediately after one short vowel at the end of a one-syllable word, as in *batch, itch, stretch, Dutch,* and *notch.*

Common exceptions to the *-tch* rule, such as *such, much, rich,* and *which,* should be memorized.

    c.   Use *-dge* to spell the /j/ sound immediately after one short vowel at the end of a one-syllable word, as in *badge, ledge, bridge, dodge,* and *fudge.*

5.   Adding suffixes to Anglo-Saxon base words

    a.   Drop final *-e* rule: When a base word ends in a final *e,* drop the *e* before adding a suffix starting with a vowel (e.g., *take, taking; fine, finer; stone, stony*).

    b.   Double-letter rule: In a one-syllable word with one short vowel (a closed syllable) ending in one consonant, double the final consonant before a suffix starting with a vowel (e.g., *-ed, -er, -ing, -y, -ish*). Do not double the final consonant before a suffix starting with a consonant (e.g., *-ful, -est, -ly, -ment, -ness*). Examples: *fit, fitted, fitful; sad, saddest, sadly; red, redder, redness;* and *ship, shipping, shipment.*

One-syllable base words that contain a vowel digraph or that end in two consonants do not need to double the final consonant, as in *heat, heater* and *help, helping.* The doubling rule for polysyllabic base and root words is covered in Chapter 7.

    c.   Change final *y* to *i* rule: When a base word ends in *y,* change the *y* to *i* before adding a suffix, unless the *y* is preceded by a vowel or unless the suffix begins with *i* (*-ing, -ish, -ist*). Examples: *cry, cried, crying; copy, copied, copyist;* and *play, player, playing.*

6.   Plural *-s* and *-es* rule

    a.   Most nouns become plural (to indicate more than one) by adding *-s* (e.g., *hat, hats; pig, pigs; girl, girls; hut, huts*).

    b.   Nouns ending in *-s, -x, -z, -ch,* and *-sh* add *-es* for the plural. Students can hear the additional syllable formed by the *-es* ending (e.g., *glass, glasses; box, boxes; waltz, waltzes; lunch, lunches; wish, wishes*).

    c.   Nouns ending in *y* form the plural according to the regular suffix addition rule. That is, change the final *y* to *i* and add *-es,* as in *fly, flies.* If the letter *y* follows a vowel, then keep the *y* and add *-s,* as in *boy, boys.*

    d.   Exceptions exist for some nouns ending in *f* or *fe;* these change to *–ves,* as in *shelf, shelves; leaf, leaves; knife, knives.*

    e.   Nouns ending in *o* sometimes add *-s* and sometimes add *-es* (e.g., *piano, pianos; tomato, tomatoes*). Students should check their dictionaries to be sure.

f.   Some plurals are completely irregular and must be learned (e.g., *foot, feet; mouse, mice; man, men; woman, women; goose, geese; moose, moose; pants, pants; deer, deer*). Most of these can be spelled correctly by using sound sequences for clues.

Children may question the use of x versus *-cks*. Singular nouns usually end in x, as in *tax, box,* and *fox,* as does the adjective *six.* Plural nouns or singular third-person verbs tend to end in *-cks* with *-s* as the suffix, as in *socks, locks,* he *picks,* and the chicken *pecks.*

Just as when learning a new pattern, children should have ample opportunities to read and spell numerous words fitting each rule. The teacher should make the rules concrete for students. The teacher may state the rules but also must work with students so that they practice and think about each rule. Working on the chalkboard or with transparencies is useful. For example, when discussing changing *y* to *i*, the teacher can easily erase and change the *y* to *i* if the conditions permit (e.g., *try, tried, trying*).

RECOMMENDATIONS FOR SPELLING

Many children continue to use invented spelling as they progress in the early grades. Yet teachers need to assist students in transferring to standard spellings. Students must learn to use conventional spelling over time. During traditional spelling instruction, words are often related by meaning or by content in a story but not by orthographic structure. Knowledge of the orthographic structure and corresponding sounds provides students with specific strategies for dealing with unfamiliar words. Think of the winners of national spelling bees. They often ask for the part of speech and the word origin to help them with their decisions.

Spelling errors are a good estimate of reading ability in many cases. Low reading rate and poor spelling usually translate into poor reading skills. Figures 6.1 and 6.2 illustrate the types of spelling errors found in the dictation of two elementary students. These two students are poor readers and spellers. They have few strategies for working out unknown words prior to intervention. Notice also the difficulty each has with letter formation. Matt is finishing third grade and has learned cursive writing (see Figure 6.1). Notice the errors in his spellings of *box, belong, door, low, how, bring, tall, ball, ask, way,* and *baby.* Furthermore, while reading a list of grade-appropriate words aloud, Matt makes no phonetic generalizations as he reads *Jack, tack,* and *sack* as *Jack, take,* and *snake.*

Dana repeated third grade and is now in Grade 5. Unfortunately, even though she has had 3 years of cursive writing instruction, her letter formation is extremely poor as she writes *Come in on time today* from dictation. Dana wrote the cursive cap-

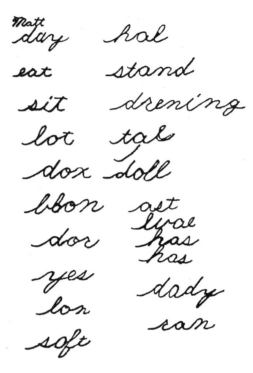

Figure 6.1. Spelling sample from a third grader.

ital *D* in her name disjointedly by drawing two circles, a line, and an arc (see Figure 6.2). Her teachers have not monitored Dana's cursive writing to check for correct letter formation.

While introducing new patterns, dictate numerous words containing the target grapheme. Be sure students sound out the word as they write it. Say the word or phrase only once or twice. Students will get used to listening. Some students benefit from saying letter names simultaneously with spelling, whereas other students say only the sound as they spell. Students should check each word by sounding it out. Try to monitor students as they spell, and cue the children promptly when an error is made. For example, when a student spells *quen* for *queen*, ask, "How do we spell /ē/ in the middle of words?" Or if a child writes *quite* for *quit*, ask, "What does the final *e* do?"

Avoid scrambled-letter exercises in which words are spelled backward, vertically rather than horizontally, or even diagonally, as such exercises are very confusing for children with reading and spelling problems. Also, giving students words that are spelled incorrectly and asking students to give correct spellings may reinforce the incorrect visual images of the words.

Figure 6.2. Spelling sample from a fifth grader.

IRREGULAR WORDS

Students need to memorize spellings for irregular words, although multisensory techniques may still be used. Irregular words (sometimes called red flag, demon, maverick, weirdo, or nonphonetic words) usually are irregular in the vowel spelling only. That is, the vowel sound does not carry its regular short or long sound. For example, *mother, laugh, cough,* and *prove* are all nonphonetic in the spelling of the vowel sound. The teacher provides a model on the students' papers. Students trace, copy, and then write from memory. During each step students say the letter names, not the sounds that the letters represent.

Some systems spend inordinate amounts of time on patterns that are better learned by rote. For example, Barnett called *ough* the "favorite scapegoat of critics of English orthography with its 'monstrous' 9 pronunciations" (1962, p. 83). He gave the following examples for the various sounds:

tough	thorough	cough
though	through	drought
thought	bough	hiccough

No wonder that although *ough* usually says /ô/ (as in *ought, bought, fought, thought, nought,* and *sought*), teachers may be apt to say that *ough* has many sounds! Try to concentrate on the most important and frequently used sound or sounds. Teach the other words as memory words. A leading basal series of the 1980s contained an exercise that asked children to identify all of the ways of spelling short /ĕ/ in the following words:

any	leopard	says	their
friend	end	bury	aerodrome
bread	said		

Actually, only the spellings *e* (as in *end*) and *ea* (as in *bread*) are used with any frequency for short /ĕ/. (An additional flaw of this list is that some of the vowel sounds in the words *bury, their,* and *aerodrome* are affected by /r/, meaning that children may have more difficulty hearing the short vowel sounds.) This type of activity and practice focuses on the exceptions rather than the regularities of the English language, something that the concepts inherent in the decoding–spelling continuum hope to prevent.

The linguist Steven Pinker noted that

> For about eighty-four percent of English words, spelling is completely predictable from regular rules. . . . The words with truly weird spellings (like *of, people, women, have, said, do, done,* and *give*) generally are the commonest in the language, so there is ample opportunity for everyone to memorize them. (1994, p. 190)

Bill Bryson (1990) pointed out the vanishing *u* in *four* when one writes *forty*. He noted that *four* (and *fourth, fourteen,* and *thirty-four*) contain the *u*. "Chaucer spelled it with a *u*, as indeed did most people until the end of the seventeenth century and some for half a century or so after that. But then, as if by universal decree, it just quietly vanished" (p. 122).

Students can learn nonphonetic words in a multisensory way. Teachers write the word on a sheet of paper as a model. Students trace the word while saying the letter names. Then students copy the word, again saying the letter names. They should then write the word by itself, in phrases, and/or in sentences, always saying the letter names.

As students learn new patterns, provide ample opportunities for them to read and spell words containing the target patterns in lists, phrases, and sentences. The resources at the end of this chapter include lists of words found in the primary grades.

SYLLABLES

Students need additional strategies in order to read and spell polysyllabic words. Accent may be difficult for some children to hear. Encourage students to tap each syllable, using different fingers for each sound. Children can tap on the opposite fist or even on a table. Some children prefer to feel the voice box in order to "feel" the accent (or stress), and still others like to clap each sound. Begin by having students count the syllables in their own names.

In Chapter 3, the types and rules for syllable division were presented. In the primary grades, the closed (VC/CVC), open (V/CV), closed (VC/V), and consonant-*le* syllables are most common. While reading multisyllabic words, students may look for the number of vowels as a cue to the number of syllables.

Only *rhythm* and the suffix *-ism* have a pronounced syllable without a vowel.

When spelling multisyllabic words, students count syllables as they say and write the word syllable by syllable.

Students can practice reading polysyllabic words and marking closed and open syllables. Remind your students that base and root words usually get the stress, whereas affixes will be schwaed. The diacritical marking for the short vowel sound is the **breve** (˘). The **macron** (¯) represents the long vowel sound. Accent is usually marked with an apostrophe or a strike (') at the end of the accented syllable.

MORPHEME PATTERNS

Readers will recall that a morpheme is the smallest meaningful unit of language. Words of Anglo-Saxon origin both compound and affix. Compound words consist of two base words.

Base Words

Base words are the short meaningful words commonly used in the primary grades. Each base word is a morpheme. Teachers should point out that the meaning of the compound word is related to its constituent words or base words. Therefore, *flashlight* is related to both *flash* and *light*. *Blackboard* refers to a *board* that is *black*. Students enjoy generating numerous compound words, such as *football, butterfly, sailboat, shoehorn,* and *playhouse.* Point out that compound words usually have the stress on the first syllable. (See Appendix C for a list of compound words.)

Anglo-Saxon base words also affix; that is, prefixes and/or suffixes can be added to them. Point out that free morphemes or free base words can stand alone and that the Anglo-Saxon base words are most often free morphemes. For example, *spell* stands alone, but prefixes and suffixes can be added to this free base word, as in *misspell* and *misspelled.* (In contrast, Latin roots, which are discussed in Chapter 7, are usually bound morphemes, and one must almost always add a prefix and/or suffix to them to make a word in English.) Remember that students do not have to completely master the letter–sound correspondences (especially the vowel digraphs) before beginning to learn spellings for the prefixes and suffixes. This is extremely important. We want to touch children with the power of word expansion, and we can do this by adding common affixes.

Prefixes

The first prefixes added are generally those found most frequently with Anglo-Saxon base words, such as *in-, un-, mis-, dis-, fore-, re-, de-, pre-,* and *a-.* In fact, words beginning with *un-, re-, in-* (meaning *not*), and *dis-* occur in more than 58% of almost 3,000 prefixed words found in textbooks for Grades 3–9 (White, Sowell, & Yanagihara, 1989). Other common prefixes, in descending order of frequency, include *en-/em-, non-, in-/im-* (meaning *in* or *into*), *over-, mis-, sub-, pre-, inter-, fore-, de-, trans-, super-, semi-, anti-, mid-,* and *under-.* Children can be given a base word and can be asked to make words with prefixes, such as with the base words *like* (e.g., *dislike, unlike*) or *read* (e.g., *reread, misread*). The prefix *a-* is one of the first uses of the schwa that students encounter. Because the base word usually retains the stress, the *a-* is unstressed; therefore, it has the schwa sound, as in *alike, around, asleep, alone, away,* and *aground.*

Suffixes

White et al. (1989) noted that *-s, -es, -ed,* and *-ing* were found in 65% of more than 2,000 common suffixed words. Another 17% of the words used *-ly, -er (-or), -ion (-tion, -ation, -ition),* and *-ible, -able.* The following suffixes were used in 1% of the group of words studied by White et al.: *-al (-ial), -y, -ness, -ty (-ity), -ment, -ic, -ous (-eous, -ious), -en,* comparative *-er, -ive (-ative, -itive), -ful, -less,* and *-est.* Other suffixes were found in 7% of the words.

The first suffixes added are generally the inflectional endings *-s, -ed, -ing, -er, -es,* and *-est.* Inflectional endings change the number, person, or tense of the base word. Derivational endings, in contrast, are those that modify the base through the addition of a suffix (e.g., *care, careless, carelessness*) or a change within the word (i.e., *song* from *sing*) to produce an affixed word that is often a different part of speech than the base word. Examples of derivational endings include *-ly, -less, -ness, -ship, -fold,* and *-ment.* Remember that suffixes usually cause a word to be a particular part of speech. Thus, *-est* is usually an adjective ending, whereas *-ly* is an adverb ending and *-ment* is a noun ending. While teaching suffixes, the teacher can introduce grammatical concepts such as noun, verb, adjective, and adverb.

The important suffix *-ed,* which signifies a past-tense verb, needs special attention because it can be pronounced three different ways. It is often a separate syllable, and because the suffix is rarely accented, the schwa sound is present. This pronunciation of /əd/ occurs after a base word ending in *d* or *t.* Thus, we have *sand, sanded* and *need, needed* or *heat, heated* and *shout, shouted.* However, the suffix *-ed* will be pronounced as /t/ after an unvoiced sound such as /k/ (*licked*), /p/ (*jumped*), /sh/ *wished,* /f/ (*cuffed*), or /s/ (*missed*). The *-ed* will also be pronounced as /d/ after a voiced sound such as /b/ (*nabbed*), /l/ (*filled*), /m/ (*aimed*), and /n/ (*loaned*).

> At a much more sophisticated level, the final syllable *-ed* in certain Early English adjectives may be pronounced, as in *barelegged, bowlegged, dogged, jagged, ragged, rugged, crooked, wretched,* and *aged.* For example: The aged man has aged a lot in the past year; Jim dogged Tom's footsteps in a dogged manner. (B. Sheffield, in press, p. 36.)

The teacher should begin with base words and suffixes that need no knowledge of suffix addition rules, such as *like, liked, likely; time, timely, untimely; blame, blameless, blamelessness; heat, heater;* and *stamp, stamping, stamped.* Once children learn common suffixes, usually in first and second grade, the teacher moves on to the suffix addition rules pertinent to Anglo-Saxon base words that are presented in the section on spelling rules in this chapter. Children need a great deal of practice as they work on these rules. Simply memorizing the rule is not enough. The teacher should discuss with the students the specific steps for adding suffixes. Here is a suggested line of questioning for dropping final *e*:

- "Here is the word *blaming*."
- "What is the base word?" [*blame*]
- "How is it spelled?" [*b-l-a-m-e*]
- "Does it end in *e*?" [*yes*]
- "If so, does the suffix begin with a vowel?" [*yes, i*]
- "If no, just add the suffix."
- "If yes, remove the final *e* before you add the suffix." [*blaming*]

Here is a line of questioning for adding suffixes to base words ending in one vowel followed by one consonant:

- "Here is the word *big*. Let's add -*est* to this word."
- "Does the word end in one consonant preceded by one vowel?" [*yes*]
- "If yes, does the suffix begin with a vowel?" [*yes, e*]
- "If no, do not double the final consonant in the base word, as in *bigness*."
- "If yes, double the final consonant in the base word." [*biggest*]

Here are lines of questioning for adding suffixes to words ending in *y*:

- "Here is the word *play*. Let's add -*ing* to this word."
- "Is there a vowel just before the *y*?" [*yes*]
- "Do we change the *y* to *i*?" [*no*]
- "If no, add the suffix." [*play + ing = playing*]
- "Here is the word *try*. Let's add -*ed* to this word."
- "Is there a vowel before the *y*?" [*no*]
- "If no, change the *y* to *i*." [*try + ed = tried*]
- "If we were to add -*ing* to try, would we change the *y* to *i*?" [*no, try + ing = trying*]

Ramsden (2001) encouraged students to make webs of base words while learning to compound and affix. The teacher and students can generate words and continue to add to the web (see Figure 6.3) as new affixes and words are identified.

The web on *friend* in Figure 6.4 was developed in a first-grade classroom in an international school in Beijing, China. Teacher Linda Brubaker and Assistant Principal Fiona Sheridan had children add prefixes and suffixes to this web. After being

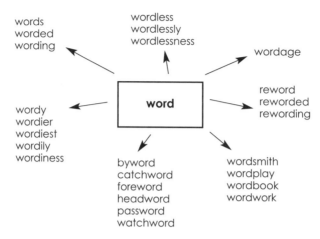

Figure 6.3. Morpheme web for the word *word*. (From Ramsden, M. [2001]. *The spelling manual in the real spelling tool box.* Retrieved March 13, 2003, from http://www.realspelling.com; adapted by permission.)

on a wordwall in the classroom, it was hung in the hallway so more children would see it.

Matrices are also helpful graphic organizers for thinking of word expansion (see Figure 6.5). Ramsden (2001) explained the power of beginning with the base word, such as *friend,* and including prefixes and suffixes that form words. Matrices give a morphologically rigorous representation of a word family. They become a

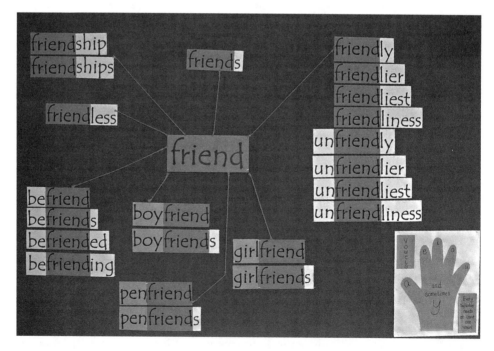

Figure 6.4. Part of classroom bulletin board of *friend* words. (Used by kind permission of Fiona Sheridan and Linda Brubaker.)

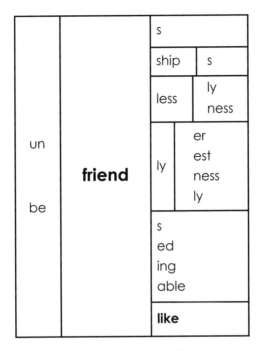

Figure 6.5. Matrix showing the addition of prefixes and suffixes to the Anglo-Saxon base *friend*. (Used by kind permission of Melvyn Ramsden.)

"machine" for word construction and provide a structural basis for reading sling words. (See http://www.realspelling.com; click on *Real Spelling RESOURCES* and then on *A word matrix*.)

Ramsden and Mira (2009) provided conventions for using matrices. These include

- Read a matrix from left to right.

- Make single complete words from a matrix.

- Use only one element from a single column at a time.

- Don't feel that you have to take an element from every column of a matrix, but do not "leapfrog" columns.

- Watch the joins! You must be on the lookout for spelling patterns when you construct a word from a matrix.

- Use the Big Suffix Checker (http://homepage.mac.com/spelling/eGroup/ check.pdf) to help.

Additional Topics

Third grade is really a year of transition. In most schools, this is when students begin to use cursive writing. As in the earlier grades, students need to trace and copy and practice cursive letters. When the children write from memory, you may ask them to say the sound or the name of the letter. As soon as several cursive letters have been taught, they can be joined in pairs or in short words. Some linkages may prove to be difficult, especially those using the bridge letters *b, o, v,* and *w,* such as *br* or *wr* in *brown*, and they should be taught explicitly. Students need practice with both upper- and lowercase letters.

Up to and during third grade, students also need to become familiar with other important concepts related to English words, such as contractions, possessives, **homonyms** and **homographs,** and antonyms and synonyms.

Contractions *Contractions* are made when two words are shortened into one word marked with an apostrophe where letters have been omitted. Here are some of the main contractions:

Long form	Contraction	Long form	Contraction
it is	it's	cannot	can't
I am	I'm	do not	don't
he is, he has	he's	would not	wouldn't
she is, she has	she's	could not	couldn't
here is	here's	should not	shouldn't
where is	where's	are not	aren't
what is	what's	were not	weren't
who is	who's	had not	hadn't
I will	I'll	you are	you're
you will	you'll	we are	we're
he will	he'll	they are	they're
she will	she'll	I have	I've
we will	we'll	you have	you've
they will	they'll	we have	we've
I would	I'd	they have	they've
you would	you'd	will not	won't
he would	he'd		
she would	she'd		
we would	we'd		
they would	they'd		

The contraction *won't* is the only truly irregular contraction. An early form of *will* was *wol,* and it is assumed that *won't* came from that early form.

Have students read phrases with contractions. Also, give students dictation phrases or sentences to practice writing contractions (e.g., *she'll run, I'd like, won't open, I'm going to the movies, Don't you wish teachers wouldn't give so much homework?*).

Possessives   Nouns and pronouns often indicate ownership or possession. Usually, possessive nouns require an apostrophe (but possessive pronouns do not). Rules for possession follow:

- Add *'s* to the singular form of the noun, as in *Jane's coats, the man's hat,* and *the dog's dish.*

- Add an apostrophe after a plural ending in *s,* as in *three boys' desks, six students' tests,* and *the cats' litters* (meaning the litters of more than one cat, in contrast to *the cat's litters,* which means the litters of only one cat).

- Most pronouns are possessive pronouns and require no apostrophe to show possession, as in *his car, her house, their mother,* and *its wings* (meaning *the bird's wings*).

 Do not use an apostrophe with the possessive pronoun *its,* as in *its dish* (meaning the *dog's dish*). Use *it's* only as the contraction of *it is,* as in *It's a nice day.*

Homonyms and Homographs   *Homonyms* (also called homophones) are words that sound the same, usually have the same spelling, but differ in meaning. For example, *bank* (embankment) and *bank* (a place for money) are homonyms; so are *die* (to stop living), *die* (a device for cutting or stamping objects), and *dye* (color).

Homographs are words that are spelled the same but that sound different and differ in meaning. Words such as *wind* (breeze) and *wind* (to wind the clock) and *bass* (a fish) and *bass* (deep tone) are homographs.

When the teacher introduces the terms *homonym* and *homograph,* students in second and third grades can even be introduced to words of Greek origin. Students can learn the meanings of *homo* (same), *nym* (name), and *graph* (writing).

Antonyms and Synonyms   The names of other concepts, such as *antonym* (opposite name) and *synonym* (same name) also contain Greek forms. *Antonyms* are words that are opposite in meaning, such as *up/down, back/front, dry/wet,* and *cold/hot. Synonyms* are words that carry like meaning, such as *sleepy* and *drowsy* or *frisky* and *lively.*

INTERVENTIONS FOR FLUENCY

By second and third grades, as strategies for decoding and spelling become more efficient, students will acquire greater fluency. Teachers can help promote fluency with several interventions that have proven successful in helping students gain fluency.

For example, repeated readings give students multiple chances to read a passage. Students first read silently, at a slow rate, then increase their rate as they become familiar with the passage. Some exercises provide lists of words to read and track the rate from day to day. Choral reading of passages may also be useful to help students to gain fluency as well as to enhance correct inflection and pauses.

Pretraining of targeted regular and irregular words is often useful. The Slingerland (1994a, 1994b, 1996) "Preparation for Reading" exercises can be adapted to any text. The teacher selects five to seven phrases that may be difficult for students and writes them on the board or on a transparency. The teacher points to and reads each phrase as the students repeat. Next the teacher reads a phrase, and one student finds the phrase among the ones displayed, points to it, and reads it. If it is read correctly, all students repeat; if it is read incorrectly, the students remain silent and the teacher reads the phrase correctly. In the next step, the teacher asks a comprehension question, such as "Find the phrase that shows a location" or "Which phrase includes an adjective?" Again, a student responds by pointing to the phrase and reading it. Finally, a student reads the phrases again as the teacher points to them. Teachers find that the passages are read much more fluently and accurately when students have practiced the phrases prior to reading aloud.

Wolf (2007) and Wolf and Katzer-Cohen (2001) discussed the RAVE-O comprehensive fluency-based reading intervention program to enhance retrieval, automaticity, vocabulary, engagement, and orthography. This program is taught in conjunction with systematic phonological analysis and blending. The program uses computer games to maximize rapid recognition and practice of the most frequent orthographic letter patterns. Preliminary data indicated that children made significant gains in word attack, word identification, oral reading rate and accuracy, and passage comprehension (see Wolf, Miller, & Donnelly-Adams, 2000).

Hasbrouck (Center for Development and Learning, 2008), however, fears that critical details from research are being overlooked as teachers "across the country are putting significant amounts of time and effort into two instructional strategies for improving fluency that the research does not support: silent reading and Round Robin Reading (RRR)" (Center for Development and Learning, 2008 p. 1). He concluded that children require more practice, support, and guided oral reading than either of these strategies can deliver.

By third grade, children should continue to expand their ability to decode and spell new words. As children move to the next level of proficiency, their knowledge of word structure will grow, they will gain new strategies for reading and spelling, and their accuracy and fluency will increase. The following sample lesson provides a model for lessons that both review previously taught patterns and teach new patterns.

Sample Lessons

| LESSON | ## Contrasting the Two Sounds of the Grapheme *oo* |

Grade 2 Prerequisites: Understanding of vowel digraphs

Opening

"Today we'll review the /o͞o/ sound of *oo* and present an alternative sound. First we'll do our visual and auditory card drills and blend some of the cards to make syllables."

Middle

Give students a group of *oo* words that contain the /o͞o/ sound on an overhead transparency, the board, or a wall chart. Ask what type of pattern *oo* is [*vowel digraph*]. Have students read the words individually or in unison.

moon	droop	spool	room
scoop	shoot	pool	stool
gloom	fool	hoop	boot
bloom	loon	tooth	boom
hoot	cool	stoop	loose
soon	smooth	spoon	
croon	boost	food	
groove	broom	goose	

Have students spell a number of these words from dictation. Also, dictate sentences that contain some of these words.

To introduce the new sound of the spelling pattern *oo*, /o͝o/, have students copy, trace, and write *oo* on paper while sounding the new sound /o͝o/, as in *book*.

Show students a new list of words on the overhead, the board, or a chart:

good	shook	wool	overtook
hook	foot	undertook	cook
brook	woodpile	stood	crook
fishhook	hood	look	nook
book	took	wood	understood

Have students note similarities and differences in the old and the new lists. [*The location of the vowel digraph is the same, i.e., in the middle; the sound is different.*] Have students read the words from the new list. Dictate several of the words from the new list; include some of the words in phrases and sentences.

As a review, ask students to write /ōō/ and /ŏŏ/ as column headings on a new piece of paper. Dictate words from either list. Students must determine column in which to place each word and then write the spelling of the word.

Closing

"Today we've worked on two sounds of the vowel digraph *oo*. What are they?" [/ōō/ *and* /ŏŏ/] "Are there other ways you know how to spell the /ōō/ sound?" [u-*consonant*-e *as in* rule, ew *as in* blew, ue *as in* true] "Are there other ways to spell the /ŏŏ/ sound?" [*There is no other common spelling;* u *as in* put, pull, push, bull, full, *and* bush *is rare.*]

Follow-Up

"Look for words that contain the *oo* pattern as you read your storybook. Make a list of those words that have the /ōō/ sound and those that have the /ŏŏ/ sound."

From Henry, M.K. (2010). *WORDS: Integrated decoding and spelling instruction based on word origin and word structure* (2nd ed., pp. 90–93). Austin, TX: PRO-ED; adapted by permission.

```
┌─────────────────────────────┐
│   Classroom Activities and  │
│   Suggested Grade Levels    │
└─────────────────────────────┘
```

The following activities are suggestions for teachers to use in reinforcing consonant and vowel patterns. The grades listed are suggested levels only; teachers may want to use the activities with students of different grades if this is more appropriate to the students' abilities.

ACTIVITIES | First Grade

Introducing Sounds

Use flip charts as you introduce new sounds to make numerous words.

Initial Phoneme Substitution

Make a new word by changing the first letter of each word:

map   __ap [cap]   jab __ab [cab]   van   __an [pan]

Medial Phoneme Substitution

Read each word. Change /ă/ to /ĭ/, and read the new word:

pan   p__n [pin]   fast   f__st [fist]   bag   b__g [big]

Word Sorting

Give student teams several cards with a word on each. Ask them to sort the cards by initial or final consonant, by short vowel sound, or by consonant blend versus consonant digraph.

Auditory Discrimination

Ask children to fold a piece of paper in half lengthwise. Have them write *i* at the top of the first column and *e* at the top of the second column. Say a word, and ask the students to write the word in the appropriate column. For example,

i	e
pin	pet
bit	set
fit	pen
slip	step

Do the same for other sets of sounds that are difficult to discriminate, such as /b/ and /p/ or /ch/ and /sh/.

Finding Orthographic Patterns

Have children underline or circle the consonant blends or consonant digraphs or other orthographic categories in a list of words. For example, ask students to underline the consonant blends in the following words:

blame   past   whale [*no blends*]   thump   clasp

belt   grind   chick [*no blends*]   sprint   gleam

Filling in the Blanks

Ask students to fill in the blanks with words containing a consonant digraph (or other type of target pattern):

The _____ sailed through the bay. [*ship*]

_____ the wood for the fire. [*Chop*]

Jaws was a famous _____. [*shark*]

_____ are the biggest mammals. [*Whales*]

I play _____ base on the team. [*third*]

We get wool from _____. [*sheep*]

Rhyming

Have students write a word in the blank that rhymes with the target word.

I found a *hat*

just as I _____ [*sat*]

next to my _____ [*cat*]

upon a _____. [*mat*]

Can you imagine _____? [*that*]

Studying Nonphonetic Words and Other Patterns

Make wall charts or word banks for nonphonetic words, for basic sight words, for adjectives describing people, for active verbs, and so forth.

Using Pocket Charts for Spelling

Place consonants and vowels in pockets on the chart. As you dictate a word for spelling, the student places the correct card in the pocket. This is an easier cognitive task than actually writing the word.

Making Sentences with Word Cards

Make short sentences with common words provided on cards.

Spelling Short and Long Vowel Sounds

Have students read each word, then add *e* to the end of the word. Have students read the new word.

tub _____ [*tube*]   glad _____ [*glade*]

scrap _____ [*scrape*]   cap _____ [*cape*]

Tim _____ [*time*]   pet _____ [*Pete*]

twin _____ [*twine*]   pin _____ [*pine*]

cut _____ [*cute*]   grim _____ [*grime*]

Finding Spelling Patterns

Have students read a passage and underline the vowel digraphs (or other target pattern):

> The girls and b<u>oys</u> planned a n<u>ea</u>t picnic. When th<u>ey</u> got to the park, th<u>ey</u> pl<u>ay</u>ed before lunch. The ch<u>ee</u>se in the c<u>oo</u>ler was sp<u>oi</u>led, but th<u>ey</u> ate the <u>oa</u>t-meal c<u>oo</u>kies and drank r<u>oo</u>t b<u>ee</u>r.

 ACTIVITY

Second and Third Grades: Letter–Sound Correspondences

Word Sorting and Auditory Discrimination

Continue **word sorting** and discrimination exercises for new, more difficult patterns.

Sorting Word Cards

Give students cards with the following words on them. Ask them to read the words and put the cards in alphabetical order:

split   mask   sport   plant   nest

jungle   flower   thorn   throat   blink

Categories

Form teams and give each team a category, such as food, game, city, animal, country, person's name, bird, and flower. Pick five or six consonants out of a hat and

Table 6.2. Topics for the Category Game

Letter	Food	Game	City	Animal	Country
S	spaghetti	soccer	San Jose	snake	Somalia
P	potato	Parcheesi	Pittsburgh	pig	Poland
T	turnip	tennis	Toledo	toad	Turkey
M	mushroom	Monopoly	Miami	monkey	Monaco
R	rhubarb	rowing	Rome	raccoon	Russia
C	corn	canasta	Cancun	cricket	Canada

have students find words beginning with those letters. These can be written in a matrix, as shown in Table 6.2. See how many words can be added to each cell.

Filling in the Blanks

Make silly stories that have blanks in place of the target sound, and ask children to choose the correct spelling pattern for the sound. Read the story to the children. For example, "Fill in each blank in the following passage with proper letters that make the /ch/ sound. Remember the general rule: If a short vowel comes right before the /ch/ sound, use *tch.* If two vowels or a consonant comes before the /ch/ sound, use *ch.*

"A mean, nasty, old wi___ [*witch*] lived in an old house with a crooked por___ [*porch*] at the bottom of a di___ [*ditch*]. One day she decided to make a ba___ [*batch*] of her famous wi___es [*witches*] brew. She went to her ki___en [*kitchen*] to fe___ [*fetch*] her biggest pot. She put a pin___ [*pinch*] of her secret ingredient into the pot with a bun___ [*bunch*] of her other wi___y [*witchy*] favorites. She lit the fire under her pot with a ma___ [*match*]. She stirred the brew with a cru___ [*crutch*] she had for her broken foot. She then sat on a ben___ [*bench*] and waited for her lun___ [*lunch*] to cook."

(Story by Mary Buzelli, Pittsburgh, PA; published by kind permission.)

Anglo-Saxon Sentences

Have students write three sentences in their notebooks using only one-syllable Anglo-Saxon words (e.g., *Come to the store with me; The horse jumps next to the stall; Her mom likes to cook and sew*). Then ask each student to read his or her sentence aloud.

| ACTIVITY | **Second and Third Grades: Syllables** |

Counting Syllables

Read the following words to students one by one. After you say each word, ask students to repeat the word and count the number of syllables in it.

| atlas [2] | simple [2] | division [3] | population [4] |
| cucumber [3] | artichoke [3] | dictionary [4] | please [1] |

Dividing Syllables

Ask students to divide the following words into syllables.

tennis [*ten/nis*]   mitten [*mit/ten*]   shuttle [*shut/tle*]   pilot [*pi/lot*]

thunder [*thun/der*]   basket [*bas/ket*]   helmet [*hel/met*]   music [*mu/sic*]

paper [*pa/per*]   lilac [*li/lac*]   velvet [*vel/vet*]   table [*ta/ble*]

| ACTIVITY | **Second and Third Grades: Morphology** |

Finding Base Words

Have students circle the base words in a list of compound words, such as the following:

cowboy   aircraft   flashlight   schoolyard   campground

lamppost   baseball   railroad   sailboat   boathouse

Adding Suffixes

Have students add suffixes to the following base words.

shape + ing = [*shaping*]   shape + ly = [*shapely*]

hope + less = [*hopeless*]   hope + ed = [*hoped*]

slide + ing = [*sliding*]   slide + er = [*slider*]

time + ly = [*timely*]   time + er = [*timer*]

Finding Suffixes

Have students underline the suffixes in the following words. Tell students, "Read carefully, there may be a trick or two."

glar<u>ing</u>   basket [*no suffixes*]   grate<u>ful</u>   slimm<u>est</u>

gold<u>en</u>   open<u>ly</u>   sleep<u>y</u>   hope<u>ful</u> <u>ness</u>

din<u>ed</u>   hundred [*no suffixes*]   care<u>less</u>   cold<u>est</u>

Matching Prefixes and Meanings

Have students match each prefix with its meaning.

[*B*]   *pre-*   A. not

[*D*]   *sub-*   B. before

[*C*]   *re-*   C. again

[*E*]   *mis-*   D. under

[*A*]   *un-*   E. wrong

Exploring Spelling and Meaning

Give students a word and ask guiding questions. For example, "Is the word *spell* an Anglo-Saxon base word?" [*yes*] "How do you know?" [*It's short, and it contains a typical Anglo-Saxon pattern: final ll.*] "Can you add prefixes and suffixes to this word?" [*respell, misspell, spelled, misspelled, misspelling*] "Why are there two s's in misspell?" [*One is at the end of the prefix; the other is at the beginning of the base word.*]

"What does *spell* mean to you?" [*I spell words as I write.*] "Do you know any other meanings?" [*It can mean a bewitched state or trance, as in* under a spell, *or it can mean to add up, as in* Their loss spelled chaos.]

You can do similar exercises for almost any interesting or unfamiliar word and can assign students to "term teams" to get as much information about the word as possible.

Making Word Webs

Have children begin developing webs for base words, as shown in Figure 6.3. For example, ask students to make a web for the word *spell*. Students work in teams and may come up with a web containing compound words, such as *spellbound, spellbind, spelldown,* and *spellchecker;* words with suffixes, such as *spells, spelled, speller,* and *spelling;* words with the prefix *re-,* such as *respell, respells, respelling,* and *respelled;* or words with the prefix *mis-,* such as *misspell, misspells, misspelled,* and *misspelling.*

Beginning Dictionary Usage

As students begin to use the dictionary, be sure they can put words in alphabetical order and use the guide words to find the target word. Students will need to learn diacritical markings for correct pronunciation. They then need practice finding precise meanings. Go through the etymology with students. Have them look up a variety of words for pronunciation and meaning. Students may study some words for their interesting histories. For example, ask guiding questions such as the following: "What does the word *nerd* mean to you? Do you think it is an Anglo-Saxon word? Why? Look up the word *nerd.* What did you learn about its history?" [*The word* nerd *is thought to be from a character in Dr. Seuss's 1950 book* If I Ran the Zoo. *See the etymology on p. 1179 of the fourth edition of* The American Heritage Dictionary, *2000.*]

"Look up the word *smog* to find its origin and how it came into the language." [Smog *was first recorded in 1905 at a Public Health Congress in London. In a paper titled "Fog and Smoke," the author used the term* smoky fog, *which was combined to make the term* smog.]

The word *scuba* is an acronym standing for *self-contained underwater breathing apparatus.* With this word, you can introduce students to the term **acronym**. Students can learn that the first letters of each word in a phrase or sentence make up an acronym, greatly shortening the phrase.

Beginning Thesaurus Activities

Encourage students to begin exploring synonyms and antonyms and the subtle differences in words. Have them think of other words that mean almost the same as *sad*, such as *unhappy, sorry, gloomy,* and *dejected*. See if students can give words that are the opposite of *sad*, such as *glad, happy,* and *joyful*.

Ask students to begin keeping their own thesaurus of words by putting each key word on an index card and adding new words as they learn them. These cards can be kept in a pencil pouch or a recipe box for vocabulary study and writing.

| ACTIVITY | **Second and Third Grades: Semantics** |

Using Semantic Categories

Have students read the words in each row and cross out the word that does not belong. Then have them try to name the category of each group of words that do belong together.

milk	cream	shirt	butter	[*dairy product*]
lemon	apple	grape	egg	[*fruit*]
bluejay	horse	robin	crow	[*bird*]
paper	crayon	pencil	rabbit	[*writing utensil*]
church	house	bus	garage	[*building*]
skirt	black	blue	yellow	[*color*]
blouse	scooter	skirt	jacket	[*clothing*]
car	truck	bus	jelly	[*vehicle*]

REINFORCEMENT AT HOME

Parents and caregivers can help with many aspects of early reading. They can read to children or listen to children reading messages, stories, letters, e-mails, and other text. They can ask children to find specific words as they are reading. Activities such as stamp spelling (in which students use wooden or rubber letter stamps and an ink pad) and word games can be enjoyable activities that reinforce reading and spelling. Parents can help children learn nonphonetic words by asking children to spell words such as *laugh, want, through,* and *busy. In* addition, parents can point out words and letters on street signs, billboards, trucks, and license plates while on errands or trips. Parents and children can search for certain letters (e.g., *q, x, z*), certain letter combinations (e.g., all vowels, double letters), or whole words.

Origins of the Words *Read, Write,* and *Spell*

The word *read* comes from the Old English *rædan,* related to the German *raāten,* and was first written down in 899. The word *write* also comes from the Old English *wrītan* and was first written down in 725. Most other languages in Western Europe derived their words for *read* from the Latin *legere* (e.g., *to read* in French is *lire*). English is the only Western European language that does not derive its word for *to write* from the Latin *scribare.*

The English word *spell* comes from the Middle English *spellen,* meaning "to read letter by letter." It came to English by way of the Old French *espeller,* which was of Germanic origin, and was first written down in 1325.

Source: The American Heritage Student Dictionary, 1998.

More Reading and Writing Words

book   The Anglo-Saxon word for the beech tree was *boc.* Early English priests scratched a variety of symbols on the smooth bark of the beech tree.

paper   The word *paper* comes from the Egyptian rush called *papyrus* (a Latin word), from which paper was first made.

pen   The Latin word for *feather* was *penna.* In Middle English, it became *penne.* Remember that the feather, or quill, was one of the first writing utensils.

Fun with Words

The word *fun* is an interesting one, and its meaning is changing. Traditionally, it has been a noun meaning *enjoyment* or *amusement.* Since the 1950s, *fun* has also been used as an adjective, as in *We had a fun time, The picnic was fun,* and so forth.

RESOURCES FOR TEACHERS

Bear, D.R., Invernizzi, M., Templeton, S., & Johnson, F. (2001). *Words their way* (2nd ed.). Upper Saddle River, NJ: Merrill.

Center for the Improvement of Early Reading Achievement. (2001, September). *Put reading first: The research building blocks for children learning to read. Kindergarten through third grade.* Washington, DC: Partnership for Reading (National Institute for Literacy, National Institute of Child Health and Human Development, & U.S. Department of Education). (Available from National Institute for Literacy at ED Pubs, P.O. Box 1398, Jessup, MD 20794-1398; 800-228-8813; e-mail: EdPub-Orders@aspensys.com

Henry, M.K. (2010). *WORDS: Integrated decoding and spelling instruction based on word origin and word structure* (2nd ed.). Austin, TX: PRO-ED.

Henry, M.K., & Redding, N.C. (2002). *Patterns for success in reading and spelling.* Austin, TX: PRO-ED.

Moats, L.C. (2003). *Speech to print workbook: Language exercises for teachers.* Baltimore: Paul H. Brookes Publishing Co.

Moats, L.C. (2010). *Speech to print: Language essentials for teachers* (2nd ed.). Baltimore: Paul H. Brookes Publishing Co.

Rome, P.D., & Osman, J.S. (1993). *Language tool kit* [Teacher's manual and cards]. Cambridge, MA: Educators Publishing Service.

Lists of One- and Two-Syllable Words

Anderson, C.W. (1980). *Workbook of resource words for phonetic reading (Books 1–3).* Lincoln, NE: Educational Tutorial Consortium. (Available from the publisher, 444 South 44th Street, Lincoln, NE 68516; 402-489-8133; http://www.etc-ne.com)

Bloom, F., & Coates, D.B. (2000). *Recipe for reading.* Austin, TX: PRO-ED.

Fry, E.B., Polk, J.D., & Fountoukidis, D.L. (1996). *The reading teacher's new book of lists* (3rd ed.). Upper Saddle River, NJ: Prentice Hall.

Slingerland, B.H. (1982). *Phonetic word lists for children's use* [Catalog No. 217-W]. Cambridge, MA: Educators Publishing Service.

Slingerland, B.H. (1987). *Teacher's word list for reference* [Catalog No. 218-W]. Cambridge, MA: Educators Publishing Service.

DICTIONARIES FOR STUDENTS

Agnes, M.E. (Ed.). (1999). *Webster's new world children's dictionary* (2nd ed.). [For grades 2–7]. New York: Wiley.

Levey, J.S. (Ed.). (1990). *Macmillan first dictionary* [For Grades K–3]. New York: Simon & Schuster.

Levey, J.S. (Ed.). (2002). *Scholastic children's dictionary* [For Grades 3–7]. New York: Scholastic Reference.

Merriam-Webster Intermediate Dictionary. (2009). [For Grades 3–7]. Springfield, MA: Merriam-Webster.

GAMES FOR STUDENTS

Educational Insights. (2009). *Blurt!* Mattel. Author.

Milton Bradley. (1999). *UpWords.* East Longmeadow, MA: Author.

CHAPTER 7

Advancing Readers

Time for the Latin and Greek Layers of Language

U pper elementary school students need to go beyond phonics, syllable knowledge, and simple prefixes and suffixes because word length and complexity change dramatically beyond third grade. Yet although federal funding for reading initiatives has increased, currently most available funds target children in preschool through third grade. It cannot be assumed that by the end of third grade, children are even ready to learn all that must be learned about the structure of language as it relates to reading and spelling. McCardle and Chhabra declared that "in international comparisons, U.S. children do not on average perform badly in the early years; if international comparisons are taken as our guide, the reading crisis is one of adolescent literacy, not one of first- to fourth-grade literacy" (2004, pp. xix–xx).

New strategies are required for decoding and spelling the multisyllabic words that upper-grade students will find in literature and in content area textbooks. The end of third grade is the time to introduce students to the Latin roots and Greek combining forms used frequently in social studies, math, and science texts. Toward the last semester of third grade, introduce some of the very common Latin roots (e.g., *form, port*) with additional prefixes and suffixes (e.g., *informal, information, formality, export, portal, important*). If third graders do not understand basic letter–

sound correspondences or syllable division, these principles must be taught. Take a month or so to introduce or review the patterns in the 2 × 3 Anglo-Saxon letter–sound correspondence matrix (see Figure 3.2 in Chapter 3). Also review the common syllable division patterns before beginning to teach roots of Latin or Greek origin. You may want to introduce your students to common roots found in social studies textbooks. For example, third-grade geography books often discuss the *exports* and *imports* of numerous countries. Therefore, *port* is a logical first root to present. Words such as *export, import, imported, important, exporting, report, porter, portal,* and *transportation* can all be taught with an emphasis on affixes and roots. The term *geography* is an interesting one for students to begin learning about Greek word roots or combining forms, with *geo* (earth) and *graph* (to write) as the main forms. Teachers of students in the upper grades can determine whether to teach the common Latin roots before introducing the Greek layer or to interweave the two.

By the time students begin to learn the Latin and Greek base elements, students are also using cursive writing. As in the primary grades, students need to trace and copy and practice cursive letters and difficult connections such as *br, ow,* and *ov.* As students write from memory, ask them to say the sound or name of each letter. As soon as several cursive letters have been taught, the letters can be joined in pairs or short words.

The Latin and Greek layers of the language acquaint students with concepts that are more abstract than the concepts portrayed by the words of Anglo-Saxon origin (Quirk, 1974). By learning the common Latin roots and Greek combining forms, students will begin to recognize the useful orthographic forms and understand the specific meanings of these base elements as well. Learning these important patterns provides strategies for not only decoding and spelling but also for expanding expressive and receptive vocabulary. The patterns may well make mind pictures for students, making word retrieval more memorable. For example, imagining a volcano as it *erupts* or knowing someone whose appendix has *ruptured* helps students recall the meanings of the root *rupt* and words that contain it. Fortunately, words of Latin and Greek origin tend to be extremely regular; that is, they follow regular letter–sound correspondences even though the words are longer than those of Anglo-Saxon origin. Teachers need to encourage their students to become *linguaphiles* (lovers of words and language) and to begin to transfer decoding skills to literature reading and content area reading.

COMMON MORPHEMES

Estimates of vocabulary knowledge vary widely. Goulden, Nation, and Read (1990) concluded that the typical educated native speaker of English has a vocabulary of approximately 17,000 words acquired at the rate of about 2 to 3 words per day. Anderson and Nagy (1992) believed that this number was greatly underestimated. They estimated that the average fifth grader may encounter more than 10,000 new words during the school year and that the average child in elementary

> ## *morph* Words
>
> A *morpheme* is the smallest unit of meaning in a word.
>
> *Morphemics* is the study and description of language in terms of morphemes.
>
> A *morphemicist* is one who studies morphemics.
>
> An **allomorph** is any variant form of a morpheme. For example, /s/ in *cats*, /z/ in *dogs*, /əz/ in *horses*, and /ən/ in *oxen* are allomorphs of the English plural morpheme. The combining form *allo* comes from the Greek word *allos*, meaning *other.*

or secondary school probably learns 2,000–3,000 words per year. By high school, he or she knows 45,000 words from the more than 88,000 word families used in elementary and secondary school. Anderson and Nagy defined *word families* as groups of words for which knowing one of the words in the family helps a reader to infer the meaning of the others when encountering them in context. For example, knowing *place* helps a reader understand *replace, replacement, misplace, placing,* and so forth. Words in English expand by compounding Anglo-Saxon base words and by adding prefixes and suffixes to Anglo-Saxon base words and to Latin roots and Greek combining forms. These affixed words abound in content area reading.

Corson suggested that the human brain may use a coding system to process words and may not register multisyllabic words in their entirety: "Words may be analyzed by access codes into units, consisting of their bases or stems with prefixes and suffixes stripped" (1985, p. 19). He also noted that, disregarding foreign phrases and slang terms, almost all words that are content specific (i.e., that come from science, social studies, mathematics, and other content areas) are of Latin and Greek origin. He suggested that these content-specific "specialist" words enter the child's "performance" vocabulary in adolescence, if at all. Teaching the roots should be part of the curriculum, he recommended, because students from some social groups may not learn these in the natural environment. He stated that "for common readers, without Latin or Greek, the more serious reading becomes remote or irritating because the language of the page is not the language of the vernacular" (p. 39).

Beck, McKeown, and Kucan (2002) wrote of categories of vocabulary that they called "vocabulary tiers." Tier 1 includes basic words that rarely need to be taught, such as *hair, always, dress,* and *grass.* Tier 2 contains high-frequency words that are important for capable language learners to have in their vocabulary, such as *remorse, distinguished, capricious,* and *devious.* Low-frequency words, which are usually specific to an academic domain and are best learned in that content area, make up Tier 3. Such words include *isotope, photosynthesis,* and *psychologist.* Note that the words in these three tiers are of Anglo-Saxon, Latin, and Greek origin, respectively.

BEYOND PHONICS

Consider Alan, an extremely bright seventh-grade student just beginning secondary school. Alan struggled with reading and spelling in the elementary grades, but because of extremely high IQ scores, he was able to compensate for his problems and complete sixth grade with only moderate difficulty. Because of severe spelling problems, he was tested by a clinical psychologist at age 12; his paragraph writing to dictation appears in Figure 7.1. (Figure 7.2 shows the correct spelling of the passage.)

Teachers gain a rich source of information regarding a student's phonological abilities, orthographic understanding, and knowledge of corresponding rules by

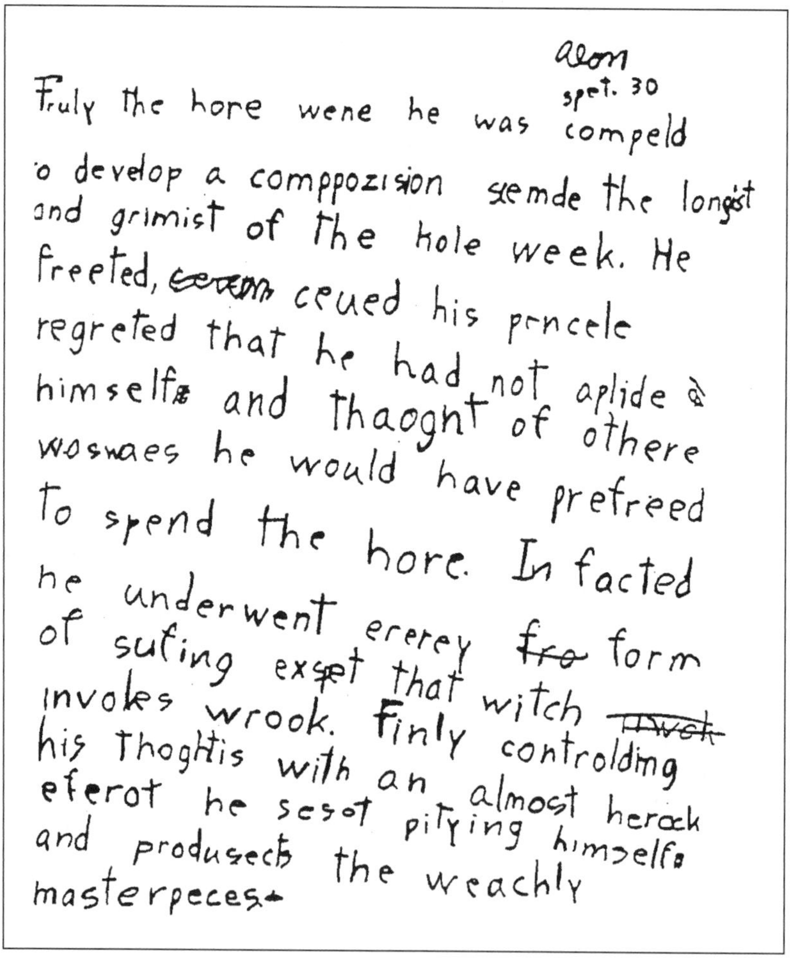
alon
spet. 30
Truly the hore wene he was compeld
o develop a comppozision semde the longist
and grimist of the hole week. He
freeted, ~~ceren~~ ceued his prncele
regreted that he had not aplide
himselfs and thaoght of othere
wosaes he would have prefreed
to spend the hore. In facted
he underwent ererey ~~fro~~ form
of sufing exset that witch
invokes wrook. Finly ~~thwek~~
his Thoghtis with an almost controlding
eferot he sesot pitying heroch
and produsects the himselfs
masterpeces weachly

Figure 7.1. Spelling from dictation by Alan, a seventh-grade student with dyslexia.

Truly, the hour when he was compelled to develop a composition seemed the longest and grimmest of the whole week. He fretted, chewed his pencil, regretted that he had not applied himself, and thought of other ways he would have preferred to spend the hour. In fact, he underwent every form of suffering except that which involves work. Finally, controlling his thoughts with an almost heroic effort, he ceased pitying himself and produced the weekly master-piece.

Figure 7.2.   Correct spelling of the dictation paragraph in Figure 7.1. This paragraph was created and used by psychologist Margaret Byrd Rawson.

looking at the student's writing samples. Look at all of the clues available from Alan's spelling. Notice that Alan seemed to understand grapheme–phoneme relationships: Some of his writing can be read phonetically (e.g., *comppozision* for *composition*, *grimist* for *grimmest*).

By the time he wrote this passage as a seventh grader, Alan had not learned many of the basic sight words needed in first and second grades, such as *hour, when, whole, ways, every, which,* and *work*. Although he did not reverse letter shapes (e.g., *b* for *d*), he did transpose the sequence of letters, as in *spet.* for *Sept., exspet* for *except,* and *wrook* for *work*. Although his speaking vocabulary was outstanding, he was not consistent in his spelling: He used *-d, -de,* and *-ed* (the correct form) for the past-tense ending. Figure 7.1 also shows that he did not understand the rules for suffix addition: He spelled *longest* as *longist, grimmest* as *grimist,* and *compelled* as *compeld*. Other errors include deleting a syllable, as in *sufing* (for *suffering*) and *herock* (for *heroic*).

So where would a teacher begin instructing students with the problems that Alan showed in his writing sample? He needed some of the basic sight words such as *when, hour, whole, thought,* and *every*. Teachers could briefly review letter–sound correspondences and the relevant rules and then immediately begin introducing the Latin word roots and affixes.

Learning the concept of schwa would be useful for students at this point, as many of the Latin-based words contain schwa sounds as unstressed affixes. Understanding morphophonemic relationships, described in Chapter 3, could also benefit students with difficulties similar to Alan's. Students need to understand that as affixes are added, sounds within syllables often change but that some of the spelling patterns of the base word remain (e.g., *house, housing; know, knowledge; remedy, remediate*).

Morphological and orthographic skills are also important, especially in longer words. Teachers need to find out what their students know about morpheme patterns. One way to assess students in the classroom is to have them mark specific patterns within a list of words. A group of students can be asked to find the suffixes in words such as *imported, tractor, instructive,* and *disruption.* Or teachers can give an individual child a card drill using common prefixes, suffixes, or Latin roots and ask the child to read the words on the cards and explain their meaning.

Prior to teaching the Latin roots, teachers should introduce additional prefixes and suffixes that are used with Latin roots. These affixes can be taught in separate prefix and suffix units or can be introduced as the individual roots are presented.

Prefixes

In a prefix unit, the teacher reviews those prefixes mentioned in Chapter 6 (e.g., *a-, de-, dis-, fore-, in-, mis-, pre-, re-, un-*). Then other prefixes with closed syllables are taught, such as *dif-, dys-, en-, ex-, il-, im-, in-, mal-, mid-, non-, sub-, suc-, suf-, sug-, sum-, sup-, sus-, trans-,* and *with-.*

 The prefix *dys-* is used with both Latin roots and Greek combining forms and contains the Greek-based pattern for *y* pronounced as short /ĭ/. The prefixes *syl-, sym-, syn-,* and *sys-* also contain *y* pronounced as short /ĭ/ and are usually taught along with the Greek combining forms.

Open-syllable prefixes include *bi-, co-, di-, e-, o-, pro-, tri-,* and *twi-,* as well as the previously taught *de-, re-,* and *pre-.* Prefixes with *r*-controlled vowels include *per-* and *fore-,* along with several of the two-syllable and **chameleon prefixes** described next. Two-syllable prefixes, including *ambi-, anti-, circum-, contra-, counter-, extra-, intra-, inter-, intro-, multi-, over-, super-,* and *ultra-,* should also be taught.

Chameleon prefixes (or assimilated prefixes) are generally taught when Latin roots are introduced. *Assimilation* is the process by which a sound is modified so that it becomes similar or identical to an adjacent or nearby sound (e.g., *inlegal* becomes *illegal*). The final letter of each of these prefixes changes depending on the first letter of the root. For example, *in-* (meaning *in* or *not*) changes to *il-* before a root beginning with *l* (e.g., *illegal*); to *ir-* before a root beginning with *r* (e.g., *irregular*); and to *im-* before a root beginning with *m, b,* or *p* (e.g., *immortal, imbibe, impede*). The prefix *con-* (meaning *together*) changes to variants *col-, cor-,* and *com-* in similar instances (e.g., *collect, correct, commute, combine, compute*). Other chameleon prefixes include *ad-* (*af-, ag-, al-, an-, ap-, ar-, as-, at-*), *sub-* (*suf-, sug-, sum-, sup-*), and *ob-* (*oc-, op-*). Teachers should tell their students that assimilation is formed because of euphony (from the Greek *eu,* meaning *well,* and the Greek *phon,* meaning *sound*). It sounds better!

Suffixes

Suffixes also need to be taught. In addition to those studied in Chapter 6 (i.e., *-able, -ed, -en, -er, -est, -fold, -ful, -hood, -ing, -less, -ling, -ly, -ment, -ness, -ship, -some,* and *-y*), which are used with Anglo-Saxon base words, the following suffixes need to be learned in approximately the order listed (i.e., column I suffixes are taught first, column II second, and column III last):

I	II	III
-ion (-tion, -sion)	-ar	-ism
-most	-ability	-ious
-ous	-ible, -ibility	-ory
-or	-ize	-ial (-cial, -tial)
-ess	-ary	-ian (-cian)
-ure, -ture	-ate	-cious
-dom	-ward	-ation
-ent, -ence	-age	-tious
-an	-al	-ile
-ant, -ance	-ify	-ade
-ist	-ity	-ium
-ic	-ee	
-ty	-fy	

Note that synthesis is likely to occur when the suffixes -ion, -ial, and -ian are added to roots ending with /s/, /t/, or /k/. In **synthesis,** two adjacent speech sounds combine to form a totally new sound, as in *congress/congressional, suspend/suspension,* and *react/reaction.* (For lists of prefixes and suffixes, along with their meanings, grammatical information, and examples of words containing them, see Appendixes D and E, respectively.)

The final spelling rule must also be learned at this time:

Doubling rule (for polysyllabic base words): When a base word ends with one consonant preceded by one short vowel, double the final consonant if the final syllable in the base word is accented, as in the following examples:

- *ad/mit':* admitting, admitted (accent is on the final syllable in the base)

- *gar'/den:* gardening, gardened (accent is on the first syllable in the base, so no doubling is necessary)

- *con/fer':* conferring, conference (accent is on the final syllable in the base, but note the shift in accent in *conference*)

 Although the past-tense forms of words such as *cancel* and *travel* traditionally have only one *l* in American English (e.g., *canceled, traveled*), newer dictionaries are giving two spellings (e.g., *canceled* or *cancelled; traveled* or *travelled*).

Here are some other interesting guidelines about suffixes:

- Use -*or* with Latin roots for nouns (as in *inventor, conductor, elevator*), but use -*ar* for adjectives (as in *popular, singular, circular*).

- Use *-or* with Latin roots (as in *spectator*), but use *-er* for Anglo-Saxon roots (as in *heater, swimmer, baker*).

- Although *-ous* and *-ess* sound alike because both are unstressed syllables that contain a schwa sound, use *-ous* for adjectives (as in *dangerous, tremendous, fabulous*) and *-ess* for feminine nouns (as in *princess, hostess, governess*). The similar sounding *-ice* is a noun suffix (as in *office, malice, practice, apprentice*).

- Use *-est* for the comparative degree of adjectives (as in *greenest, loveliest, smallest*), but use *-ist* for people nouns (as in *dentist, pianist, socialist*)

- Although not always the case, *-able* is usually added to Anglo-Saxon base words (as in *likable, reasonable, eatable*) and *-ible* is usually added to Latin roots (as in *credible, edible, impossible*).

- Although *-ent* and *-ant*, as well as *-ence* and *-ance*, sound alike because of the schwa, *-ent* and *-ence* are used somewhat more often than *-ant* and *-ance*. If in doubt, before you check the dictionary or spell checker, use *-ent* or *-ence*. Also, the suffix *-ant* often indicates a person noun (as in *tenant, sergeant, complainant*).

 When working with morphemes, be sure that students are not finding "false" morphemes in words. For example, students should not conclude that *sister* contains the comparative suffix *-er* or that *hundred* contains the past-tense suffix *-ed*. Students can consult the dictionary for etymologies together or independently to clear up confusion.

LATIN ROOTS

Teach each Latin root directly. Remember that the spelling of each Latin root is reliable in scores of words. Edmund H. Henderson noted that the Latin roots and Greek combining forms are stable elements of word knowledge and that "they are like the meaning characters in Chinese and Japanese. They provide meaning efficiency for reading across a shifting surface of sound" (1990, p. 74). Moreover, more than 50% of English words contain Latin word roots (King, 2000).

As students begin to learn the Latin roots, the teacher should incorporate etymology study in the curriculum. Etymology is the study of the history of words and the development of the structures and meanings of words. Corson said that "marked educational improvements have been reported for children who have followed programmes focusing on the etymology and word relationship of English" (1985, p. 28). Students learn to analyze the etymology of a word by looking in the dictionary. For example, students can look up the word *inspire* in the fourth edition of *The American Heritage Dictionary* (2000). They will find an etymology that shows that the word goes back to the Latin and prefixes the root *spir* with *in-*. The teacher can ask students to use a thesaurus to find synonyms of *inspire* or can ask them to generate other words with the root *spir*.

The sequence of presentation of Latin roots is based on both the frequency of words containing them and the regularity of their spellings. The first roots learned have only one or two forms (e.g., *tract; dic, dict; stru, struct*). Next, roots with three and four variants can be learned (e.g., *duc, duce, duct; fac, fact, fect, fic*). Two or three groups of roots can be taught in each lesson. The teacher should give ample opportunities for students to generate words and to read and spell them in lists, phrases, and sentences. (See the end of this chapter for other practice activities.)

Here is one logical sequence of presentation, reading across rows. See Appendix F for the Latin roots, their meanings, and examples of words. (Brown, 1947, suggested that the 12 Latin roots marked by asterisks, along with the Greek combining forms *graph* and *ology*, provide clues to the meanings of more than 100,000 words.)

form (to shape)

rupt (to break or burst)

scrib, script (to write)*

stru, struct (to build)

flect, flex (to bend or curve)

fer (to bear or yield)*

duc, duce, duct (to lead)*

vers, vert (to turn)

fac, fact, fect, fic (to make or do)*

tend, tens, tent (to stretch or strain)*

ped (foot)

aud (to hear or listen)

leg (law)

capit, capt (head or chief)

cap, ceit, ceive, cep, cept, cip (to take, catch, seize, hold, or receive)*

voc, vok, voke (to call)

lit, liter, litera (letters)

ten, tain, tin, tinu (to hold)*

sist, sta, stat, stit (to stand)*

pon, pose, pound (to put, place, or set)*

mob, mot, mov (to move)

cide (to kill)

plic, ply (to fold)*

port (to carry)

tract (to draw or pull)

spec, spect, spic (to see, watch, or observe)*

dic, dict (to say or tell)

mit, miss (to send)*

cred (to believe)

pel, puls (to drive or push)

pend, pens (to hang or weigh)

jac, jec, ject (to throw or lie)

cur, curs (to run or go)

vid, vis (to see)

vit, vita, viv, vivi (to live)

greg (group, crowd, flock, or herd; to assemble)

spir, spire (to breathe)

grad, gred, gress (step, degree; to walk)

lect, leg, lig (to choose, pick, read, or speak)

cede, ceed, cess (to go, yield, or surrender)

feder, fid, fide, feal (trust or faith)

cad, cas, cid (to fall or befall)

cern (to separate), *cert* (to decide)

gen, genus (race, kind, or species; birth)

cise (to cut)

cogn (to know)

Because the spellings of Latin roots are so phonetic, the teacher may present the roots in almost any order. The teacher may wish to determine which roots are found in the literature and textbooks that his or her students read and develop a customized sequence.

The teacher can ask students to generate morpheme webs using roots as they are presented. Ramsden (2001) illustrated this web activity (see Figure 7.3). Matrices are also good visual reinforcement for many roots. Again, Ramsden (2001) illustrated a matrix that shows the affixes that can be added to a target root (see Figure 7.4).

The teacher should consciously direct students to the spelling–meaning connection. Remember that accent often shifts and that vowel sounds become schwa. The teacher should show the relationship of words in word families. For example, the teacher can help students notice that in *sign*, the *g* is not heard that but that in *signal, signify*, and *signature*, the *g* has its hard sound. Students can be asked to compare the vowel sounds in the following words: *melody, melodic,* and *melodious*. In *melody*, the *o* is pronounced as schwa; in *melodic* the *o* says short /ŏ/, and in *melodious* the *o* says long /ō/. Similar compare/contrast examples include word pairs such as *condemn, condemnation; compete, competition; image, imagine;* and *local, locality*. Students should mark the accent and vowel sounds in each word.

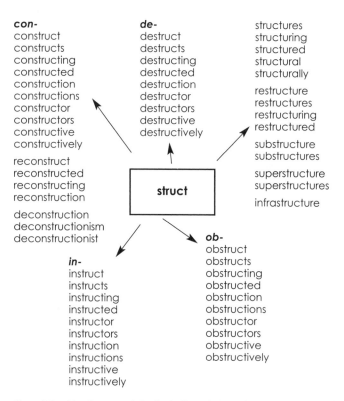

Figure 7.3. Morpheme web for the Latin root *struct*. (From Ramsden, M. [2001]. *The spelling manual in the real spelling tool box.* Retrieved March 7, 2003, from http://www.realspelling.com; adapted by permission.)

re de	con		s ed ing	
			ive	ly
de in ob sub super infra		**struct**	or	s
			ion	s ism ist
			ure	s ed ing
				al / ly

Figure 7.4. Matrix showing the addition of prefixes and suffixes to the Latin root *struct*. (Used by kind permission of Melvyn Ramsden.)

The teacher should point out to students that some Latin roots require "connectives" between the root and the suffix. The *u* in *contemptuous* is a connective, as is the *i* in *solitude*. Other examples, with connectives underlined, include *monument, conspicuous, convenient, ingenious,* and *editorial.*

After students learn several Latin roots, the teacher connects these roots to content area reading to ensure transfer. The teacher selects phrases or sentences from a social studies text that contain words with the target roots. Students read or write the selected groups of words. (See Appendix H for content area words related to upper elementary and middle school subject areas.)

While working with Latin word roots, the teacher should remember that affixes generally contain the schwa sound. Students cannot just depend on phonological clues for decoding and spelling these multisyllabic words but must know the words' grammatical function as well. For example, in spelling the word *governess*, students need to know that both *-ous* and *-ess* say /əs/. But knowing that *-ess* is used for feminine nouns and that *governess* is a feminine noun, whereas *-ous* is used only for adjectives (e.g., *mountainous, adventurous*), brings students to the correct solution.

WORD WISDOM

The Influence of French on English

Many English words are influenced by the French language. For example, most words with the grapheme *ch* sounding like /sh/ come from French:

chef	cache	chenille	chamois
machine	mustache	sachet	brochure
champagne	chute	chiffon	parachute
chandelier	chivalry	nonchalant	chauvinist
chaise	chanteuse	charade	chivalrous

Many French-based words include the grapheme *ou*:

adjourn	sojourn	journey	journal
flourish	courage	encourage	nourish
courier	couple	courtesy	courteous

The spelling pattern *eau* is also a convention from French:

flambeau	bandeau	rondeau	tableau
trousseau	bureau	chateau	plateau
beau	chapeau	portmanteau	gateau

In addition, the word-final -*que*, sounding like /k/, is from French:

oblique	antique	technique	pique
perique	physique	unique	critique
clique	cinque	baroque	equivoque
Basque	masque	arabesque	Romanesque
humoresque	picturesque	grotesque	cheque

| LESSON | **Introducing Latin Word Roots** |

Opening

"Today we're going to continue breaking words apart to make them easier to read and spell. We've worked on Anglo-Saxon root words and numerous prefixes and suffixes. For the next several days, we will talk about Latin roots. Who remembers what a root is?" [*The root is the main part of the word, the part to which prefixes and suffixes are added. The root usually receives the accent or stress in Latin-based words.*] "Roots are valuable as patterns not only for decoding and spelling but also for learning new vocabulary to enhance your reading, writing, listening, and speaking. Thousands of words—more than half of the words in the dictionary—come from Latin roots. Each root has a specific meaning; we change the meaning by adding prefixes and suffixes."

Middle

Write the root *rupt* on the board. Ask students to generate a number of words with *rupt* as the root. Write the words on the board. See if students can pick up the meaning of *rupt* (to break, to burst) from the words on the board. Here are some words containing *rupt*:

rupture	interrupts	disrupted	irrupt
abrupt	disruptive	corruption	eruptive
disrupt	corrupting	eruption	interruption
corrupted	erupt	interrupted	corruptible
abruptly	interrupting	corrupt	bankrupt

Add additional words containing *rupt* and affixes. For each word, have students read the word and identify the common word part (*rupt*). Have students note the placement of the root (at the beginning if there is no prefix, the end if there is no suffix, the middle if there are prefixes and suffixes).

Dictate several words containing *rupt* and sentences containing these words.

Closing

Probe for content, structure, and process. Review why learning these roots is valuable for students.

Follow-Up

Have students look for words of Latin origin in newspapers or in their social studies textbook.

In a format similar to this lesson, continue to present new, frequently used roots, such as *port* (to carry); *form* (to shape); *tract* (to pull); *stru, struct* (to build); *dic, dict* (to say, tell); *flect, flex* (to bend); *mit, miss* (to send); *fer* (to bear, carry); and so forth.

From Henry, M.K. (2010). *WORDS: Integrated decoding and spelling instruction based on word origin and word structure* (2nd ed., pp. 153–155). Austin, TX: PRO-ED. Copyright (c) 2010 by PRO-ED; and Henry, M.K., & Redding, N.C. (2002). *Patterns for success in reading and spelling* (2nd ed., pp. 281–284). Austin, TX: PRO-ED. Copyright (c) 2002 by PRO-ED; adapted by permission.

GREEK COMBINING FORMS

Many of the Latin roots were actually borrowed from Greek. Some of the Greek words had themselves been borrowed from the language of still earlier people, the Phoenicians. Greek-based words in English tend to be related to math and science. Words such as *biology, geology, archaeology, physics, chemistry,* and *geography* all contain Greek combining forms, and the words used in these domains are often of Greek origin.

Teachers may want to finish introducing the majority of Latin roots before presenting the Greek combining forms. Or teachers may wish to teach some of the common Greek forms along with the Latin roots, especially in fifth grade, when science and math texts begin to depend on Greek-based words as the key content words.

When introducing Greek-based words, first teach those letter–sound correspondences that are exclusive to Greek (i.e., *ph* for /f/ as in *photograph, ch* for /k/ as in *chemotherapy,* and *y* for /ĭ/ as in *symphonic*). Other Greek-based letter combinations include *y* as long /ī/ as in *hydrogen, ps* as in *psychology, rh* as in *rhinoceros, pn* as in *pneumonia, pt* as in *pterodactyl,* and *mn* as in *mnemonic.* If a word begins with *x,* such as *xylophone* or *Xerxes,* students can assume it is from Greek.

Because Greek-based word parts compound, the parts are usually called combining forms. Some teachers, however, use the term *root,* which is fine as long as the term is used consistently. Note also that some teachers use the term *prefix* for Greek combining forms that appear at the beginnings of words (e.g., *auto, tele*) and the term *suffix* for those forms that appear at the ends of words (e.g., *ology, logue*). Again, this is fine as long as the terms are applied consistently.

Words of Greek origin often contain the connective letter *o.* For example, in the word *phonology,* the first combining form is *phon* and the second is *log/logy.* The *o* is used to connect the two word parts. In the word *oceanographer,* the *o* connects *ocean* (from the Greek *okeanos*) and *graph,* and the suffix *-er* is added.

Give approximately four to six Greek combining forms in any lesson. This way, scores of words can be generated from each combining form. A possible sequence for presenting the Greek combining forms, based primarily on grade level and frequency, follows, reading across rows:

phon, phono (sound)

photo (light)

gram, graph (written or drawn)

meter, metr (measure)

tele (distant)

bio (life)

micro (small or minute)

hydr, hydra, hydro (water)

therm, thermo (heat or hot)

cracy, crat (rule)

scope (to watch or see)

metro (mother city; measure)

biblio (book)

dem, demo (people)

geo (earth)

hypo (under)

pol, polis, polit (city; method of government)

cycl, cyclo (wheel or circle; circular)

chrom (color)

derm (skin)

techn (skill, art, or craft)

chron, chrono (time)

psych (mind or soul)

hyper (over, above, or excessive)

gno, gnosi (know)

phys (nature)

mech (machine)

path (feeling, suffering, or disease)

arch (chief or ruler)

lex (word)

phil, phila, phile, philo (love or affinity for)

mega (large or great)

meta (beside, after, later, or beyond)

soph (wisdom or cleverness)

kine, cine (movement)

phobia, phobic; phobe (irrational fear or hatred; one who fears or hates)

the, theo (god)

mania (madness, frenzy, abnormal desire, or obsession)

andr, anthr (man)

poly (many)

ast, astro (star)

hemi, semi, demi (half)

archae, arche, archi (primitive or ancient)

mon, mono (one)

auto (self)

gon (angle)

logy (study; from *logos, logue* [speech or word])

sphere (sphere, circle)

A combined unit on Latin- and Greek-based number words is recommended for upper-grade students, as such terms appear over and over in math and science textbooks at this level. (See "Number Prefixes from Latin and Greek" in Appendix D for the related number words.)

| LESSON | **Introducing Greek Combining Forms** |

Opening

"Today we will switch from working on words of Latin origin to learning words of Greek origin. You may remember that these words are often used in science classes and textbooks. Different people use different terms to describe the Greek word parts. In some dictionaries and books they are called *roots*, in some they are called *combining forms*, in others some Greek-based word parts are known as *prefixes* and *suffixes*. We will call them all *combining forms* because usually there are two parts of equal stress and importance that are combined, almost as in Anglo-Saxon compound words. Some of the parts come only at the beginning of a word, and others come at the end. Some forms can be used in either position. The connective letter *o* often connects the two combining forms."

Middle

On the board, write a number of word parts. Point out that some parts usually come at the beginning or at the end of words. Among the first combining forms to be learned are *auto, phono, photo, biblio, hydro, hyper, tele, chron, chrom, arch, phys, psych, micro, peri, bi, semi, hemi, mono, meta, mega, metro, philo, soph, theo, techni, graph, gram, meter, ology, sphere, scope, crat, cracy,* and *polis.*

 Alert students to the Greek letter–sound correspondences that predominate in these combining forms, such as *ph; ch; y* as medial vowel; silent *p* in *ps, pt,* and *pn;* and, rarely, *rh, mn,* and *x* that sounds like /z/.

Have students generate Greek-based words, such as the following:

chronometer	perimeter	microscope	hyperactive
physiology	physician	periscope	archeology
bibliography	physiologist	telescope	phonograph
telegraph	zoology	autograph	architect
autobiography	metropolis	metropolitan	hemisphere
hydrogen	philosophy	philharmonic	theology
psychology	pterodactyl	pneumonia	metaphysics

Have students read words from flipcharts or from word lists that you have prepared.

Dictate a number of words with Greek word parts for students to spell.

Closing

Review the terminology and origin of these Greek combining forms. Let students know that in the next lesson, they will deal with the specific meanings of many of these combining forms.

Follow-Up

Have students look in their science textbooks for words that contain Greek combining forms. Continue to teach several specific combining forms in following lessons. The format will remain the same. See Appendix G for the Greek combining forms, their meanings, and examples. Also, provide plenty of practice in working with content area words such as those found in Appendix H.

From Henry, M.K. (2010). *WORDS: Integrated decoding and spelling instruction based on word origin and word structure* (2nd ed., pp. 164–166). Austin, TX: PRO-ED. Copyright (c) 2010 by PRO-ED; and Henry, M.K., & Redding, N.C. (2002). *Patterns for success in reading and spelling* (2nd ed., pp. 281–284). Austin, TX: PRO-ED. Copyright (c) 2002 by PRO-ED; adapted by permission.

PRACTICE READING AND SPELLING LONGER WORDS

As students read unfamiliar words, the teacher should ask the students to try to identify the language of origin of each word. Next, students should look for the morpheme units (e.g., prefixes, roots, and suffixes; combining forms). If they cannot find morphemes in a word, or if they can find morphemes but still cannot read the entire word, students should break the word into syllables using the common options for syllable division. If syllable division does not work or works for only part of the word, students should use letter–sound correspondences to read the word.

Activities to Reinforce Latin- and Greek-Based Morphemes

The following are examples of activities that are designed to reinforce students' familiarity with Latin- and Greek-based morphemes.

ACTIVITY | **Counting Morphemes**

Have students count the number of syllables and morphemes in each of the words in Table 7.1.

Table 7.1. Counting syllables and morphemes

Word	Number of syllables	Number of morphemes
prediction	3	3
illegality	5	4
resistant	3	3
autobiography	6	4
photograph	3	2
hydrology	4	2
popularize	4	3 (*ul* is a connective)

ACTIVITY | **Matching Prefixes and Meanings**

Have students match prefixes and their meanings:

trans-	[B]	A.	forward
pro-	[A]	B.	across
mid-	[E]	C.	under
non-	[F]	D.	out
sub-	[C]	E.	between
ex-	[D]	F.	not
ultra-	[I]	G.	between
contra-	[K]	H.	around
intro-	[J]	I.	beyond
inter-	[G]	J.	inward
intra-	[F]	K.	against
circum-	[B]	L.	within

ACTIVITY | Matching Suffixes and Meanings

Have students match suffixes and their parts of speech.

-or	[C]	A.	adverb
-ess	[D]	B.	adjective
-ist	[E]	C.	noun
-ly	[A]	D.	feminine noun
-ous	[B]	E.	noun, person

ACTIVITY | Finding Morphemes in Words

Have students read the following words and list the root and any prefixes and/or suffixes. Have them analyze the following Latin-based words for word structure and pronunciation:

Word	Prefix(es)	Root	Suffix(es)
reflection	[*re*]	[*flect*]	[*ion*]
disrupted	[*dis*]	[*rupt*]	[*ed*]
attractive	[*at*]	[*tract*]	[*ive*]
collective	[*col*]	[*lect*]	[*ive*]
subtracting	[*sub*]	[*tract*]	[*ing*]
prescriptions	[*pre*]	[*script*]	[*ion, s*]
reconstructionist	[*re, con*]	[*struct*]	[*ion, ist*]
pendant	[*no prefixes*]	[*pend*]	[*ant*]
congregation	[*con*]	[*greg*]	[*ation*]
inspector	[*in*]	[*spect*]	[*or*]

ACTIVITY | Finding Latin Roots

Have students underline the Latin word roots in the following words:

nonde<u>script</u>	in<u>struct</u>ive	con<u>vert</u>ible	con<u>fer</u>ence
at<u>tract</u>ive	ad<u>vers</u>ary	unin<u>tent</u>ionally	con<u>duct</u>or
ex<u>pell</u>ed	<u>spect</u>acular	re<u>flect</u>ion	con<u>ject</u>ure

ACTIVITY | Matching Roots and Meanings

Have students match the Latin root with the letter of the correct meaning.

[C]	*rupt*	A. to say or tell
[F]	*spect*	B. to breathe
[A]	*dict*	C. to break or burst
[E]	*flect*	D. to pull
[B]	*spire*	E. to bend
[D]	*tract*	F. to see

ACTIVITY | Matching Words and Meanings

Ask students to match the correct meaning of each of these words containing the root *dic, dict* (meaning *to say or tell*):

[F]	malediction	A. an absolute ruler
[D]	benediction	B. to express the opposite
[B]	contradict	C. to point out
[G]	prediction	D. a blessing
[A]	dictator	E. a reference book for words
[C]	indicate	F. a curse
[E]	dictionary	G. something foretold

ACTIVITY | Defining Roots

Ask students to write the Latin root that corresponds with each of the following:

to pull [*tract*]	to build [*struct*]
to write [*scribe* or *script*]	to bend [*flect* or *flex*]
to see [*spect*]	to break [*rupt*]
to hear [*aud*]	to run [*cur* or *curs*]
to stretch [*tend* or *tens*]	to turn [*vert* or *vers*]
to believe [*cred*]	to bear [*fer*]

ACTIVITY | Identifying Affixes

Ask students to underline the prefixes and circle the suffixes in the following passage:

The active conductor took the elevator to the fifth floor. There he walked briskly to the composer's attractive apartment. Mr. Musician the conductor, was furious that Mr. Composition had forgotten to deliver the latest manuscript to the auditorium for the rehearsal.

Mr. Musician: "How can the orchestra possibly play this piece at tonight's performance? We have been unable to rehearse. The violinists are fuming the trombonists are seething and the percussionists are almost insane."

Mr. Composition: "The latest corrections have been included in this final draft. Your musicians are so talented and precocious they can play anything. Take this folder containing the symphony and leave me alone!"

ACTIVITY | Finding Target Morpheme Cards

Using 3 × 5 cards with prefixes, roots, and suffixes on them, ask students to find target cards, such as the cards that mean *before, against, build, turn,* and so forth (*pre, ante, struct, vert*).

ACTIVITY | Using Words in Context

Ask students to write each word in a sentence:

exports   [*The United States exports grain to many countries.*]

bankrupt   [*Numerous companies may go bankrupt during a recession.*]

transformed   [*The darkness transformed our memory of the forest.*]

ACTIVITY | Filling in the Blanks

Ask students to fill in the missing word in each sentence with the best word from the following choices:

interrupted	spectators	information	supported
formality	report	convertible	formula

My _____ card had mostly As.   [*report*]

My sister _____ our telephone conversation.   [*interrupted*]

The building was _____ by heavy beams.   [*supported*]

Give me new _____ on the research.   [*information*]

I have a new yellow _____ .   [*convertible*]

The _____ cheered at the football game.   [*spectators*]

ACTIVITY | Substituting Latin-Based Words

For each italicized word or phrase, have students choose a substitute term from the three choices given. This substitute term should contain a Latin-based root.

My *teacher* helped the principal at lunchtime.
  informer   [*instructor*]   reporter

Turn in your *research paper* tomorrow.
  [*manuscript*]   prescription   protractor

Sign the *business agreement* soon.
  [*contract*]   inscription   export

He had a new mathematical *equation* to study.
  informal   conductor   [*formula*]

ACTIVITY | Adding Suffixes

Review the doubling rule for polysyllabic base words. Ask students to underline the accented syllable in the following base words and write the words with the given suffixes added:

con<u>struct</u> + ed   [*constructed*]

ex<u>pel</u> + ing   [*expelling*]

<u>gov</u>ern + or   [*governor*]

pre<u>vent</u> + ive   [*preventive*]

com<u>mit</u> + ee   [*committee*]

ad<u>mit</u> + ance   [*admittance*]

<u>sum</u>mon + ed   [*summoned*]

for<u>bid</u> + en   [*forbidden*]

ACTIVITY | Identifying the Language of Origin

Have students identify the language of origin (Anglo-Saxon, Latin, or Greek) of the following words:

philharmonic   [*Greek*]

extraction   [*Latin*]

introspective   [*Latin*]

bookish   [*Anglo-Saxon*]

expeditious   [*Latin*]

psychology   [*Greek*]

hopelessness   [*Anglo-Saxon*]

laughing   [*Anglo-Saxon*]

manufactured   [*Latin*]

hydrophobia   [*Greek*]

ACTIVITY | Finding Greek Combining Forms

Have students circle the Greek combining forms in the following words:

chron ology   micro scope   tele graph   hydro sphere

poly gon   mono gram   thermo meter   philo sophy

ACTIVITY | Matching Combining Forms

Have students match the letter of the correct meaning with the Greek combining form.

[F]	*micro*	A.	sound
[G]	*ology*	B.	life
[D]	*auto*	C.	look or see
[J]	*graph, gram*	D.	self
[I]	*therm*	E.	distant
[E]	*tele*	F.	small
[B]	*bio*	G.	study
[A]	*phon, phono*	H.	water
[C]	*scope*	I.	heat
[H]	*hydro*	J.	written or drawn

ACTIVITY | Identifying Parts of Speech

Ask students to give the part of speech (noun, verb, adjective, or adverb) for each word:

geology [*noun*]   geologist [*noun*]

geologize [*verb*]   geologizer [*noun*]

geologizing [*noun*]   geologic [*adjective*]

geological [*adjective*]   geologically [*adverb*]

geologian [*noun*]

ACTIVITY | Making Words

Give pairs of children a Greek-based word with two combining forms, such as *biology*. Have the students identify the two combining forms [*bio* and *logy*], give the forms' meanings, and make words with those two forms.

biology

bio (life)	*logy* (study of)
biosphere	geology
biodegradable	dermatology
biochemistry	phonology
biography	zoology
autobiography	pathology
	mythology

ACTIVITY | Finding Words in Context

Astro is a Greek combining form meaning *star*. Ask students to find as many *astro* words as possible in their science book, in the dictionary, or on the Internet. [*astrophysics, astrochemistry, astrobiology, astrogeology,* and so forth]

ACTIVITY | Making Morpheme Webs

Ask students to draw a web for the root *rupt* using the blank web shown in Figure 7.5 as a model. Students should use as many prefixes and suffixes as they can. This can be a group or individual activity.

ACTIVITY | Brainstorming Greek-Based Words

Have students write as many words as they can containing each Greek combining form. This can be a group or solo activity.

micro

chron

photo

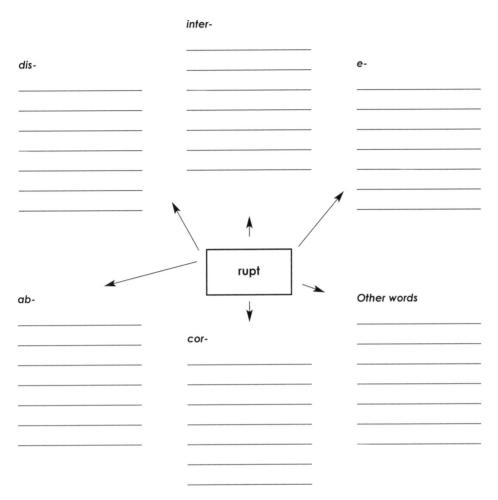

Figure 7.5. Blank morpheme web for the Latin root *rupt*.

| ACTIVITY | **Guided Questioning** |

Have students answer the following types of questions about words of interest:

photosynthesis: "What is the word's origin? [*Greek*] What are the clues?" [*The letters* ph *saying* /f/ *and* y *saying* /ĭ/] "What do you think this word means? What is the dictionary definition?"

interruption: "What is the word's origin?" [*Latin*] "What are the clues?" [*prefix* inter-, *root* rupt, *suffix* -ion] "What is the meaning?" [*a hindering or stopping of some action by someone breaking in*] "What is the literal definition?" [*to break between*]

Table 7.2. Comparing Anglo-Saxon, Latin, and Greek words

Anglo-Saxon	Latin	Greek
teacher	instructor, professor	philosopher
earth	terrain	geography
watery	aquatic	hydraulic
fear	trepidation	phobia

ACTIVITY | Anglo-Saxon, Latin, and Greek Contrasts

Ask students to compare Anglo-Saxon, Latin, and Greek words with similar meanings. See if they can add to the list in Table 7.2.

ACTIVITY | Contrasting Meaning

Have children contrast word pairs, as in the following examples. Students should try to figure out the meaning of the target words, and they can check their answers by using the dictionary. This is a good activity for small groups of students working together.

"Describe a person with *megapods* and *megadonts*." [*A person with megapods and megadonts has large feet and large teeth.*]

"Compare the behavior of an *extrovert* and an *introvert*." [*An extrovert is outgoing and gregarious, whereas an introvert turns inward.*]

"How do *intrastate* and *interstate* highways differ?" [*Intrastate highways exist within a state, whereas interstate highways run between states.*]

ACTIVITY | Playing Word Games

Games are useful for reinforcing concepts learned. Activities based on popular games such as Bingo, Concentration, Jeopardy!, Wheel of Fortune, and Charades can be adapted to practice with word roots and combining forms.

The Letter *i* as Consonant /y/

When the letter *i* comes after *ll* or word-medial *l* or *n*, the *i* is often pronounced as the consonant sound /y/:

alien	billiards	bunion	familiar
million	companion	civilian	billion
onion	peculiar	trillion	union

RESOURCES FOR TEACHERS

Bebko, A.R., Alexander, J., & Doucet, R. (n.d.). *LANGUAGE!: Roots* (2nd ed.). Longmont, CO: Sopris West.

Blanchard, C. (n.d.). *Word root series* (Level A: grades 4–6, Level B: grades 7 to adult). Pacific Grove, CA: Critical Thinking Books and Software.

Ebbers, S.M. (2004). *Vocabulary through morphemes.* Longmont, CO: Sopris West.

Ehrlich, I. (1988). *Instant vocabulary* (Reissue ed.). New York: Pocket Books.

Fifer, N., & Flowers, N. (1990). *Vocabulary from classical roots.* Cambridge, MA: Educators Publishing Service.

Henry, M.K. (2010). *WORDS: Integrated decoding and spelling instruction based on word origin and word structure* (2nd ed.). Austin, TX: PRO-ED.

Henry, M.K., & Redding, N.C. (2002). *Patterns for success in reading and spelling* (2nd ed.). Austin, TX: PRO-ED.

Johnson, K., & Bayrd, P. (1998). *Megawords series.* Cambridge, MA: Educators Publishing Service.

Marcellaro, E.G., & Ostrovsky, G.R. (1988). *Verbal vibes series.* Sacramento, CA: Lumen.

Morgan, K. (2002). *Dynamic roots.* Albuquerque, NM: Morgan Dynamic Phonics.

Quinion, M. (2002). *Ologies and isms: Beginnings and endings of words.* Oxford, England: Oxford University Press.

Rome, P.D., & Osman, J.S. (2000). *Advanced language tool kit* [Teacher's manual and cards]. Cambridge, MA: Educators Publishing Service.

Steere, A., Peck, C.Z., & Kahn, L. (1971). *Solving language difficulties.* Cambridge, MA: Educators Publishing Service.

Dictionaries and Thesauri

The American heritage student dictionary. (1998). Boston: Houghton Mifflin. (For grades 6–9)

The American heritage student thesaurus. (1999). Boston: Houghton Mifflin. (For grades 7–10)

Barnhart, R.K. (Ed.). (1988). *The Barnhart dictionary of etymology.* New York: The H.W. Wilson Company.

Bollard, J.K. (1998). *Scholastic children's thesaurus.* New York: Scholastic.

Crutchfield, R.S. (1997). *English vocabulary quick reference: A comprehensive dictionary arranged by word roots.* Leesburg, VA: LexaDyne. (Also available online: http://www.quickreference.com/order.htm)

Halsey, W.D. (Ed.). (2001). *Macmillan dictionary for children.* New York: Simon & Schuster.

Latimer, J.P., & Nolting, K.S. (2001). *Simon & Schuster thesaurus for children* [ages 9–12]. New York: Simon & Schuster.

Merriam-Webster's school dictionary. (2004). Springfield, MA: Merriam-Webster. (For upper elementary and secondary grades)

Merriam-Webster thesaurus. (2005). Springfield, MA: Merriam-Webster. (For upper elementary and secondary grades)

Web Sites

A.Word.A.Day, http://www.wordsmith.org/awad/index.html

Children of the Code, http://www.childrenofthecode.org

Confusing Words, http://www.confusingwords.com

Critical Thinking Books and Software, http://www.criticalthinking.com

Dictionary.com, http://www.dictionary.com

Explore English Words by Focusing on Words, http://www.wordexplorations.com

Morgan Dynamic Phonics, http://www.dynamicphonics.com/advanced.htm

Online Etymology Dictionary, http://www.etymonline.com

Real Spelling, http://www.realspelling.com

Vocabulogic: A Weekly Blog, http://www.vocablog-plc.blogspot.com/

Word Root Quick Reference, http://www.espindle.org/roots.html

Word Searcher, http://www.neilramsden.co.uk/spelling

WordsWorth Compendium, http://www.dictionary-thesaurus.com

WordWorks, http://www.wordworkskingston.com

World Wide Words, http://www.worldwidewords.org/index.htm

GAME FOR STUDENTS

Johnson, P.F. (1999). *Word scramble 2.* East Moline, IL: LinguiSystems.

CHAPTER 8

Competent Readers

Extending the Latin and Greek Layers of Language

Many teachers and curriculum developers believe that reading instruction is the purview of the elementary school. Yet many students need other strategies to analyze and comprehend the more difficult words and concepts found in their high school and college textbooks and literature. Langer (2001) found that 60% of 12th graders could not interpret or analyze text in more than superficial ways, according to the 1998 National Assessment of Educational Progress. Since then, little has improved for graduating seniors. Shanahan (2007) noted that the "Nation's Report Card" published by National Assessment of Educational Progress showed an overall decline in reading test scores since 1992 for 12th graders. Students have difficulty making inferences and understanding figurative language. A California State University (2008) report on English and math proficiency noted that in the fall of 2008, of slightly more than 50,000 incoming freshman, only 53% were considered proficient. The students came from many ethnicities; unfortunately, no data were available on the number of students who were English language learners.

Except where noted otherwise, the dictionary definitions in the activities in this chapter are paraphrased from *The American Heritage Dictionary* (2000).

Langer urged the embracing of Vygotsky's sociocultural framework, according to which learning occurs "within an environment in which both [teacher and student] can participate in thoughtful examination and discourse about language and content" (2001, p. 839). Langer noted the importance of providing students with challenging literary tasks and explicitly teaching skills. She found that in those English classrooms where students performed highest in writing assignments, students learned how language works in context: "[Students] were learning grammar, spelling, vocabulary, and organizational structure—sometimes in context but also with carefully planned activities that focused directly on the structure and use of language" (p. 856).

Consider Alan, whose seventh-grade writing sample is presented in Figure 7.1 in Chapter 7. After little more than 5 months of instruction, 1 hour per week, in the common affixes, Latin roots, and Greek combining forms, Alan provided another writing sample from dictation (see Figure 8.1).

During instruction, Alan did not work on these words directly; instead, he learned the important orthographic structures and rules. After a review of letter–sound correspondences and syllable patterns, Alan immediately began learning about affixes and roots. Notice also that Alan learned to use cursive writing. Using

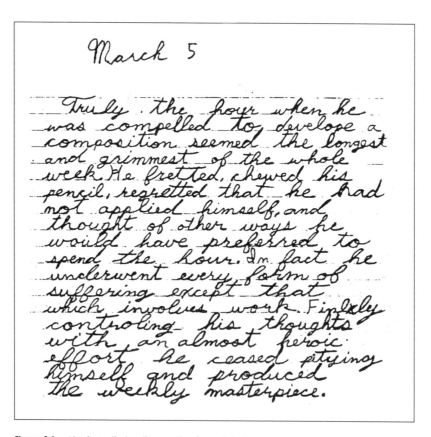

Figure 8.1. Alan's postinstruction spelling from dictation.

cursive was part of the instruction, and he balked at this initially. Alan learned the linguistic information presented in the preceding chapters of this book. He also learned other less common Latin roots and Greek combining forms.

LESS COMMON LATIN ROOTS

After learning the more common Latin affixes and roots and Greek combining forms suggested in Chapter 7, students are ready for less common forms. Such less common Latin roots include the following:

civ (citizen)

claim, clam (to declare, call out, or cry out)

claus, clois, clos, clud, clus (to shut or close)

corp, corpor (body)

crea (to create)

dent (tooth)

dorm (to sleep)

fin, finis (end)

flu, fluc, fluv, flux (flowing)

forc, fort (strong)

grat, gre (thanks; pleasing)

grav, gravi (heavy)

hab, habit (to have or live)

hum, human (earth, ground, or man)

intellect, intellig (power to know and think)

join, junct (to join)

jud, judi, judic (judge)

jur, jus (law)

liber, liver (free)

lic, licit (permit)

loc, loqu (to speak)

luc, lum, lus (light)

matr, matri (mother)

numer (number)

patr, pater (father)

pict, picto (paint)

plac, plais (please)

plu, plur, plus (more)

portio (a part or a share)

poten, poss (power)

prim, prime (first)

punct (point or dot)

put (to think)

rect, recti (straight or right)

rog, roga (to ask or beg)

sat, satis (enough)

sign, signi (to sign, mark, or seal)

simil, simul (like or resembling)

sume, sump (to take, use, or waste)

tact, tag, tang, tig, ting (to touch)

tempo, tempor (time)

trib (to pay or bestow)

tui, tuit, tut (to guard or teach)

ultima (last)

vac (empty)

vale, vali, valu (strength, worth, or valor)

ver, veri (true or genuine)

vore (to devour)

Lesson formats for these roots are the same as those presented in earlier chapters.

Activities Related to Less Common Latin Roots

Older students require more intellectually challenging activities to reinforce concepts and patterns. For example, older students may do some of the following.

ACTIVITY | Studying Shakespeare

Study the words of William Shakespeare. These words are notable for surviving for more than 400 years. Shakespeare used Anglo-Saxon words such as *lonely* and *bump* but also introduced Latin-based words such as *assassination, accommodation, reliance, dexterously, submerged,* and *obscene;* the Greek words *apostrophe* and *misanthrope;* and many others (Klausner, 1990). Students can look for unfamiliar words in the works of Shakespeare and investigate their origin and meaning.

ACTIVITY | Comparing and Contrasting

Have students compare and contrast *luxuriant* and *luxurious.* "How are these words similar in meaning?" [*Both contain the root* luxor, *meaning* excess; *both are adjectives.*] "How are they different?" [Luxuriant *means* characterized by rich or profuse growth, *whereas* luxurious *means* fond of or given to luxury.]

Compare and contrast *ingenious* and *ingenuous.* "What are their similarities?" [*Both are adjectives.*] "How do they differ?" [*Although the roots look alike, they are different; therefore meaning differs.* Ingenious *comes from the Latin* ingenium *and means* inborn talent marked by inventive skill, imagination, or cleverness, *whereas* ingenuous *comes from Latin* ingenuus, *meaning* lacking in cunning or artless.]

ACTIVITY | Creating Word Webs

Have students make webs of words related to newly learned Latin roots, such as *dent, poten,* or *dorm.*

ACTIVITY | Using Thematic Units

Thematic units provide students with listening, speaking, reading, and writing opportunities based on numerous topics. Teachers in the secondary grades can plan thematic units that enhance knowledge of Latin roots and Greek combining forms. For example, teachers might facilitate units on the environment, on citizenship, or on other topics related to Latin roots, such as the branches of government. (Several types of thematic units are discussed later in this chapter.) Students can read in their social studies textbook about the *judicial, legislative,* and *executive* branches and can identify the origins of these words and their meanings. [*All are Latin;* judicial *comes from* judic, *meaning* judge; legislative *comes from* legis, *meaning* law, *and* lator, *meaning* bearer *or* proposer; *and* executive *comes from* sequi, *meaning* to follow.] As students continue reading and complete further research, they can identify other words of Latin or Greek origin.

LESS COMMON GREEK COMBINING FORMS

Greek combining forms less common than those presented in Chapter 7 also require instruction. They include the following:

drome, dromos (course or running)

dyn, dynamo (power, strength, or force)

eco (house or home)

ecto (outside, external, or beyond)

helio (sun)

hema, hemo (blood)

hypn, hypno (sleep)

lith, litho (stone)

log, logo, logue (speech or word; *logy,* meaning *study,* comes from this word family)

macro (large, long, or great)

morph (form, shape, or structure)

neo (new or recent)

nym, onym (name)

ortho (straight, correct, or upright)

pan (all)

phyll (leaf or leaves)

pneumon, pneuma (breath or lung)

proto (earliest, original, or first in time)

saur (lizard or serpent)

stereo (solid, firm, or hard)

zo, zoo (animal)

Not only will learning Latin and Greek word parts enhance reading and spelling, but it will also enhance performance on the SATs and other verbal achievement tests. (See Appendix H for words found in middle school and high school social studies and psychology textbooks.)

WORD WISDOM

A Unique Greek Letter Combination

The Greek grapheme *ph* is sometimes found before *th.* Usually, the *ph* and *th* occur in separate syllables, as in *diphthong, diphtheria, ophthalmology, exophthalmos, naphtha,* and *aphtha,* and are pronounced as /f/ and /th/, respectively. Sometimes, however, *ph* is followed by *th* in the syllable, especially in words denoting chemicals or disease, such as *phthalic, phthalein,* and *phthisic.* In this latter group of words, the letters *phth* are pronounced either as /th/ or as /t/.

Activities Related to Less Common Greek Combining Forms

Older students need activities to reinforce their learning of the less common Greek combining forms, much as they do for learning the less common Latin roots. The following activities provide opportunities for this kind of practice with Greek combining forms.

ACTIVITY | **Adding Words to a Bulletin Board**

Design bulletin boards to which students can add words that contain the primary word parts listed on the boards. For example, Pete Bowers built a bulletin board with his fourth-grade students to show words containing the Greek combining form *graph* (see Figure 8.2).

Bowers used whole-class and individual brainstorming sessions with his students. Using dictionaries, students were able to come up with an amazing number of words that use the Greek form *graph*: 92 different words using 15 prefixes and 18 suffixes. The students studied the meanings of all of the words. Students added

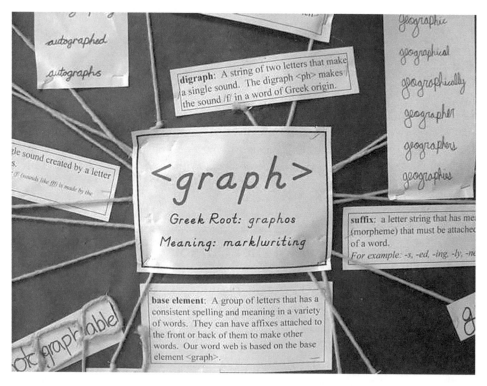

Figure 8.2. Part of Pete Bowers's class bulletin board of *graph* words. Students found 92 words containing the Greek combining form *graph*; words used 15 prefixes and 18 suffixes. (Used by kind permission of Pete Bowers.)

rare words, found in a variety of texts, on a separate "challenge" list. These words included *paragraphic, graphitic, biogeography, biostratigraph,* and *orthograph*. (Can you guess the meanings of these words by looking at their parts?) Bowers sent a letter to parents describing the *graph* bulletin board and how it was formed. He encouraged students to explain this word work to their parents.

ACTIVITY | Exploring *-nym* Words

The Greek combining forms *nym* and *onym* mean *name*. Have students find as many words as possible ending in *nym* or *onym*. Ask them to use their dictionaries to define and give examples of the following words.

acronym [*A word formed from the initial letters of a name or phrase, such as* RADAR *from **ra**dio **d**etecting **a**nd **r**anging or* WAC *from **W**omen's **A**rmy **C**orps*]

anonym [*A false or assumed name*]

antonym [*A word having a meaning opposite to that of another word.* Hot *and* cold, tall *and* short, *and* sweet *and* sour *are antonyms.*]

aptronym [*A name that is especially suited to the profession of its owner. Examples include* Sally Ride, *the astronaut;* William Wordsworth, *the poet;* Margaret Court, *the former tennis player; and* Tiger Woods, *the golfer—a wood is a type of golf club.*]

characteronym [*A name of a fictional character that suggests the personality traits of that character.* Daddy Warbucks *(a war profiteer in the comic strip "Little Orphan Annie");* Mr. Bumble *and* Mr. Sowerberry *(the undertaker) in* Oliver Twist *by* Charles Dickens; *and* Alfie Doolittle, *the constantly unemployed dad in* Pygmalion *and* My Fair Lady, *are all characteronyms (also spelled charactonyms).*]

eponym [*A person whose name is or is thought to be the source of the name of something, such as a city or era.* Romulus *is the eponym of* Rome; Vulcanian, *after* Vulcan, *the god of fire and metalworking, relates to a volcanic eruption.*]

heteronym [*One of two or more words that have the same spelling but different meanings and pronunciations. For example,* row *(a fight) and* row *(a line) are heteronyms.*]

homonym [*One of two or more words that have the same pronunciation and often the same spelling but differ in meaning; a synonym of the term* homophone. Bank, *a place where money is kept, and* bank, *an embankment, are homonyms.*]

mononym [*A one-word name, such as* Madonna, Oprah, *or* Bono.]

numeronyn [*A telephone number that spells a word or words. For example, to purchase tickets for Stanford University athletic events in the 1980s, fans dialed* 1-800-BEAT-CAL. *CAL denotes the rival University of California–Berkeley Bears.*]

oronym [*A sequence of words that sound the same as a different sequence of words, such as* ice cream *and* I scream. *Steven Pinker (1994) in* The Language Instinct *offered* The good can decay many ways *versus* The good candy came anyways *as well as* Some others I've seen *versus* Some mothers I've seen.]

paronym [*A cognate; a word derived from the same root as another; for example,* heal *is a* paronym *of* health.]

pseudonym [*A fictitious name, especially a pen name. Samuel Clemens used the pseudonym* Mark Twain.]

synonym [*A word having the same or nearly the same meaning as another word or words.* Large *and* big, *as well as* run *and* jog, *are synonyms.*]

tautonym [*A scientific name in which the genus and the species names are the same. For example, the scientific name for one kind of greenfinch is* Chloris chloris; *for the bank swallow is* Riparia riparia; *for the black rat is* Rattus rattus; *and for the gorilla is* Gorilla gorilla.]

toponym [*A place name or a word derived from a place such as Paris, Illinois, Champagne, and Pennsylvania.*]

ACTIVITY | Studying Unfamiliar Words

Select an unfamiliar word, such as *pterodactyl*. Ask students guiding questions such as the following.

"Analyze the word *pterodactyl*. What is its origin?" [*Greek*] "How do you know?" [*The* pt *and* y *for short* /ĭ/ *are clues; the word sounds scientific.*] "What are the two combining forms?" [ptero *and* dactyl] "What are the meanings of *ptero* and *dactyl*?" [Ptero *means* wing, *and* dactyl *means* digit *or* finger.] "In what subject area might you find this word?" [*history, archaeology, paleontology*] "Can you find other related words?" [pterosaur, pteranodon, pteropod, dactylitis, dactylology, *and so forth*]

ACTIVITY | Comparing and Contrasting *dermatology* and *psychology*

Have students compare and contrast the words *dermatology* and *psychology*. [*Both contain* ology, *meaning* study of, *as one combining form. The first combining forms differ; one is* derma, *meaning* skin, *and the other is* psych, *meaning* mind.] "What word origin do they share?" [*Greek*] "How are the words related?" [*Both are medical terms; both deal with people.*]

ACTIVITY | Asking the Experts at http://www.askoxford.com

Invite students to ask the experts for answers to questions such as the following:

"Do any English words have all five vowels in any order, with no intervening consonants?" (Ask the Experts knows of "only one word in anything like standard use which has five consecutive vowels, and that is *Rousseauian* 'pertaining to Rousseau or his views on religion, politics, education, etc.' Apart from this, and the large vowel clusters in *queuing/queueing*, there are only the Greek-derived words of the *pharmacopoeia* type.")

"What words contain the vowels in alphabetical order?" [*abstemious* and *facetious*]

"What are some common one-syllable words with nine letters?" [*screeched, strengths, scratched, stretched*, and *scrounged*]

| ACTIVITY | ## Exploring the Term *euphemism* |

Have students analyze the word *euphemism*. "What is its part of speech?" [*noun*] "What is its meaning?" [*A mild, indirect, or vague term used in place of one considered harsh, blunt, or offensive*] "What are its parts and their meanings?" [Eu *means* good, pheme *means* speaking, *and* ism *is a noun suffix.*] "Give examples of several euphemisms." [pass away *for* die, sanitation worker *for* garbage collector, budget *for* cheap, reception centers *for* concentration camps in World War II]

| ACTIVITY | ## Exploring the Term *pneumono-ultramicroscopicsilicovolcanoconiosis* |

At 45 letters, this is the longest word in any English-language dictionary! Garg (2006) called it a "trophy word," as its only job is to serve as the longest word. It is a lung disease caused by inhaling fine particles of silica. Garg said, "Its nine-letter synonyms 'silicosis' or 'black lung' work just as well, and the latter is more descriptive."

Most of the very long words in English are medical terms consisting of Greek combining forms.

| ACTIVITY | ## Exploring the Term *etymology* |

"What is the meaning of the term *etymology?* Find the etymology of the word *etymology*."

| ACTIVITY | ## Studying Manias and Phobias |

Older students are often intrigued with learning *mania* and *phobia* words. See if students can figure out the meanings of the following manias:

Anglomania	monomania	bibliomania	pyromania
demonomania	dipsomania	Gallomania	kleptomania
theomania	logomania	melomania	egomania

See how many of these phobias students can identify before checking in the dictionary. Students enjoy doing this type of exercise in teams.

arachnophobia	chromophobia	hydrophobia	pyrophobia
ichthyphobia	scriptophobia	agoraphobia	claustrophobia
kenophobia	tachophobia	Anglophobia	thermophobia
astrophobia	cyclophobia	limnophobia	toxiphobia
microphobia	verbophobia	auroraphobia	verminophobia

(See The Phobia List, http://www.phobialist.com, compiled by Fredd Culbertson, for more phobias.)

WORD WISDOM

Interesting *gram* Words

Common metric measures, such as kilogram and milligram, contain the Greek combining form *gram*; other *gram* words relate to written language:

pictogram: Images representing objects or ideas rather than words. Egyptian hieroglyphs are pictograms.

logogram (also called *ideogram*): A sign or character representing a word. Chinese writing consists of logograms.

phonogram: A written character or symbol representing a common sound (e.g., *b* is a phonogram representing the phoneme /b/)

anagram: A word or phrase made by transposing or rearranging the letters of another word or phrase. For example, *dirty room* is an anagram for *dormitory*. Can you think of anagrams for *the Morse code* or for *slot machines*? [*here comes dots* and *cash lost in 'em*]

isogram: A word without repeated letters

pangram: A sentence that makes use of all the letters of the alphabet (from the Greek *pan*, meaning *all*, and *gram*, meaning *something written*). The most well-known pangram is the one used to study the typewriter or computer keyboard: *The quick brown fox jumps over a lazy dog.* Others include *By Jove, my quick study of lexicography won a prize* and *Pack my box with five dozen liquor jugs.*

epigram A short expression or observation (often a poem) that is usually witty

Palindromes

A *palindrome* is any word or phrase that is spelled the same forward and backward. *Palindrome* comes from the Greek combining forms *palin*, meaning *again* and *backwards*, and *dromos*, meaning *course* or *running*. Here are some palindromes:

eye	deed	peep	kayak	level
Eve	radar	redder	civic	racecar
noon	toot	rotator	reviver	Madam

must sell at tallest sum	evil olive	senile felines
never odd or even	Anna	Renner
Madam, I'm Adam.	Poor Dan is in a droop.	Was it a rat I saw?

A man, a plan, a canal, Panama!

Try to find other palindromes. Barbara Kingsolver's book *The Poisonwood Bible* has one character who speaks only in palindromes!

Google "Weird Al Yankovic" and get the lyrics to his song *Bob*. Performed in a style resembling that of Bob Dylan, the four verses are all in palindromes, including *A Toyota's a Toyota* and *A dog, a panic in a pagoda*.

Portmanteau Words

The term *portmanteau* comes from the name of a large traveling case for carrying clothes. The term *portmanteau word* was invented by Lewis Carroll in 1872 and can be found in *Alice Through the Looking Glass and What She Saw There* (Humpty Dumpty chapter, 2005). Portmanteau words are formed by merging the sounds and meanings of two separate words. Carroll said, "'Slithy' means 'lithe and slimy' . . . You see it's like a portmanteau—there are

(continued)

Portmanteau *(continued)*

two meanings packed up into one word (p. 83)." And, "'Mimsy' is 'flimsy and miserable' (there's another portmanteau for you. (p. 83)"

Common portmanteau words and their components include the following:

brunch	breakfast and lunch
bit	binary and digit
motel	motor and hotel
squish	squirt and swish
blurt	blow and spurt
chortle	chortle and snort
smog	smoke and fog
splatter	splash and spatter
squawk	squall and squeak

ACTIVITY | **Thematic Units**

Thematic units are useful for integrating several content areas as students read, write, and speak on a variety of related topics. Several examples of possible units follow.

Calendar Unit

Students themselves often raise the question "Why are the last four months of the year, actually the 9th, 10th, 11th, and 12th months, named September, October, November, and December, the roots of which mean 7, 8, 9, and 10, respectively?" This question leads to some interesting research for the students to find out why, indeed. In their research they find that the Roman calendar consisted of 10 months and 304 days. In 702 B.C.E., two more months were added, with Januarius as the first month and Februarius as the last month.

In 46 B.C.E., Julius Caesar developed the Julian calendar of 12 months, with January as the first month, February as the second, and so forth. The Gregorian calendar, introduced in 1582 C.E., was modified slightly to add a leap year, but the order of the months remained the same. This calendar is used today throughout most of the world.

This unit examines interesting historical, mathematical, and linguistic concepts. Subunits can be designed based on the names of the months and the days of the week. In English, the names of the months retain their Roman origin. Students can learn the Roman origins for the names of the months, such as Janus, the god of beginning and endings, for January; Mars, the god of war, for March; Augustus, the first Roman emperor (who was originally called Sextilius), for August (the sixth month of the Roman calendar); and so forth.

The Romans associated a cycle of 7 days with the sun, the moon, and the five known planets (i.e., Sunday comes from *dies solis*, meaning *sun's day*; Monday comes from *dies lunae*, meaning *moon's day*; Saturday comes from *dies Saturni*, meaning *Saturn's day*). The other days of the week are based on Germanic names for Mars, Mercury, Jupiter, and Venus (i.e., Tuesday from *Tiw's day*, Wednesday from *Woden's day*, Thursday from *Thor's day*, and Friday from *Frigg's day*).

Unit on *An Exaltation of Larks*

Provide each student with a copy of *An Exaltation of Larks: The Ultimate Edition* by James Lipton (1968/1993). Lipton provided terms denoting crowds or flocks of animals, such as an *exaltation* of larks, a *herd* of swine, a *kindle* of kittens, a *skulk* of foxes, a *nye* of pheasants, a *parliament* of owls, a *swarm* of eels, and a *gam* of whales. Most of these collective terms came to us from the 15th century, during the time of Middle English. Students can work in groups or individually to study these terms. Lipton's book also includes terms for people, places, things, professions, sports, and medicine.

Dictionary Unit

Introduce high school students to a variety of dictionaries and reference sources. Have students look for similarities and differences in pronunciation, definitions, and so forth. For example, use the word *bury* or *burial* as the target word. Various dictionaries list different pronunciations and meanings for each of these words. See, for example, *Webster's II New College Dictionary* (1995), *World Book Millennium 2000: The World Book Dictionary* (2000), and *Webster's Third New International Dictionary* (1981).

Ask students to read *The Professor and the Madman: A Tale of Murder, Insanity, and the Making of the* Oxford English Dictionary, by Simon Winchester (1998). This outstanding book tells the remarkable story of the writing of the *Oxford English Dictionary* and two of the extraordinary men who made it possible. Students will become immersed in new words, etymology, and an amazing tale.

Mythology Unit

Students can study Greek, Roman, German, and Scandinavian mythology. They can find the etymology of the word *mythology*. Students can define the common term in the term's root word, *myth*. Students can find the names of gods and goddesses prevalent in mythology, such as Dionysus, the Greek god of wine and grape growing; Terpsichore, the muse of dancing and choral song; Vulcan, the Roman god of fire and craftsmanship; Frija, the Germanic goddess of marriage and fertility; and Thor, the Norse god of thunder. Students can research the battles, the objects of art, the symbols, and other key elements of these mythical tales.

Word Analysis in Advanced Thematic Units

Thematic units at this more advanced level contain words from all three major languages of origin. As students read and investigate, they can categorize the words in text according to their language of origin. For example, a unit on prehistoric times may include the following words:

Anglo-Saxon	*Latin*	*Greek*
earthquake	ancestors	tectonics
embedded	evolution	anthropology
hunter	extinct	geologist
tar pit	culture	archaeology
Stone Age	aggregate	dinosaur
spearhead	minerals	pterodactyl
toolmaker	volcano	technology
imprint	fossilize	paleoarchaeology

Other activities related to reading and spelling include looking up unknown words in a textbook's glossary or the dictionary; writing reports; reading supplemental texts; developing a time line; and contrasting related terms, such as *anthropologist, archaeologist,* and *paleoarchaeologist.*

NEW WORDS ENTERING THE ENGLISH LANGUAGE

Barnett noted, "It is clear that the English language in America today differs from that of the past primarily with respect to its vocabulary" (1965, p. 15). He observed that "its underlying architecture remains the same, and its mechanisms of inventions and expansion have not changed" (p. 15). The same is true today. New words and phrases are being coined, but they generally use familiar word parts or are proper names that become familiar because of world events. An examination of the fourth edition of *The American Heritage Dictionary* (2000) reveals that many newly invented words have actually been formed by extension of the use of Latin and Greek word parts.

For example, Soukhanov described *compunication,* "a coupling of the technologies for transmission and manipulation of information" (1995, p. 293), and *criticality,*

> an item of hardware or a system on a spacecraft or on the rocket launching the spacecraft, for which there is no backup, the loss or failure of which will result in a catastrophic accident involving the loss of crew, craft, and payload. (p. 294)

In these two terms, bases are combined or suffixes are added to form new words.

Barnett stated, "Throughout the long history of the English tongue, the challenge of new concepts and experiences has repeatedly forced new words into being" (1965, p. 15). While learning more about the structure of written English and gaining new strategies for both reading and spelling words from *abecedarian* to *zymosis*, students will enhance their academic and personal success.

SUMMARY

In writing this book, I hope I have conveyed the joys of learning to read and write words in the English language. When teachers and their students understand some of the historical forces that have influenced the development of English, they find that English is not a language of exceptions, but rather is a stable and learnable language. As Ramsden stated so well, "The English spelling system is tidy, behaves itself and has a high degree of order" (2001b, p. 6).

The structure of the majority of English words is based on historical events and influences from the origin languages, primarily Anglo-Saxon, Latin, and Greek. I strongly encourage teachers to move beyond phonics at the Anglo-Saxon layer of language to the Latin affixes and roots and Greek combining forms that are used in upper elementary and secondary texts. Without learning the contributions of the Latin and Greek languages, students will be unable to read text much beyond the primary-grade level.

As teachers present letter–sound correspondences, affixes, roots, and combining forms, students need numerous opportunities to read and spell words. Just as in learning to play a musical instrument or a new sport successfully, students need extensive practice while learning to read and spell. My hope is that this book gives teachers and tutors the background necessary to teach decoding and spelling, along with effective instructional strategies and activities for student practice.

RESOURCES FOR TEACHERS AND STUDENTS

Osborne, E. (2003). *Vocabulary from Latin and Greek roots: A study of word families.* Clayton, DE: Prestwick House.

See also the resources at the end of Chapter 7.

Calendar Unit

Burns, M. (1987). The calendar story. In V.A. Arnold & C.B. Smith (Eds.), *Tapestries* (pp. 528–537). New York: Macmillan.

Calendars. (2002). *World book* (Vol. 3, pp. 28–32). Chicago: World Book.

History of Our Calendar, http://www.webexhibits.org/calendars/year-history.html

Calendars, http://www.infoplease.com/ipa/A0875653.html

Calendars Through the Ages, http://www.webexhibits.org/calendars

Unit on *An Exaltation of Larks*

Lipton, J. (1993). *An exaltation of larks: The ultimate edition* (Rev. ed.). New York: Penguin. (Original work published 1968)

Dictionary Unit

Winchester, S. (1998). *The professor and the madman: A tale of murder, insanity, and the making of the* Oxford English Dictionary. New York: HarperCollins.

High school students can use almost any college or adult dictionary. One possible dictionary for the transition from children's to adult dictionaries is

Merriam-Webster's intermediate dictionary. (1999). Springfield, MA: Merriam-Webster.

Mythology Unit

Cotterell, A. (1989). *The Macmillan illustrated encyclopedia of myths and legends.* New York: Macmillan.

Graves, R. (1988). *The Greek myths.* Mount Kisco, NY: Moyer Bell.

Greek Mythology, http://www.Greekmythology.com

Mythology. (2002). *World book* (Vol. 13, pp. 973–990). Chicago: World Book.

Vinge, J.D. (1999). *The Random House book of Greek myths.* New York: Random House.

Web Sites

See the web sites listed at the end of Chapter 7.

References

Aaron, P.G., Joshi, R.M., & Quatroche, D. (2008). *Becoming a professional reading teacher.* Baltimore: Paul H. Brookes Publishing Co.

Abbott, S., & Berninger, V. (1999). It's never too late to remediate: A developmental approach to teaching word recognition. *Annals of Dyslexia, 49,* 223–250.

Adams, M.J. (1990). *Beginning to read: Thinking and learning about print.* Cambridge, MA: The MIT Press.

Adams, M.J., Foorman, B.R., Lundberg, I., & Beeler, T. (1998). *Phonemic awareness in young children: A classroom curriculum.* Baltimore: Paul H. Brookes Publishing Co.

The American heritage dictionary (4th ed.). (2000). Boston: Houghton Mifflin.

The American heritage student dictionary. (1998). Boston: Houghton Mifflin.

American Speech-Language-Hearing Association. (2002). *How does your child hear and talk?* Retrieved January 3, 2002, from http://www.asha.org/public/speech/development/chart.htm

Anderson, R.C., Hiebert, E.H., Scott, J.A., & Wilkinson, I.A.G. (Eds.). (1985). *Becoming a nation of readers: The report of the Commission on Reading.* Washington, DC: National Academy of Education, Commission on Education and Public Policy.

Anderson, R.C., & Nagy, W.E. (1992). The vocabulary conundrum. *American Educator, 16*(4), 14–18, 44–47.

Arnbak, E., & Elbro, C. (2000). The effects of morphological awareness training on the reading spelling skills of young dyslexics. *Scandinavian Journal of Educational Research, 44*(3), 229–251.

AskOxford online dictionary. (n.d.). Retrieved November 20, 2009, from http://www.askoxford.com/asktheexperts/faq/aboutenglish/numberwords?view=uk

Ayto, J. (1999). *Twentieth century words.* New York: Oxford University Press.

Badian, N. (1997). Dyslexia and the double deficit hypothesis. *Annals of Dyslexia, 47,* 69–87.

Ball, E.W. (1993). Phonological awareness: What's important and to whom? *Reading and Writing, 5*(2), 141–160.

Balmuth, M. (1982). *The roots of phonics: A historical introduction.* Timonium, MD: York Press.

Balmuth, M. (2009). *The roots of phonics: A historical introduction* (Rev. ed.). Baltimore: Paul H. Brookes Publishing Co.

Barnett, L. (1962, March 2). The English language. *LIFE, 52*(9), 74–77, 79–80, 83.

Barnett, L. (1964). *The treasure of our tongue.* New York: Alfred A. Knopf.

Barnett, L. (1965). History of the English language. *LIFE Educational Reprints,* Reprint 54. New York: Time Inc.

Barnhart, R.K. (Ed.). (1988). *The Barnhart dictionary of etymology.* New York: H.W. Wilson Company.

Bear, D. (1992). The prosody of oral reading and stage of word knowledge. In S. Templeton & D. Bear (Eds.), *Development of orthographic knowledge and the foundations of literacy: A memorial Festschrift for Edmund H. Henderson* (pp. 137–186). Mahwah, NJ: Lawrence Erlbaum Associates.

Beck, I.L., McKeown, M.G., & Kucan, L. (2002). *Bringing words to life.* New York: Guilford Press.

Berninger, V.W. (2000). Dyslexia the invisible, treatable disorder: The story of Einstein's ninja turtles. *Learning Disability Quarterly, 23*(3), 175–195.

Berninger, V.W., Nagy, W.E., Carlisle, J., Thomson, J., Hoffer, D., Abbott, S., et al. (2005). Effective treatment for children with dyslexia in grades 4–6: Behavioral and brain evidence. In B. Foorman (Ed.), *Preventing and remediating reading disabilities: Bringing science to scale* (pp. 355–379). Timonium, MD: York Press.

Berninger, V.W., & Wolf, B.J. (2009). *Teaching students with dyslexia and dysgraphia: Lessons from teaching and science.* Baltimore: Paul H. Brookes Publishing Co.

Birsh, J. (2005). Research and reading disability. In J.R. Birsh (Ed.), *Multisensory teaching of basic language skills* (2nd ed., pp. 1–21). Baltimore: Paul H. Brookes Publishing Co.

Blachman, B.A., Ball, E.W., Black, R., & Tangel, D.M. (2000). *Road to the code: A phonological awareness program for young children.* Baltimore: Paul H. Brookes Publishing Co.

Blok, H., Oostdam, R., Otter, M.E., & Overmaat, M. (2002). Computer-assisted instruction in support of beginning reading instruction: A review. *Review of Educational Research, 72*(1), 101–130.

Bodmer, F. (1944). *The loom of language.* New York: W.W. Norton.

Bourassa, D., & Treiman, R. (2008, Summer). Linguistic factors in spelling development. *Toward a Common Goal, 1,* 11, 13, 17.

Bowers, P.G., Sunseth, K., & Golden, J. (1999). The route between rapid naming and reading progress. *Scientific Studies in Reading, 3*(1), 31–53.

Bowers, P.G., & Wolf, M. (1993). Theoretical links among naming speed, precise timing mechanisms and orthographic skill in dyslexia, *Reading and Writing: An Interdisciplinary Journal, 5*(1), 69–85.

Bowers, P.N., & Kirby, J.R. (2010). Effects of morphological instruction on vocabulary acquisition. *Reading and Writing: An Interdisciplinary Journal, 23,* 515–537.

Bowers, P.N., Kirby, J.R., & Deacon, S.H. (in press). The effects of morphological instruction on literacy skills: A systematic review of the literature. *Review of Educational Research, 80*(2).

Boyanova, M. (n.d.). *A brief history of the English language.* Retrieved September 10, 2009, from http://www.studyenglishtoday.net/english-language-history.html,

Brady, S., & Moats, L. (1997). *Informed instruction for reading success: Foundations for teacher preparation.* Baltimore: International Dyslexia Association.

Brown, J.I. (1947). Reading and vocabulary: 14 master words. In M.J. Herzberg (Ed.), *Word study, 1–4.* Springfield, MA: G & C Merriam.

Bruck, M., & Waters, G.S. (1990). An analysis of the component spelling and reading skills of good readers–good spellers, good readers–poor spellers, and poor readers–poor spellers. In T.H. Carr & B.A. Levy (Eds.), *Reading and its development: Component skills approaches* (pp. 161–206). San Diego: Academic Press.

Bryson, B. (1990). *The mother tongue: English and how it got that way.* New York: William Morrow.

Burridge, K. (2002). *Blooming English.* Cambridge, England: Cambridge University Press.

Butler, K.G., & Silliman, E.R. (2002). *Speaking, reading and writing in children with learning disabilities.* Mahwah, NJ: Lawrence Erlbaum Associates.

Calfee, R.C., & Baldwin, L.S., Chambliss, M., Curley, R., Henry, M., Munson, R., et al. (1981–1984). *The book: Components of reading instruction.* Unpublished manuscript, Stanford University, Stanford, CA.

Calfee, R.C., & Henry, M.K. (1986). Project READ: An inservice model for training classroom teachers in effective reading instruction. In J.V. Hoffman (Ed.), *The effective teaching of reading: Research into practice* (pp. 199–229). Newark, DE: International Reading Association.

Calfee, R.C., Henry, M.K., & Funderburg, J.A. (1988). A model for school change. In S.J. Samuel & P.D. Pearson (Eds.), *Building exemplary reading programs and initiating change* (pp. 120–141). Newark, DE: International Reading Association.

California State University Board of Trustees. (2008, Fall). *Report on English proficiency.* Retrieved August 21, 2009, from http://www.asd.calstate.edu/proficiency/2008/Prof_Sys_fall2008.htm

Carlisle, J.F. (1987). The use of morphological knowledge in spelling derived forms by learning-disabled and normal students. *Annals of Dyslexia, 37,* 90–108.

Carlisle, J.F. (1995). Morphological awareness and early reading achievement. In L.B. Feldman (Ed.), *Morphological aspects of language processing* (pp. 189–209). Mahwah, NJ: Lawrence Erlbaum Associates.

Carlisle, J.F., & Stone, C.A. (2005). Exploring the role of morphemes in word reading. *Reading Research Quarterly, 40*(4), 428–449.

Carney, E. (1994). *A survey of English spelling.* London: Routledge.

Carreker, S. (2005). Teaching spelling. In J.R. Birsh (Ed.), *Multisensory teaching of basic language skills* (2nd ed., pp. 257–296). Baltimore: Paul H. Brookes Publishing Co.

Carroll, L. (2005). *The complete stories and poems of Lewis Carroll.* New Lanark, Scotland: Geddes & Grosset.

Catts, H., & Kamhi, A. (1999). *Language and reading disabilities.* Boston: Allyn & Bacon.

Center for Development and Learning. (2008). *For students who are not yet fluent, silent reading is not the best use of classroom time.* Retrieved March 18, 2009, from http://www.cdl.org/resource-library/pdf/students_not_fluent.pdf

Chall, J.S. (1967). *Learning to read: The great debate.* New York: McGraw-Hill.

Chall, J.S. (1983). *Stages of reading development.* New York: McGraw-Hill.

Chall, J.S., & Popp, H.M. (1996). *Teaching and assessing phonics.* Cambridge, MA: Educators Publishing Service.

Chall, J.S., & Squire, J.R. (1991). The publishing industry and textbooks. In R. Barr, M.L. Kamil, P. Mosenthal, & P.D. Pearson (Eds.), *Handbook of reading research* (Vol. 2, pp. 120–146). New York: Longman.

Cicci, R. (1995). *What's wrong with me? Learning disabilities at home and school.* Timonium, MD: York Press.

Claiborne, R. (1983). *Our marvelous native tongue: The life and times of the English language.* New York: Times Books.

Connor, C.M. (2009). Individualizing reading instruction in early elementary classrooms. *Perspectives on Language and Literacy, 35*(5), 33–38.

Cooke, G. (2008a, Summer). Phono-logic: A treatise on the schwa, part 1. *Toward a Common Goal,* 7–8.

Cooke, G. (2008b, Fall). Phono-logic: A treatise on the schwa, part 2. *Toward a Common Goal,* 7–8.

Cooke, G. (2008c, Winter). Phono-logic: A treatise on the schwa, part 3. *Toward a Common Goal,* 7–8.

Cooper, E.K., Blackwood, P.E., Boeschen, J.A., Giddings, M.G., & Carin, A.A. (1985). *HBJ Science* (Purple ed.). Orlando, FL: Harcourt.

Corson, D. (1985). *The lexical bar.* Oxford: Pergamon Press.

Coulmas, F. (1996). *The Blackwell encyclopedia of writing systems.* Malden, MA: Blackwell.

Crystal, D. (2006). *The fight for English.* Oxford: Oxford University Press.

Cunningham, A. (2009, November). *The cognitive consequences of reading volume: Implications for comprehension and vocabulary.* Paper presented at the 60th Annual Conference of the International Dyslexia Association, Orlando, FL.

Denckla, M., & Rudel, R. (1976). Rapid automatized naming (R.A.N.): Dyslexia differentiation from other learning disabilities. *Neuropsychologia, 14,* 471–479.

DeStefano, J.S. (1972). *Some parameters of register in adult and child speech.* Louvain, Belgium: Institute of Applied Linguistics.

Dickinson, D.K. (2001). Putting the pieces together: Impact of preschool on children's language and literacy development in kindergarten. In D.K. Dickinson & P.O. Tabors (Eds.), *Beginning literacy with language: Young children learning at home and school* (pp. 257–287). Baltimore: Paul H. Brookes Publishing Co.

Dickinson, D.K., & Tabors, P.O. (Eds.). (2001). *Beginning literacy with language: Young children learning at home and school.* Baltimore: Paul H. Brookes Publishing Co.

Downing, J. (1979). *Reading and reasoning.* New York: Springer-Verlag.

Ebbers, S.M. (2008). Morphological word families in narrative and informational text. In Y. Kim, V.J. Risko, D.L. Compton, D.K. Dickinson, M.K. Hundlley, R.T. Jimenez, et al. (Eds.), *57th Yearbook of the National Reading Conference* (pp. 203–218). Oak Creek, WI: National Reading Conference.

Ebbers, S.M., & Denton, C.A. (2008). A root awakening: Vocabulary instruction for older students with reading difficulties. *Learning Disabilities Research & Practice, 23*(2), 90–102.

Ehri, L.C. (1985). Effects of printed language acquisition on speech. In D.R. Olson, N. Torrance, & A. Hildyard (Eds.), *Literacy, language, and learning* (pp. 333–367). Cambridge, England: Cambridge University Press.

Ehri, L.C. (1987). Learning to read and spell words. *Journal of Reading Behavior, 19,* 5–31.

Ehri, L.C. (1989). The development of spelling knowledge and its role in reading acquisition and reading disability. *Journal of Learning Disabilities, 22,* 356–365.

Ehri, L.C. (1991). Development of the ability to read words. In R. Barr, M. Kamil, P. Mosenthal, & P.D. Pearson (Eds.), *Handbook of reading research* (Vol. 2, pp. 383–417). New York: Longman.

Ehri, L.C. (1998). Research on learning to read and spell: A personal-historical perspective. *Scientific Studies in Reading, 2*(2), 97–114.

Ehri, L.C. (2004). Teaching phonemic awareness and phonics: An explanation of the National Reading Panel meta-analyses. In P. McCardle & V. Chhabra (Eds.), *The voice of evidence in reading research* (pp. 153–186). Baltimore: Paul H. Brookes Publishing Co.

Ehri, L.C. (2006). Alphabetics instruction helps students learn to read. In R.M. Joshi & P.G. Aaron (Eds.), *Handbook of orthography and literacy* (pp. 649–678). Mahwah, NJ: Lawrence Erlbaum Associates.

Ehri, L., & Soffer, A.G. (1999). Graphophonemic awareness development in elementary students. *Scientific Studies in Reading, 3*(1), 1–30.

Elbro, C., & Arnbak, E. (1996). The role of morpheme recognition and morphological awareness in dyslexia. *Annals of Dyslexia, 46,* 209–240.

Elkind, J. (1998). Computer reading machines for poor readers. *Perspectives, 24*(2), 9–14.

Elkind, K., & Elkind, J. (2007, Summer). Text-to-speech software for reading. *Perspectives on Language and Literacy, 33*(3), 11–16.

Engstrom, E., & Hecker, L. (2005). Assistive technology and individuals with dyslexia. In J.R. Birsh (Ed.), *Multisensory teaching of basic language skills* (2nd ed.). Baltimore: Paul H. Brookes Publishing Co. Available at http://textbooks.brookespublishing.com/birsh/21/fulltext.htm

Felton, R.H. (1993). Effects of instruction on the decoding skills of children with phonological-processing problems. *Journal of Learning Disabilities, 26,* 583–589.

Fernald, G.M., & Keller, H. (1921). The effect of kinaesthetic factors in the development of word recognition in the case of non-readers. *Journal of Educational Research, 4,* 355–377.

Feynman, R.P., Leighton, R.B., & Sands, M. (1970). *The Feynman lectures on physics (Vols. I–III).* Reading, MA: Addison-Wesley.

Fielding-Barnsley, R. (1999). How preschools can contribute to identifying and helping children at risk for dyslexia. *Perspectives, 25*(4), 6–9.

Firmage, R.A. (1993). *The alphabet abecedarium: Some notes on letters.* Boston: David R. Godine.

Flavell, J. (1985). *Cognitive development* (2nd ed.). Upper Saddle River, NJ: Prentice Hall.

Foorman, B.R., Francis, D.J., Beeler, T., Winikates, D., & Fletcher, J.M. (1997). Early interventions for children with reading problems: Study designs and preliminary findings. *Learning Disabilities, 8,* 63–71.

Forrest-Pressley, D.L., & Waller, T.G. (1984). *Cognition, metacognition, and reading.* New York: Springer-Verlag.

Frith, U. (Ed.). (1980). *Cognitive processes in spelling.* London: Academic Press.

Fromkin, V., & Rodman, R. (1998). *An introduction to language* (6th ed.). Orlando, FL: Harcourt.

Garg, A. (2006, June 8). *A.Word.A.Day: Pneumonoultramicroscopicsilicovolcanoconiosis.* Retrieved September 21, 2008, from http://wordsmith.org/words/pneumonoultramicroscopic silicovolcanoconiosis.html

Garg, A. (2009, September 10). *A.Word.A.Day: Devious.* Retrieved September 12, 2009, from http://wordsmith.org/words/devious.html

Gillingham, A., & Stillman, B.W. (1956). *Remedial training for children with specific disability in reading, spelling and penmanship* (5th ed.). Cambridge, MA: Educators Publishing Service.

Gillingham, A., & Stillman, B.W. (1997). *The Gillingham manual: Remedial training for children with specific disability in reading, spelling and penmanship* (8th ed.). Cambridge, MA: Educators Publishing Service.

Goodman, K. (1967). Reading: A psycholinguistic guessing game. *Journal of the Reading Specialist, 6*(1), 126–135.

Goodman, K. (1976). Reading: A psycholinguistic guessing game. In H. Singer & R. Ruddell (Eds.), *Theoretical models and processes of reading* (2nd ed., pp. 497–508). Newark, DE: International Reading Association.

Gough, P.B., & Tunmer, W.E. (1986). Decoding, reading, and reading disability. *Remedial and Special Education, 7*(1), 6–10.

Goulden, R., Nation, P., & Read, J. (1990). How large can a receptive vocabulary be? *Applied Linguistics, 11*(4), 341–363.

Groff, P. (1971). *The syllable: Its nature and pedagogical usefulness.* Portland, OR: Northwest Regional Educational Laboratory.

Hammill, D.D., Mather, N., Allen, E.A., & Roberts, R. (2002). Using semantics, grammar, phonology, and rapid naming tasks to predict word identification. *Journal of Learning Disabilities, 35*(2), 121–136.

Hanna, P.R., Hodges, R.E., & Hanna, J.S. (1971). *Spelling: Structure and strategies.* Boston: Houghton Mifflin.

Hart, B., & Risley, T.R. (1995). *Meaningful differences in the everyday experience of young American children.* Baltimore: Paul H. Brookes Publishing Co.

Henderson, E.H. (1990). *Teaching spelling* (2nd ed.). Boston: Houghton Mifflin.

Henderson, L. (1982). *Orthography and word recognition in reading.* London: Academic Press.

Henderson, L. (1985). Toward a psychology of morphemes. In A.W. Ellis (Ed.), *Progress in the psychology of language* (Vol. 2, pp. 15–72). Mahwah, NJ: Lawrence Erlbaum Associates.

Henry, M.K. (1988a). Beyond phonics: Integrated decoding and spelling instruction based on word origin and structure. *Annals of Dyslexia, 38,* 259–275.

Henry, M.K. (1988b). Understanding English orthography: Assessment and instruction for decoding and spelling. *Dissertation Abstracts International, 48,* 2841A. (University Microfilms No. 8800951)

Henry, M.K. (1989). Children's word structure knowledge: Implications for decoding and spelling instruction. *Reading and Writing: An Interdisciplinary Journal, 2,* 135–152.

Henry, M.K. (1990). *Words: Integrated decoding and spelling instruction based on word origin and word structure.* Austin, TX: PRO-ED.

Henry, M.K. (1993). Morphological structure: Latin and Greek roots and affixes as upper grade code strategies. *Reading and Writing, 5*(2), 227–241.

Henry, M.K. (1997). The decoding/spelling curriculum: Integrated decoding and spelling instruction from pre-school to early secondary school. *Dyslexia, 3,* 178–189.

Henry, M.K. (1998). *Just the facts series: Multisensory teaching.* Baltimore: International Dyslexia Association.

Henry, M.K. (1999). A short history of the English language. In J.R. Birsh (Ed.), *Multisensory teaching of basic language skills* (pp. 119–140). Baltimore: Paul H. Brookes Publishing Co.

Henry, M.K. (2010). *Words: Integrated decoding and spelling instruction based on word origin and word structure* (2nd ed.). Austin, TX: PRO-ED.

Henry, M.K., Calfee, R.C., & Avelar-LaSalle, R.A. (1989). A structural approach to decoding and spelling. In S. McCormick & J. Zutell (Eds.), *Thirty-eighth yearbook of the National Reading Conference* (pp. 155–163). Chicago: National Reading Conference.

Henry, M.K., & Redding, N.C. (2002). *Patterns for success in reading and spelling* (2nd ed.). Austin, TX: PRO-ED.

Henshilwood, C.S., d'Errico, F., Yates, R., Jacobs, Z., Tribolo, C., Duller, G.A.T., et al. (2002, February 15). Emergence of modern human behavior: Middle stone age engravings from South Africa. *Science, 295,* 1278–1280.

Herron, J. (2008). Why phonics teaching must change. *Educational Leadership, 66*(1), 77–81.

Holdaway, D. (1986). The visual face of experience and language: A metalinguistic excursion. In D.B. Yaden, Jr., & S. Templeton (Eds.), *Metalinguistic awareness and beginning literacy* (pp. 65–78). Portsmouth, NH: Heinemann.

Johnston, R.S., & Watson, J.E. (2006). The effectiveness of synthetic phonics teaching in developing reading and spelling skills in English-speaking boys and girls. In R.M. Joshi & P.G. Aaron (Eds.), *Handbook of orthography and literacy* (pp. 679–691). Mahwah, NJ: Lawrence Erlbaum Associates.

Kemmer, S. (2009). *Chronology of events in the history of English.* Retrieved October 14, 2009, from http://www.ruf.rice.edu/~kemmer/Words/chron.html

King, D.H. (2000). *English isn't crazy!* Timonium, MD: York Press.

Klausner, J.C. (1990). *Talk about English: How words travel and change.* New York: Thomas Y. Crowell.

Krensky, S. (1996). *Breaking into print: Before and after the invention of the printing press.* Toronto: Little, Brown.

Langer, J.A. (2001). Beating the odds: Teaching middle and high school students to read and write well. *American Education Research Journal, 38,* 837–880.

Lederer, R. (1991). *The miracle of language.* New York: Pocket Books.

Lewis, M.P. (2009). (Ed.). *Ethnologue: Languages of the world* (16th ed.). Dallas, TX: SIL International.

Liberman, I.Y. (1973). Segmentation of the spoken word and reading acquisition. *Bulletin of the Orton Society, 23,* 65–77.

Liberman, I.Y., & Liberman, A.M. (1990). Whole language vs. code emphasis: Underlying assumptions and their implications for reading instruction. *Annals of Dyslexia, 40,* 51–78.

Liberman, I.Y., & Mann, V. (1981). Should reading instruction vary with the sex of the child? In A. Ansara, N. Geschwind, A. Galaburda, M. Albert, & N. Gartrell (Eds.), *Sex differences in dyslexia* (pp. 151–167). Baltimore: International Dyslexia Association.

Liberman, I.Y., & Shankweiler, D. (1991). Phonology and beginning reading: A tutorial. In L. Rieben & C.A. Perfetti (Eds.), *Learning to read: Basic research and its implications* (pp. 3–17). Mahwah, NJ: Lawrence Erlbaum Associates.

Liberman, I.Y., Shankweiler, D., Fischer, F.W., & Carter, B. (1974). Explicit syllable and phoneme segmentation in the young child. *Journal of Experimental Child Psychology, 18,* 201–212.

Lipton, J. (1993). *An exaltation of larks: The ultimate edition* (Rev. ed.). New York: Penguin. (Original work published 1968)

Logan, R.K. (1986). *The alphabet effect.* New York: St. Martin's Press.

Lyon, G.R. (1995). Research initiatives in learning disabilities: Contributions from scientists supported by the National Institute of Child Health and Human Development. *Journal of Child Neurology, 10,* 120–126.

Lyon, G.R. (1996). The future of children: Learning disabilities. *Special Education for Students with Disabilities, 6*(1), 54–76.

Lyon, G.R. (2004, March). *The NICHD research program in reading development, reading disorders, and treading instruction initiated: 1965.* Paper presented at the 31st annual conference of the New York Branch of the International Dyslexia Association, New York City.

Lyon, G.R., Fletcher, J.M., & Barnes, M.C. (2003). Learning disabilities. In E.J. Mash & R.A. Barkley (Eds.), *Child psychopathology* (2nd ed., pp. 520–588). New York: Guilford Press.

Macaruso, P., & Hook, P.E. (2007, Summer). Computer assisted instruction: Successful only with proper implementation. *Perspectives on Language and Literacy, 33*(3), 43–46.

Male, M. (2003). *Technology for inclusion* (4th ed.). Boston: Allyn & Bacon.

Manguel, A. (1996). *A history of reading.* New York: Viking.

McCardle, P., & Chhabra, V. (Eds.). (2004). *The voice of evidence in reading research.* Baltimore: Paul H. Brookes Publishing Co.

McCrum, R., Cran, W., & MacNeil, R. (1992). *The story of English* (2nd ed.). New York: Penguin.

McGuinness, D. (2004). *Early reading instruction.* Cambridge, MA: The MIT Press.

McIntyre, C., & Pickering, J. (1995). *Clinical studies of multisensory structured language education for students with dyslexia and related disorders.* Salem, OR: International Multisensory Structured Language Education Council.

Moats, L. (1994). The missing foundation in teacher education: Knowledge of the structure of spoken and written language. *Annals of Dyslexia, 44,* 81–102.

Moats, L.C. (1995). *Spelling: Development, disability, and instruction.* Timonium, MD: York Press.

Moats, L.C. (1998, Spring/Summer). Teaching decoding. *American Educator, 22*(1 & 2), 42–49, 95–96.

Moats, L.C. (2000). *Speech to print: Language essentials for teachers.* Baltimore: Paul H. Brookes Publishing Co.

Moats, L.C. (2003). *Speech to print workbook: Language exercises for teachers.* Baltimore: Paul H. Brookes Publishing Co.

Moats, L.C. (2005/2006, Winter). How spelling supports reading. *American Educator, 29*(4), 12–22, 42–43.

Moats, L.C. (2009a). Knowledge foundations for teaching reading and spelling. *Reading and Writing, 22,* 379–399.

Moats, L.C. (2009b). Still wanted: Teachers with knowledge of language. *Journal of Learning Disabilities, 42*(5), 387–391.

Moats, L.C., & Farrell, M.L. (2005). Multisensory structured language education. In J.R. Birsh (Ed.), *Multisensory teaching of basic language skills* (2nd ed., pp. 23–41). Baltimore: Paul H. Brookes Publishing Co.

National Committee for Latin and Greek. (2009). SAT updates for 2008. Retrieved October 21, 2009, from http://www.promotelatin.org/SAT%20Updates%20for%202008.pdf

National Institute of Child Health and Human Development. (2000). *Report of the National Reading Panel. Teaching children to read: An evidence-based assessment of the scientific research literature on reading and its implications for reading instruction* (National Institutes of Health Publication No. 00-4754). Washington, DC: U.S. Government Printing Office. Also available online at http://www.nichd.nih.gov/publications/nrp/smallbook.cfm

Nist, J. (1966). *A structural history of English.* New York: St. Martin's Press.

Nunes, T., & Bryant, P. (2006). *Improving literacy by teaching morphemes.* London: Routledge.

Oller, J., Oller, S., & Badon, L. (2006). *Milestones: Normal speech and language development across the life span.* New York: Plural Publishing.

Orton, J.L. (1966). The Orton-Gillingham approach. In J. Money (Ed.), *The disabled reader: Education of the dyslexic child* (pp. 119–145). Baltimore: The Johns Hopkins University Press.

Orton, S.T. (1937). *Reading, writing, and speech problems in children.* New York: W.W. Norton.

Paulesu, E., Démonet, J.-F., Fazio, F., McCrory, E., Chanoine, V., Brunswick, N., et al. (2001, March 16). Dyslexia: Cultural diversity and biological unity. *Science, 291,* 2165–2167.

Perfetti, C. (1984). Reading acquisition and beyond: Decoding includes cognition. *American Journal of Education, 93,* 40–60.

Perfetti, C. (1985). *Reading ability.* New York: Oxford University Press.

Perfetti, C. (1986). Continuities in reading acquisition, reading skill and reading disability. *Remedial and Special Education, 7*(1), 11–21.

Pinker, S. (1994). *The language instinct: How the mind creates language.* New York: William Morrow & Co.

Pratt, C., & Grieve, R. (1984). The development of metalinguistic awareness: An introduction. In W. Tunmer, C. Pratt, & M. Herriman (Eds.), *Metalinguistic awareness in children* (pp. 2–11). New York: Springer-Verlag.

Pressley, M. (1998). *Reading instruction that works: The case for balanced teaching.* New York: Guilford Press.

Pressley, M., Disney, L., & Anderson, K. (2007). Landmark vocabulary instructional research and the vocabulary instructional research that makes sense now. In R.K. Wagner, A.E. Muse, & K.R. Tannenbaum (Eds.), *Vocabulary acquisition: Implications for reading comprehension* (pp. 205–232). New York: Guilford Press.

Pyles, T., & Algeo, J. (1982). *The origins and development of the English language.* New York: Harcourt Brace Jovanovich.

Quirk, R. (1974). *The linguist and the English language.* London: Arnold.

Ramsden, M. (2001). *The spelling manual in the real spelling tool box.* Retrieved March 17, 2008, from http://www.realspelling.com

Ramsden, M., & Mira, P. (2009). *70 word matrices.* DVD available at www.realspelling.com

Read, C. (1971). Pre-school children's knowledge of English phonology. *Harvard Educational Review, 41*(1), 1–34.

Reid, J.F. (1966). Learning to think about reading. *Educational Research, 9,* 56–62.

Rome, P.D., & Osman, J.S. (1993). *Language tool kit* [Teacher's manual and cards]. Cambridge, MA: Educators Publishing Service.

Samoyault, T. (1996). *Alphabetical order: How the alphabet began.* New York: Viking.

Sampat, P. (2001, May–June). Last words. *World-Watch,* 34–40.

Scanlon, D.M., & Vellutino, F.R. (1996). Prerequisite skills, early instruction and success in first grade reading. *Mental and Developmental Disabilities Research Reviews, 2,* 54–63.

Scarborough, H. (1998). Early identification of children at risk for reading disabilities: Phonological awareness and some other promising predictors. In B. Shapiro, P. Accardo, & A. Capute (Eds.), *Specific reading disability: A view of the spectrum* (pp. 75–119). Timonium, MD: York Press.

Seidenburg, M.S., & McClelland, J.L. (1989). A distributed developmental model of word recognition and naming. *Psychological Review, 96,* 523–568.

Shanahan, T. (2007, April). "Nation's Report Card" shows overall decline in reading test scores for 12th graders since 1992. *Reading Today, 24*(5), 3.

Shaywitz, S. (2003). *Overcoming dyslexia.* New York: Alfred A. Knopf.

Sheffield, B. (in press). *Teacher training manual.* Cincinnati, OH: Sheffield Press.

Singson, M., Mahony, D., & Mann, V. (2000). Reading ability and sensitivity to morphological relations. *Reading and Writing: An Interdisciplinary Journal, 12,* 191–218.

Slingerland, B.H. (1994a). *Basics in scope and sequence of a multi-sensory approach to language arts for specific language disability children: A guide for primary teachers* (Book 2, Rev. ed.). Cambridge, MA: Educators Publishing Service.

Slingerland, B.H. (1994b). *A multi-sensory approach to language arts for specific language disability children: A guide for elementary teachers* (Book 3, Rev. ed.). Cambridge, MA: Educators Publishing Service.

Slingerland, B.H. (1996). *A multi-sensory approach to language arts for specific language disability children: A guide for primary teachers* (Book 1). Cambridge, MA: Educators Publishing Service.

Smelt, E. (1976). *Speak, spell and read English.* Melbourne: Longman Australia.

Snow, C.E., Burns, M.S., & Griffin, P. (Eds.). (1998). *Preventing reading difficulties in young children.* Washington, DC: National Academies Press.

Soukhanov, A.H. (1995). *Word watch: The stories behind the words of our lives.* New York: Henry Holt & Co.

Stahl, S.A., & Miller, P.D. (1989). Whole language and language experiences approaches for beginning reading. *Review of Educational Research, 59,* 87–116.

Stanback, M.L. (1992). Syllable and rime patterns for teaching reading: Analysis of a frequency-based vocabulary of 17,602 words. *Annals of Dyslexia, 42,* 196–221.

Stanovich, K.E. (1980). Toward an interactive-compensatory model of individual differences in the development of reading fluency. *Reading Research Quarterly, 16,* 32–71.

Stanovich, K.E. (1986). Matthew effects in reading: Some consequences of individual differences in the acquisition of literacy. *Reading Research Quarterly, 21,* 360–407.

Stanovich, K.E. (1996). Romance and reality. *The Reading Teacher, 47,* 280–291.

Stanovich, K.E., West, R.F., & Feeman, D.J. (1981). A longitudinal study of sentence context effects in second-grade children: Tests of an interactive-compensatory model. *Journal of Experimental Child Psychology, 32,* 185–199.

Steere, A., Peck, C.Z., & Kahn, L. (1971). *Solving language difficulties.* Cambridge, MA: Educators Publishing Service.

Tangel, D.M., & Blachman, B.A. (1995). Effect of phoneme awareness instruction on the invented spelling of first-grade children: A one-year follow-up. *Journal of Reading Behavior, 27,* 153–185.

Templeton, S. (1986). Metalinguistic awareness: A synthesis and beyond. In D.B. Yaden, Jr., & S. Templeton (Eds.), *Metalinguistic awareness and beginning literacy* (pp. 293–309). Portsmouth, NH: Heinemann.

Templeton, S. (1995). *Children's literacy: Contexts for meaningful learning.* Boston: Houghton Mifflin.

Templeton, S. (2004). The spelling-vocabulary connection: Orthographic development and morphological knowledge at the intermediate grades and beyond. In J.F. Baumann & E.J. Kame'enui (Eds.), *Vocabulary instruction: Research to practice* (pp. 118–138). New York: Guilford Press.

Templeton, S., & Morris, D. (1999). Theory and research into practice: Questions teachers ask about spelling. *Reading Research Quarterly, 34,* 102–112.

Torgesen, J.K. (2000). Individual differences in response to early intervention in reading: The lingering problem of treatment resisters. *Learning Disability Research and Practice, 15,* 55–64.

Torgesen, J.K. (2004). Avoiding the devastating downward spiral. *American Educator, 28*(3), 6–9, 12–13, 17–19, 45–47.

Torgesen, J.K., Wagner, R.K., & Rashotte, C.A. (1997). Prevention and remediation of severe reading disabilities: Keeping the end in mind. *Scientific Studies in Reading, 1*(3), 217–234.

Treiman, R. (1993). *Beginning to spell: A study of first-grade children.* New York: Oxford University Press.

Treiman, R. (2006). Knowledge about letters as a foundation for both reading and spelling. In R.M. Joshi & P.G. Aaron (Eds.), *Handbook of orthography and literacy* (pp. 581–599). Mahwah, NJ: Lawrence Erlbaum Associates.

Tunmer, W.E., & Herriman, M. (1984). The development of metalinguistic awareness: A conceptual overview. In W. Tunmer, C. Pratt, & M. Herriman (Eds.), *Metalinguistic awareness in children* (pp. 12–35). New York: Springer-Verlag.

Uhry, J.K. (2005). Phonemic awareness and reading: Research, activities, and instructional materials. In J.R. Birsh (Ed.), *Multisensory teaching of basic language skills* (2nd ed., pp. 83–111). Baltimore: Paul H. Brookes Publishing Co.

Vaughn, S., Wanzek, J., Woodruff, A.L., & Linan-Thompson, S. (2007). Prevention and early identification of students with reading disabilities: A research review of the three-tier model. In D. Haager, J. Klingner, & S. Vaughn (Eds.), *Evidence-based reading practices for response to intervention* (pp. 11–27). Baltimore: Paul H. Brookes Publishing Co.

Venezky, R. (1999). *The American way of spelling: The structure and origins of American English orthography.* New York: Guilford Press.

Webster's new universal unabridged dictionary (2nd ed.). (1983). New York: Simon & Schuster.

Webster's third new international dictionary. (1981). Springfield: Merriam-Webster.

Webster's II new college dictionary. (1995). Boston: Houghton Mifflin.

West, R.F., & Stanovich, K.E. (1978). Automatic contextual facilitation in readers of three ages. *Child Development, 49,* 717–727.

West, T. (1998). Words to images: Technological change redefines educational goals. *Perspectives, 24*(2), 27–31.

Westbrook, A. (2002). *Hip hoptionary.* New York: Harlem Moon-Broadway.

White, T.G., Sowell, J., & Yanagihara, A. (1989). Teaching elementary students to use word-part clues. *The Reading Teacher, 42,* 302–308.

Winchester, S. (1998). *The professor and the madman: A tale of murder, insanity, and the making of the* Oxford English Dictionary. New York: HarperCollins.

Wise, B.W. (1998). Computers and research in learning disabilities. *Perspectives, 24*(2), 4–6.

Wise, B.W., Olson, R.K., & Ring, J. (1997). Teaching phonological awareness with and without the computer. In C. Hulme & M. Snowling (Eds.), *Dyslexia: Biology, cognition and intervention* (pp. 254–275). London: Whurr.

Wise, B.W., & Raskind, M.H. (2007, Summer). Technology and reading difficulties: Theme editors' summary. *Perspectives on Language and Literacy, 33*(3), 7–8.

Wise, B.W., & Van Vuuren, S. (2007, Summer). Choosing software gems to improve children's reading. *Perspectives on Language and Literacy, 33*(3), 34–38.

Wolf, M. (1991). Naming speed and reading: The contribution of the cognitive sciences. *Reading Research Quarterly, 26*(2), 123–141.

Wolf, M. (2007). *Proust and the squid: The story and science of the reading brain.* New York: HarperCollins.

Wolf, M. (2009, October). *Implications of an evolving brain for reading, dyslexia, intervention and the future reader.* Keynote address presented at the annual conference of the Rocky Mountain Branch of the International Dyslexia Association, Beaver Creek, CO.

Wolf, M., & Bowers, P.G. (1999). The double-deficit hypothesis for developmental dyslexia. *Journal of Educational Psychology, 91,* 415–438.

Wolf, M., & Katzer-Cohen, T. (2001). Reading fluency and its intervention. *Scientific Studies in Reading, 5*(3), 211–239.

Wolf, M., Miller, L., & Donnelly-Adams, K. (2000). Retrieval, automaticity, vocabulary elaboration, orthography (RAVE-O): A comprehensive fluency-based reading intervention program. *Journal of Learning Disabilities, 33,* 375–386.

World Book millennium 2000: The World Book dictionary. (2000). Chicago: World Book.

Yaden, D.B., Jr., & Templeton, S. (1986). Metalinguistic awareness: An etymology. In D.B. Yaden, Jr., & S. Templeton (Eds.), *Metalinguistic awareness and beginning literacy* (pp. 3–10). Portsmouth, NH: Heinemann.

Appendixes

Surveys of Language Knowledge

The following surveys of language knowledge are intended to help teachers become aware of their own strengths and weaknesses. The surveys vary in difficulty and may challenge even experienced teachers who may already have a strong background in language structure. A word of caution, however: The questions and the way they are posed require a deeper and more explicit level of knowledge than many "teacher tests" that are used to test superficial knowledge of phonics. Critics have argued that such knowledge is not required to teach reading. Those professionals who have deepened their knowledge, however, will be better at explaining concepts, individualizing instruction, choosing examples, and making language study come alive even for children who are struggling.

_____

Answers appear at the end of Appendix A.

From Moats, L.C. (2003). *Speech to print workbook: Language exercises for teachers* (pp. 1–10). Baltimore: Paul H. Brookes Publishing Co.; adapted by permission.

Brief Survey of Language Knowledge

Phoneme Counting

Count the number of speech sounds or phonemes that you perceive in each of the following spoken words. Remember, the speech sounds may not be equivalent to the letters. For example, the word *spoke* has four phonemes: /s/, /p/, /ō/, and /k/. Write the number of phonemes to the right of each word.

thrill	ring	shook
does	fix	wrinkle
sawed	quack	know

Syllable Counting

Count the number of syllables that you perceive in each of the following words. For example, the word *higher* has two syllables, the word *threat* has one, and the word *physician* has three. Write the number of syllables to the right of each word.

cats	capital	shirt
spoil	decidedly	banana
recreational	lawyer	walked

Phoneme Matching

Read the first word in each line and note the sound that is represented by the underlined letter or letter cluster. Then select the word or words on the line that contain the same sound.

1. pu<u>sh</u>	although	sugar	duty	pump
2. w<u>eigh</u>	pie	height	raid	friend
3. doe<u>s</u>	miss	nose	votes	rice
4. in<u>t</u>end	this	whistle	baked	batch
5. ri<u>ng</u>	sink	handle	signal	pinpoint

Recognition of Sound–Symbol Correspondence

Find in the following words the letters and letter combinations that correspond to each speech sound in the word. For example, the word *stress* has five phonemes, each of which is represented by a letter or letter group: s / t / r / e / ss. Now try these:

best   fresh   scratch

though   laughed   middle

chirp   quaint

Definitions and Concepts

Write a definition or explanation for each of the following:

Vowel sound (vowel phoneme)

Consonant digraph

Prefix

Inflectional (grammatical) morpheme

Why is phonemic awareness important?

How is decoding skill related to reading fluency and comprehension?

Comprehensive Survey of Language Knowledge (Form A)

1. From the list below, find an example of each of the following (answer will be a word or part of a word):

   Inflected verb

   Compound noun

   Bound root

   Derivational suffix

   Greek combining form

peaches	incredible	slowed	although	shameful

bicycle	neuropsychology	sandpaper	vanish

2. For each word in the following list, determine the number of syllables and the number of morphemes:

	Syllables	*Morphemes*
bookworm		
unicorn		
elephant		
believed		
incredible		
finger		
hogs		
telegram		

3. A closed syllable is one that _____.

   An open syllable is one that _____.

   _____

   _____

   _____

From *Speech to Print Workbook: Language Exercises for Teachers* by Louisa Cook Moats.
Copyright © 2003 by Paul H. Brookes Publishing Co. • www.brookespublishing.com • 1-800-638-3775
Do not reproduce without permission of Paul H. Brookes Publishing Co.

4. How many speech sounds are in the following words?

sigh	thrown	scratch
ice	sung	poison
mix	shrink	know

5. What is the third speech sound in each of the following words?

joyful	should	patchwork
tinker	rouge	talk
square	start	shower
protect		

6. Underline the schwa vowels:

telephone	along	imposition
addenda	precious	unless

7. Underline the consonant blends (not all words have blends):

knight	napkin	springy
climb	squished	first
wreck		

8. Underline the consonant digraphs (not all words have digraphs):

spherical	numb	thought
church	shrink	whether

9. When is *ck* used in spelling?

10. What letters signal that *c* is pronounced /s/?

11. List all of the ways you know to spell long /ō/.

12. List all of the ways you know to spell the consonant sound /f/.

13. When adding a suffix to a word ending with silent *e*, what is the spelling rule?

14. How can you recognize an English word that came from Greek?

Comprehensive Survey of Language Knowledge (Form B)

What is your professional role at present?

How many years have you taught?

What is your most advanced degree?

1. From the list below, find an example of each of the following (answer may be a word or part of a word):

    Inflected verb

    Compound noun

    Bound root

    Derivational suffix

revise	already	carpetbag	trilogy
released	behind	complexity	flower

2. For each word in the following list, determine the number of syllables and the number of morphemes:

	Syllables	*Morphemes*
caterpillar		
attached		
contracts		
butter		
spring		
preacher		
telemeter		

3. How many speech sounds (phonemes) are in the following words?

exit	flung	boil	sledge
thrash	shocks	through	gnawed

4. Underline the schwa vowels:

amend	complicate	correlation
alumnus	compare	position

5. Underline the consonant blends (not all words have blends):

   autumn   gnaw   square   burst
   cloak   shepherd   twang

6. Underline the consonant digraphs (not all words have digraphs):

   asphyxiate   thigh   shrunk
   nimble   chunk   whistle

7. When is *tch* used in spelling?

8. What letters signal that *g* is pronounced /j/?

9. List all of the ways you know to spell long /o͞o/.

10. List all of the ways you know to spell the consonant sound /k/.

11. Why does *bible* have one *b* and *bubble* have two?

12. If a child writes the word *dress* as *JRS,* what hypotheses can you make about the child's approach to spelling?

13. Describe the sound, spelling, and meaning structure of this word: *metamorphosis*

Answers for the Surveys of Language Knowledge

Brief Survey: Phoneme Counting

Number of speech sounds or phonemes:

thrill [4]	ring [3]	shook [3]
does [3]	fix [4]	wrinkle [5]
sawed [3]	quack [4]	know [2]

Brief Survey: Syllable Counting

Number of syllables:

cats [1]	capital [3]	shirt [1]
spoil [1 or 2]	decidedly [4]	banana [3]
recreational [5]	lawyer [2]	walked [1]

Brief Survey: Phoneme Matching

1. pu<u>sh</u> [*sugar*]

2. w<u>eigh</u> [*raid*]

3. doe<u>s</u> [*nose*]

4. in<u>t</u>end [*baked*]

5. ri<u>ng</u> [*sink*]

Brief Survey: Recognition of Sound–Symbol Correspondence

The letters and letter combinations that correspond to each speech sound:

b / e / s / t	f / r / e / sh	s / c / r / a / tch
th / ough	l / au / gh / ed	m / i / dd / le
ch / i / r / p	q / u / ai / n / t	

From *Speech to Print Workbook: Language Exercises for Teachers* by Louisa Cook Moats.
Copyright © 2003 by Paul H. Brookes Publishing Co. • www.brookespublishing.com • 1-800-638-3775
Do not reproduce without permission of Paul H. Brookes Publishing Co.

Brief Survey: Definitions and Concepts

A vowel sound (vowel phoneme) is an open speech sound that is the nucleus of a syllable.

A consonant digraph is a letter combination corresponding to one unique sound.

A prefix is a morpheme (meaningful part), usually of Latin origin, that is added before a root and that changes the meaning of the whole word.

An inflectional (grammatical) morpheme is a grammatical ending added to a verb, adjective, or noun that changes the number, degree, or tense of the word but does not change the meaning of the word.

Phonemic awareness is one (but not the only) necessary skill in learning to read an alphabetic writing system.

The ability to decode words accurately will not of itself support good reading. In addition to decoding, one needs to read words fluently so that attention can be relegated to comprehension.

Comprehensive Survey (Form A)

1. Inflected verb [*slowed*]

   Compound noun [*sandpaper*]

   Bound root [*cred, cyc, psych*]

   Derivational suffix [*-ful, -ible*]

   Greek combining form [Any of the following are correct: *neuro, psych, ology*]

2.

	Syllables	*Morphemes*
bookworm	2	2
unicorn	3	2
elephant	3	1
believed	2	3
incredible	4	3
finger	2	1
hogs	1	2
telegram	3	2

3. *A closed syllable is one that contains a short vowel and ends in one consonant. An open syllable is one that contains a long vowel sound spelled with one vowel letter that ends the syllable.*

4. Number of speech sounds in the following words:

sigh [2]	thrown [4]	scratch [5]
ice [2]	sung [3]	poison [5]
mix [4]	shrink [5]	know [2]

5. The third speech sound in the following words:

joyful /f/	should /d/	patchwork /ch/
tinker /ng/	rouge /zh/	talk /k/
square /w/	start /ŏ/	shower /w/
protect /ō/		

6. Schwa vowels:

tel<u>e</u>phone	<u>a</u>long	imp<u>o</u>sit<u>io</u>n
<u>a</u>ddend<u>a</u>	preci<u>ous</u>	<u>u</u>nless

7. Consonant blends:

knight [*none*]	napkin [*none*]	<u>spr</u>ingy
<u>cl</u>imb	<u>squ</u>ished	fir<u>st</u>
wreck [*none*]		

8. Consonant digraphs:

s<u>ph</u>erical	numb [*none*]	<u>th</u>ought
chur<u>ch</u>	<u>sh</u>rink	<u>wh</u>e<u>th</u>er

9. *The spelling* ck *is used when a* /k/ *sound follows a stressed, short sound.*

10. Letters that signal that *c* is pronounced /s/: *e, i,* or *y* following the *c.*

11. Ways to spell long /ō/: *o, oa, ow, oe, o-e (o-consonant-e), ough*

12. Ways to spell the consonant sound /f/: *f, ff, gh, ph*

13. When adding a suffix to a word ending with silent *e,* the spelling rule is: *Drop the* e *if the suffix begins with a vowel; keep the* e *if the suffix begins with a consonant.*

14. *An English word that came from Greek might have* ph *for* /f/, ch *for* /k/, *or* y *for* /i/; *it is likely to be constructed from two or more combining forms; and it is likely to be a mythological* (myth), *scientific* (chlorophyll), *or mathematical* (dyscalculia) *term.*

Comprehensive Survey (Form B)

1. Inflected verb [*released*]

   Compound noun [*carpetbag*]

   Bound root [Any of the following are correct: *vis, lease, ready, complex, logy, flower*]

   Derivational suffix [*-ity*]

2.

	Syllables	Morphemes
caterpillar	4	1
attached	2	3
contracts	2	3
butter	2	1
spring	1	1
preacher	2	2
telemeter	4	2

3. Number of speech sounds (phonemes) in the following words:

exit [4]	flung [4]	boil [3]	sledge [4]
thrash [4]	shocks [4]	through [3]	gnawed [3]

4. Underline the schwa vowels:

   a̲mend   compli̲cate   corre̲lati̲on

   a̲lumnu̲s   co̲mpare   po̲siti̲on

5. Consonant blends:

   autumn [*none*]   gnaw [*none*]   s̲q̲uare   bur̲s̲t̲

   c̲l̲oak   shepherd [*none*]   t̲w̲ang

6. Consonant digraphs:

   asp̲h̲yxiate   t̲h̲igh   s̲h̲runk

   nimble [*none*]   c̲h̲unk   w̲h̲istle

7. *The spelling* tch *is used when a* /ch/ *sound follows a stressed, short vowel.*

8. Letters that signal that *g* is pronounced /j/: *e, i,* or *y* following the *g* (exception: *get, give, gynecologist*)

9. Ways to spell long /o͞o/: *u, oo, ou, oe, ue, ew, ough, o, u-e (u-consonant-e)*

10. Ways to spell the consonant sound /k/: *k, -ck, c, -que, ch*

11. *The first syllable in* bible *is open (it ends in a long vowel). The last syllable is* -ble. *The first syllable in* bubble *is closed (it ends with the consonant* b*):* bub + ble = bubble.

12. *The child is showing the beginnings of phonetic spelling but does not yet have conventional use of symbols to represent speech sounds. He or she has phoneme awareness but does not have complete knowledge of grapheme–phoneme correspondence.*

13. *The word* metamorphosis *has five syllables, 11 phonemes, and two morphemes* (meta + morphosis)*. It is of Greek origin (clues are the Greek combining form* meta, *the fact that it is a scientific word, and the use of* ph *to spell the* /f/ *sound. The word means* transformation, *and the morphemes in the word mean* change *and* form.

Nonphonetic Rote Memory Word Lists

A pproximately 150 commonly used words have nonphonetic spellings, primarily in the vowel sounds. These words need to be memorized by rote for both reading and spelling. List A includes those words that should be taught in first and second grades. List B includes those words that should be taught by third or fourth grade. Students should memorize 3–5 words at a time. Students should write the words, saying the letter names (not the sounds represented by the letters) out loud as they form the letters. Frequent review is necessary for reading and spelling accuracy.

Groups of words that contain similar letter–sound correspondences (or similar patterns) should be taught together as suggested.

Sources: Henry, M.K., & Redding, N.C. (2002). *Patterns for success in reading and spelling* (2nd ed.). Austin, TX: PRO-ED. Rome, P.D., & Osman, J.S. (1993). *Language tool kit* [Teacher's manual and cards]. Cambridge, MA: Educators Publishing Service.

LIST A

a	are	could	door
again	bear	do	friend
against	been	does	from
always	both	done	give
any	come	don't	goes
gone	have	nothing	one
guess	hour	of	only
guest	live	off	other
guide	love	often	pear
guy	much	once	people
pretty	said	sure	there
pull	says	talk	they
push	should	tear	though
put	son	the	through
rich	such	their	to
too	want	where	would
toward	was	which	you
two	wear	who	your
very	were	whom	youth
walk	what	whose	

Groups to Be Taught Together

once	who	could	such
one	whom	should	much
only	whose	would	rich
			which
to	you	bear	
too	your	pear	
two	youth	tear	
		wear	

LIST B

among	build	clothes	enough
another	built	cough	eye
blood	busy	debt	flood
break	buy	double	floor
broad	calf	doubt	four
fourth	guard	honest	listen
front	half	honor	many
gauge	heart	iron	month
great	hearth	island	move
group	height	laugh	muscle
ninth	sew	sugar	trouble
ocean	soft	swore	truth
pint	some	sworn	usual
prove	steak	thorough	Wednesday
rough	straight	tough	whole

wolf
won
wore
worn

Groups to Be Taught Together

great	blood	wore	calf
break	flood	worn	half
steak		swore	
		sworn	
rough	hour	double	guard
tough	honest	trouble	guess
enough	honor		guest
			guide
			guy
group	heart		
soup	hearth		

Compound Words

Compound words can be read when students have learned most consonant and vowel patterns. The teacher explains that two short words of Anglo-Saxon origin often combine, or compound, to form a new word that is based on the meanings of the two constituent words. Students should try to generate as many compound words as they can before reading the words listed in this appendix.

Activities Using
Compound Words

The compound words in this appendix can be used in the activities mentioned in Chapter 6. The compound words can also be used in the following activities.

Phonological Awareness: Syllable Deletion

Ask students to say a compound word, and then ask them to delete one part of it. For example, "Say *skywalk*. Now say it without *sky*," or "Say *housecoat*. Now say it without *coat*."

Adding Words to a Bulletin Board

Have children add new compound words to a bulletin board of compound words. The words can be divided into categories such as the ones used in this appendix.

Compound Invention

Ask children to invent new compound words and draw pictures representing the words.

Discussion

Discuss with students how the meanings of the constituent words in a compound relate to the meaning of the compound word. Remind them also that compounds usually have their stress on the first syllable.

COMPOUND WORDS

People

grandchild	stepdaughter	skycap	dishwasher
grandparent	schoolgirl	statesman	bookkeeper
grandmother	dogcatcher	bookworm	granddaughter
grandfather	salesperson	scatterbrain	watchmaker
housemother	bodyguard	firefighter	babysitter
stepmother	housekeeper	scapegoat	lifeguard
stepfather	stagehand	glassmaker	blacksmith
stepson	cowboy	grandson	silversmith

Animals

butterfly	shellfish	firefly
bluebird	jellyfish	honeybee
starfish	hookworm	horsefly
blackbird	tadpole	skylark
snowbird	rattlesnake	walleye

Actions

slipstitch	sleepwalk	sleighride

Objects

bookbag	snowball	turntable	firecracker
lunchbox	snowboard	checkbook	diskdrive
blackboard	flashlight	spitball	toothpick
chalkboard	housecoat	slingshot	notebook
floorboard	pillowcase	trapdoor	paycheck
skateboard	tablecloth	chairlift	keyboard
mailbox	wallpaper	backpack	bookmark
shoebox	hardware	bookcase	
shoelace	stepladder	saucepan	
snowshoe	snapshot	plaything	

Games

baseball	basketball	handball	volleyball
football	tetherball	softball	

Buildings/Places

classroom	warehouse	haystack	campfire
boardroom	lighthouse	railroad	skyline
stockroom	treehouse	airport	seawall
playground	smokehouse	graveyard	waterfall
playhouse	smokestack	campground	riverhead

headwall	bookstore	seashore	township
skywalk	ballroom	airfield	wheelhouse
sweatshop	crosswalk	grandstand	schoolyard
fishpond	schoolhouse	headquarters	showplace
bedroom	hometown	household	

Vehicles

sailboat	motorbike	airplane	truckload
speedboat	motorcycle	spacecraft	lifeboat
motorboat	steamship	shipwreck	fireboat

Food

buttermilk	strawberry	shortbread	centercut
cheeseburger	cheesecake	fruitcup	jellybean
blueberry	butterscotch	peppermint	horseradish

Abstract Concepts

trademark	humpback	viewpoint	homemade
showtime	horseback	northwest	elsewhere
seasick	homework	southeast	widespread
homesick	paperwork	lifetime	

Weather

sunrise	starlight	sandstorm	rainstorm
sunset	whirlwind	thunderstorm	earthquake

Prefixes

The prefixes in this appendix are listed alphabetically, not in order of presentation. See Chapters 6 and 7 for logical sequences of presentation. In most cases, numerous other words containing the target prefixes can be added to these lists. Prefixes generally have specific meanings, and these are given in parentheses after the prefix. The prefixes in this appendix are of Latin origin unless noted otherwise. (Number prefixes are listed at the end of this appendix.) Suffixes can be added to many of the words in this appendix.

PREFIXES

a- (*on* or *in; to;* **Anglo-Saxon and Latin**)

abeam	across	alone	around
abed	adrift	along	aside
abet	afire	aloud	asleep
abide	afoot	among	aswarm
abound	ahead	amuse	await
above	alight	anoint	awake
abroad	alike	apart	away
abut	alive	arise	awoke

The prefix *a-* can also mean *without* or *not*, as in *amoral* and *asocial*.

ab- (*from* or *away*)

abdicate	ablation	abrupt	absorption
abdication	ablative	abscess	abstain
abduct	ablution	abscissa	abstinence
abduction	abnegate	absence	abstract
aberration	abnegation	absent	abuse
abjection	abrade	absentee	abusive
abjuration	abrasion	absenteeism	
abjure	abrogate	absorb	

ad- (*to, toward, in,* or *near*)

adapt	adhesion	administrator	advent
adaptation	adhesive	admiration	adverb
adapter	adjacent	admire	adverse
adaptive	adjectival	admirer	advertise
addict	adjective	admission	advertisement
address	adjunct	admit	advertiser
adduct	adjust	admonish	advice
adduction	administer	adopt	advise
adhere	administration	advance	adviser
adherence	administrative	advantage	advisor

Variants of *ad-*

ac- (used before roots beginning with *c, k,* or *q*)

accede	accolade	account	accustomed
accelerant	accommodate	accountant	acknowledge
accelerate	accommodation	accretion	acquaint
accent	accompany	accrual	acquaintance
accept	accomplice	accrue	acquiesce
access	accomplish	accumulate	acquire
accessory	accord	accuracy	acquisition
accident	accordance	accurate	acquit
acclaim	accost	accuse	acquittal

af- (used before roots beginning with *f*)

affair	affiliate	afflict	affright
affect	affiliation	affliction	affront
affectation	affinity	affluent	affusion
affection	affirm	afflux	
affidavit	affix	afford	

ag- (used before roots beginning with *g*)

agglomerate	aggrandize	aggression	aggrieved
agglutinate	aggravate	aggressive	
aggrade	aggregate	aggressor	

al- (used before roots beginning with *l*)

allegation	alleviate	allot	allure
allege	alliance	allotment	allusion
allegiance	alliterate	allow	alluvial
allegory	alliteration	allowance	
allergic	allocate	alloy	
allergy	allocation	allude	

an- (used before roots beginning with *n*)

annex	annotate	annul
annexation	announce	annulment
annihilate	announcement	annunciate

 The prefix *an-* can also mean *without* or *not,* as in *anhydride.*

ap- (used before roots beginning with *p*)

appall	append	applicant	apprehend
apparatus	appendage	application	apprehension
apparent	appendicitis	applicator	apprentice
apparition	appendix	apply	apprise
appeal	apperceive	appoint	approach
appear	appertain	apportion	appropriate
appearance	applaud	apposite	approve
appease	applause	appraisal	approximate
appellate	appliance	appreciate	approximation
appellation	applicable	appreciation	

ar- (used before roots beginning with *r*)

arraign	arrangement	arrest	arrogant
arraignment	array	arrival	
arrange	arrears	arrogance	

as- (used before roots beginning with *s*)

assail	assessment	assimilation	assortment
assault	assessor	assist	assuage
assemble	asset	assistance	assume
assembler	assiduous	assistant	assumption
assembly	assign	associate	assurance
assent	assignation	association	assure
assert	assignment	assonance	
assess	assimilate	assonant	

at- (used before roots beginning with *t*)

attach	attend	attire	attribute
attachment	attention	attitude	attribution
attack	attenuate	attorney	attrition
attain	attenuation	attract	attune
attainment	attest	attraction	
attempt	attestation	attractive	

ambi- (*both*)

ambidextrous	ambiguous	ambivalent
ambiguity	ambivalence	ambiversion

ante- (*before*)

ante	antecessor	antefix	anteroom
antebellum	antechamber	antemeridian	anteversion
antecede	antechoir	antenatal	anteverted
antecedence	antedate	antependium	
antecedent	antediluvian	antepenultimate	

anti- (*opposite* or *against*)

antiabortion	antianxiety	antibody	anticlimax
antiaircraft	antiapartheid	anticancer	anticoagulant
antiallergic	antiart	antichoice	anticonvulsant
antiantibody	antibiotic	anticlerical	anticrime

antidepressant	antihistamine	antilock	antipope
antifeminist	anti-inflammatory	antimagnetic	antismog
antifreeze		antinomy	antismoking
antihero	anti-intellectual	antinoise	antisocial

be- (*completely, thoroughly,* or *excessively;* **used as an intensive; Anglo-Saxon)**

becalm	bedraggled	beguiling	besotted
became	befoul	belabor	betray
becloud	befriend	belay	betrayal
become	befuddle	belittle	betrayer
bedeck	begrudge	beloved	between
bedevil	beguile	beset	

bene- (*well* or *good*)

| benediction | beneficent | benefit | benevolent |
| benefactor | beneficial | benevolence | |

circum- (*around* or *about*)

circumambulate	circumference	circumlocute	circumspect
circumcise	circumfix	circumlocution	circumstance
circumcision	circumflex	circumnavigate	circumstantial
circumduct	circumfluent	circumpolar	circumvent
circumduction	circumfuse	circumscribe	circumvention

con- (*together, with, joint,* or *jointly*)

concatenate	concrete	confer	confusion
concatenation	concur	confess	congest
concave	condemn	confessor	congestion
conceit	condemnation	confidant	congregate
concentrate	condense	confide	congress
concentration	condition	confident	congressional
concentric	condole	confiscate	congruent
concern	conduct	conflict	conjecture
concert	conduction	conform	conjunction
concise	conductor	conformance	connect
conclave	confection	conformist	connection
conclude	confectioner	confront	connotation
conclusion	confederacy	confrontation	connote
concord	confederate	confuse	conscript

conscription	constitute	consummation	contrast
consecrate	constitution	contact	contribute
consecration	constrain	contain	contribution
consider	constraint	containment	convene
considerate	construct	continuation	convention
consideration	construction	continue	converge
consolation	consult	contract	conversation
console	consultant	contraction	converse
consonant	consultation	contracture	conversion
conspire	consume	contraption	convert
constellation	consummate	contrary	convince

Variants of *con-*

**   *co-* (usually used before a vowel or *h*)**

co-anchor	coexist	coherent	cooperate
co-author	cohabit	cohesion	coordinate
coeducation	cohere	cohesive	copilot
coerce	coherence	cohort	

**   *col-* (used before roots beginning with *l*)**

collaborate	collateral	collector	collision
collaboration	colleague	college	colloquium
collaborator	collect	collegiate	colloquy
collapse	collection	collide	collude
collate	collective	collinear	collusion

**   *com-* (used before roots beginning with *m, b,* or *p*)**

combat	commerce	communism	comparison
combatant	commercial	community	compartment
combative	commiserate	commutation	compassion
combination	commiseration	commutative	compatible
combine	commission	commute	compatriot
command	commit	compact	compel
commander	commitment	compaction	compendium
commandment	committee	companion	compensate
commence	commode	companionship	compete
commencement	commodious	company	competence
commentate	communal	comparable	competition
commentator	commune	compare	compilation

compile	compliment	comprehension	computation
complain	complimentary	compress	compute
complainant	compose	compression	computer
complaint	composer	comprise	
complement	composition	compulsion	
complementary	comprehend	compunction	

cor- (used before roots beginning with r)

corrade	correspondence	corroborate	corrupt
correlate	correspondent	corrode	corruption
correspond	corrigible	corrosion	

contra- (against, opposite, contrasting)

contraband	contradict	contrapuntal
contrabass	contradiction	contravene
contrabassoon	contrapositive	contravention

counter- (contrary, opposite)

counterargument	counterexample	counterpart
counterattack	counterfeit	counterplea
counterbalance	counterfeiter	counterplot
counterblow	counterforce	counterpoint
countercharge	counterintelligence	counterproposal
countercheck	counterintuitive	counterrevolution
counterclaim	countermand	countersue
counterclockwise	countermarch	counterterrorism
counterculture	countermeasure	
counterdemonstration	counterpane	

de- (down or away from)

debark	declaim	defeat	deflection
debarkation	decline	defect	defog
debate	decode	defection	deform
debrief	decoding	defenestrate	delight
debug	decompose	defenestration	depilatory
decamp	decomposition	defer	deplace
decampment	deduce	deferral	deplane
decay	deduct	defile	deport
decease	deduction	deflect	deportation

dis- (not, absence of, or apart)

disability	disfavor	disorder	distance
disable	disfigure	displace	distant
disarm	disgrace	disposal	distend
disband	dishonest	dispose	distention
disbar	dishonesty	dispute	distract
discharge	dishonor	disrupt	distraction
disclose	disinterest	disruption	distrust
discount	disjoint	dissolution	
discuss	dislike	dissolve	
discussion	dislodge	distal	

Variant of dis-
dif- (used before roots beginning with f)

differ	difficult	diffident	diffuse
different	difficulty	diffract	diffusion
differentiate	diffidence	diffraction	diffusive

dys- (bad or difficult; Latin from Greek)

dyscalculia	dysgraphia	dysphagia	dysthymia
dysenteric	dyskinesia	dysphasia	dystonia
dysentery	dyslexia	dysphonia	dystrophy
dysfunction	dyslexic	dysplasia	
dysfunctional	dyspepsia	dyspnea	
dysgenic	dyspeptic	dysrhythmia	

ex- (out)

exact	except	execute	existential
exalt	exchange	execution	exit
exaltation	excise	executive	expand
example	excision	executor	expatriate
excavate	excite	exemplify	expect
excavation	excitement	exempt	expectorant
exceed	exclude	exemption	expectorate
excel	exclusive	exercise	expedite
excellency	exclusivity	exhilarate	expedition
excellent	excursion	exhilaration	expeditious
excelsior	excuse	exist	expel

expense	expiration	explosion	extend
expensive	expire	explosive	extension
experience	explain	export	extensive
experiential	explanation	exportation	extensor
experiment	explicate	exporter	extent
experimenta-tion	explication	express	extract
experimenter	explode	expression	extraction
expert	exploration	expressive	extrication
expertise	explore	expulsion	extricate
	explorer	extant	extrication

 The prefix *ex-* is usually pronounced /ĕgz/ when followed by a vowel or silent *h* and /ĕks/ when followed by a consonant.

Variant of *ex-*
   e-

ebullient	elapse	erase	evaluate
eclectic	elect	erect	evaluation
eclipse	electric	erode	evaporate
edict	electron	eruct	event
effluent	elide	erupt	eviscerate
egress	elision	evacuate	evoke
eject	emit	evacuation	

fore- (*before;* **Anglo-Saxon**)

forearm	forefather	foreman	foreshadow
forebear	forefoot	foremast	foreshock
forebode	forego	foremost	foresight
forebrain	foregone	forename	forestall
forecast	foreground	forepaw	foretell
forecaster	forehand	forepeak	forethought
foreclose	forehead	forereach	forewarn
foreclosure	foreleg	forerunner	foreword
forecourt	forelimb	foresail	
foredeck	forelock	foresee	

in- (*in, on,* or *toward*)

inbreed	incubation	ingress	inspiration
incandescence	incubator	inhabit	inspire
incandescent	incumbency	inhabitant	install
incarcerate	incumbent	inherent	installation
incarceration	incur	inhibit	institute
incarnate	indebted	inhibition	institution
incarnation	indeed	inject	instruct
incentive	indent	injection	instruction
inception	indentation	inlay	insult
incident	indenture	innate	insurance
incinerate	indicate	innovate	insure
incineration	indication	innovation	insurer
incinerator	indict	innovative	intense
incise	indictment	innovator	intensive
incision	individual	input	intent
incite	induce	inquire	intention
inclination	inductance	inquisition	intrude
incline	induction	inquisitive	intrusion
include	indulge	insect	inure
inclusion	indulgent	insert	invent
inclusive	infect	insertion	invention
income	infection	inset	inventive
incorporate	infer	inside	inventor
incorporation	inference	insider	inversion
increase	infield	insist	invert
incriminate	inflate	insistence	invest
incrimination	inflation	inspect	investment
incriminatory	ingrained	inspection	invitation
incubate	ingredient	inspector	invite

Variants of *in-* (*in, on,* or *toward*)
  il- (used before roots beginning with *l*)

illuminate	illumine	illustration	illustrious
illumination	illustrate	illustrative	

im- (used before roots beginning with *b*, *m*, or *p*)

imbibe	impale	import	imprint
immerge	impalement	important	imprison
immerse	impart	importer	imprisonment
immigrant	impeach	impose	improve
immigrate	impeachment	imposition	improvement
immigration	implant	impress	
imminence	implantation	impression	
imminent	implore	impressive	

ir- (used before roots beginning with *r*)

irradiate	irrigate	irrupt
irradiation	irrigation	irruptive

in- (*not*)

inability	incompliant	ineffective	inorganic
inaccuracy	inconclusive	ineffectiveness	insane
inaccurate	inconsiderate	inelastic	insanity
inactive	inconsideration	inelasticity	insensibility
inactivity	inconsistent	ineluctable	insensible
inadequacy	incorrupt	inept	insensitive
inadequate	incurability	ineptitude	insensitivity
inadvertent	incurable	inexact	insignificance
inadvisable	indecency	infant	insignificant
inappreciative	indecent	infantile	insolent
inarticulate	indecision	infelicitous	insolvency
inartistic	indecisive	infinite	insolvent
inattentive	indelible	infinity	insufficiency
inattentiveness	independence	infirm	insufficient
incapable	independent	infirmary	insupportable
incognito	indestructible	infirmity	intrepid
incognizant	indifference	inharmonious	invalid
incomparability	indifferent	injustice	invariable
incomparable	indignity	innocence	involuntary
incomplete	indirect	innocent	
incompletion	indiscreet	inobservant	

Variants of *in-* (*not*)

il- (used before roots beginning with *l*)

illegal	illegible	illicit	illusion
illegality	illegitimacy	illiteracy	illusory
illegibility	illegitimate	illiterate	

im- (used before roots beginning with *b, m,* or *p*)

imbalance	immodest	impatient	impingement
imbecile	immoral	impeccable	implement
immaterial	immorality	impedance	implementation
immature	immortal	impede	implication
immaturity	immortality	impel	imply
immediacy	immovable	impenetrability	impossible
immediate	immune	impenetrable	impossibility
immemorial	immunity	imperfect	improper
immense	impair	impersonal	impulse
immethodical	impairment	impertinent	impure
immiscible	impartial	imperturbable	imputation
immitigable	impartiality	impetuous	impute
immobile	impassability	impetus	
immoderate	impassable	impinge	

ir- (used before roots beginning with *r*)

irrational	irrelevant	irresistible	irretrievable
irreclaimable	irreligious	irresoluble	irreverent
irreconcilable	irremovable	irresolute	irritate
irreducible	irreparable	irrespective	irritation
irregular	irreplaceable	irresponsible	
irregularity	irreproachable	irresponsive	

inter- (between)

interact	intercession	interdict	interlace
interaction	interchange	interdiction	interlope
interactive	interchangeabil-ity	interest	interloper
interbreed		interfere	intermediary
intercede	interchangeable	interference	intermediate
intercept	intercom	interject	intermix
interception	intercontinental	interjection	interpersonal

interplay · interpreter · interrogation · interstate
interpolate · interregnum · interrogative · interstice
interpolation · interrelate · interrogator · intervene
interpose · interrelation · interrupt · intervention
interposition · interrelation- · interruption · interview
interpret · ship · intersect · interviewee
interpretation · interrogate · intersection · interviewer

intra- (*within*)

intracellular · intramural · intraocular · intrastate
intradermal · intramuscular · intrapersonal · intravenous

intro- (*in* or *inward*)

introduce · introjection · introspect · introversion
introduction · intromission · introspection · introvert
introject · intromit · introspective

mal- (*bad* or *badly; abnormal*)

maladaptation · malcontent · malevolent · malodorous
maladaptive · maldistribution · malfeasance · malpractice
maladjusted · malediction · malfeasant · malversation
maladjustment · maleficence · malformation
maladminister · maleficent · malfunction
malapropism · malevolence · malnutrition

mid- (*middle;* Anglo-Saxon)

midline · midsection · midterm · midwinter
midnight · midshipman · midtown
midpoint · midstream · midway
midriff · midsummer · midweek

mis- (*bad* or *badly; wrong* or *wrongly;* Anglo-Saxon and Latin)

misadventure · miscreant · mismatch · mistaken
misbecome · misdirect · misname · mistook
misbehave · misfire · misplace · mistreat
misbelieve · misgive · misprint · mistrial
miscall · mishandle · misread · misuse
miscast · mishap · misspell
mischief · mishear · misspent
miscount · mislead · mistake

multi- (*many* or *much*)

multicellular	multilevel	multiply
multicolor	multilingual	multiport
multidirectional	multimedia	multipurpose
multifaceted	multimillionaire	multiracial
multifamily	multinational	multisensory
multifold	multinuclear	multisport
multiform	multiparty	multistage
multigenerational	multiped	multistory
multilateral	multiplex	multivariable
multilayered	multiplication	multivitamin

non- (*not* or *negative*)

nonconformist	nonfood	nonreader	nonstop
nondairy	nonhero	nonsense	non-union
nondrinker	nonjuror	nonskid	nonverbal
nonfat	nonperson	nonstick	

ob- (*down, against,* or *facing; to*)

obituary	obligation	obsequious	obsession
object	oblige	observation	obsolescence
objectification	obliterate	observe	obsolete
objectify	obliteration	observer	obstreperous
objection	oblong	obsess	obverse

 The prefix *ob-* can also be used as an intensive, as in *obfuscate*.

Variants of *ob-*

    oc- (**used before roots beginning with** *c*)

occult	occupy	occupant

    of- (**used before roots beginning with** *f*)

offense	offer

    op- (**used before roots beginning with** *p*)

opponent	opposition	oppression	oppressor
oppose	oppress	oppressive	opprobrium

per- (*through* or *completely;* **also used as an intensive**)

perceive	perfume	perpetuity	persuade
perception	perfuse	perplex	persuader
percolate	perfusion	perquisite	persuasion
percolation	perjure	persecute	persuasive
percussion	perjurer	persecution	pertain
percussive	perjury	persecutor	perturb
perennial	permeate	perseverance	pervade
perfect	permeation	perseverate	pervasive
perfection	permission	perseveration	pervasiveness
perform	permissive	persevere	
performance	permit	persist	
performer	perpetual	persistence	

post- (*after, behind,* or *following*)

postclassical	posthypnotic	postlude	postpone
postdate	postimpression-	postmark	postscript
posthaste	ism	postmortem	postwar

pre- (*before* or *earlier*)

preamble	prediction	prejudice	presentiment
prearrange	predictor	prejudicial	preservation
precaution	predispose	preliminary	preservative
precede	predominance	premeditate	preserve
precinct	predominant	premeditation	preserver
precipice	predominate	premix	presold
precipitate	prefabricate	prename	pretend
precipitation	prefabrication	prepackage	pretest
precipitous	prefabricator	preparation	pretext
precise	prefer	prepare	prevail
precision	preferable	preparedness	prevalence
preclude	preference	prepay	prevalent
precognition	preferential	preplan	prevent
precondition	preflight	prerecord	preventative
precursor	preform	prescribe	prevention
predate	preheat	prescription	preview
predetermine	prehistorical	presell	
predicament	prehistory	present	
predict	prejudge	presenter	

pro- (*forward, earlier,* or *prior to*)

problem	profane	progress	protector
problematic	profanity	progression	protectorate
procedural	profess	progressive	protest
procedure	profession	proliferate	protestation
proceed	professional	prologue	protester
process	professionality	promise	proverb
procession	professor	promote	provide
proclaim	professorial	promoter	provider
proclamation	profile	promotion	province
procure	profit	pronoun	provincial
procurement	profiteering	pronounce	provision
procurer	profligate	pronunciation	provocation
produce	profuse	proscribe	provoke
producer	profusion	proscription	
production	program	protect	
productive	programmatic	protection	

re- (*back* or *again;* also used as an intensive)

rebind	recover	refresh	rejoice
rebirth	recuperate	refreshment	rejoin
rebound	recuperation	refusal	rejuvenate
rebuild	refer	refuse	rejuvenation
rebuke	reference	regain	relapse
rebut	referential	regard	relate
rebuttal	refine	regardless	relation
recall	refinement	regress	relationship
recapture	reflect	regression	relative
recast	reflection	rehearsal	relativity
recent	reflective	rehearse	relax
reciprocal	reflector	reinforce	relaxation
reciprocation	reflex	reinforcement	release
reciprocity	reflexive	reinvest	relegate
reclaim	reform	reinvestment	relieve
recollection	reformation	reissue	relinquish
record	reformer	reject	relocate
recount	refrain	rejection	remain

remand · replacement · restain · retrace

remark · reprint · restoration · retract

remission · reproach · restorative · retraction

remit · reproachful · restore · retrain

remittance · reproduce · restorer · return

remote · reproduction · restrain · reversal

removal · reproductive · restrict · reverse

remove · require · restriction · reversion

renounce · resign · restrictive · revert

renunciation · resignation · restructure · revival

reorder · respect · retell · revive

repay · respectful · rethink · rework

repel · respond · retire · rewrite

repellent · respondent · retirement

replace · responder · retouch

se- (*apart* or *aside, without*)

secede · sedate · segregate · separation

secession · sedation · segregation · sever

seclude · sedition · segregationist · several

secrecy · seditious · select · severe

secret · seduce · selection · severity

secrete · seducer · selective

secure · seduction · selector

security · seductive · separate

sub- (*under, beneath,* or *below; secondary*)

subaltern · subject · submissive · subservient

subalternate · subjection · submit · subside

subclass · subjective · subnormal · subsidiary

subcontract · subjugate · suboceanic · subsidy

subcontractor · subjugation · subordinate · subsist

subdivide · subjunctive · subplot · subsoil

subdivision · sublease · subscribe · substage

subdue · submarine · subscription · substitute

subgroup · submerge · subsequent · substitution

subhuman · submission · subserve · substrate

substruction	subtract	suburban	subversive
subterminal	subtraction	suburbanite	subvert
subterranean	suburb	subversion	subway

Variants of *sub-*

suc- (used before roots beginning with *c*)

| succeed | succession | succinct | succumb |
| success | successive | succor | |

suf- (used before roots beginning with *f*)

suffer	sufficiency	suffrage	suffusion
sufferable	sufficient	suffragist	
sufferance	suffix	suffuse	

sug- (used before roots beginning with *g*)

| suggest | suggestible | suggestion | suggestive |

sup- (used before roots beginning with *p*)

supplant	supply	suppose	suppressive
suppliant	support	supposition	suppressor
supplicant	supporter	suppress	
supplication	supportive	suppression	

sus- (used before roots beginning with *p* or *t*)

suspect	suspense	suspicious	sustenance
suspend	suspension	suspire	
suspenders	suspicion	sustain	

syn- (*together* or *with;* Greek)

synagogue	synchronous	syncretism	synecdoche
synapse	syncline	syndicate	synergy
synchronic	syncopate	syndication	synthetic
synchronize	syncopation	syndrome	

Variants of *syn-*

syl- (used before roots beginning with *l*)

| syllabary | syllabicate | syllabus | syllogism |
| syllabic | syllable | syllepsis | |

sym- (used before roots beginning with *b, m,* or *p*)

symbiosis	symmetry	symphony	symptomatic
symbol	sympathetic	symphysis	symptomize
symbolize	sympathy	symposium	
symmetrical	symphonic	symptom	

trans- (*across* or *beyond*)

transact	transcription	translate	transportation
transaction	transfer	translation	transporter
transcend	transference	translator	transpose
transcendence	transfix	transmission	transposition
transcendental	transform	transmit	transverse
transcribe	transformation	transpire	
transcriber	transformer	transport	

un- (*to undo* or *to reverse;* **Anglo-Saxon and Latin**)

unarm	unearth	unlash	unseat
unbend	unfold	unlatch	unsnarl
unbind	unglue	unlearn	unstick
unchain	unhand	unload	unwrap
unclothe	unhitch	unlock	unyoke
uncoil	unlace	unpack	unzip

un- (*not* or *opposite of;* **Anglo-Saxon and Latin**)

unable	uneasy	unlawful	unskilled
unabridged	unfair	unlike	unsound
unasked	unfaithful	unlucky	unthinkable
unaware	unfit	unmanly	untruthful
unawares	unfounded	unmindful	unusual
unbidden	unhappy	unpaid	unwilling
uncertain	unhealthy	unready	unwise
unclean	unjust	unrest	
undaunted	unkempt	unruly	
undying	unknown	unsafe	

NUMBER PREFIXES FROM LATIN AND GREEK

1

uni- (**Latin**)

unicorn	unicycle	uniform	universe

mono- (Greek)

monochromatic	monocycle	monolith	mononucleosis
monochrome	monodynamic	monolithic	monopoly
monochronic	monogram	monologue	
monocle	monograph	monomania	

 See Appendix G for more *mono-* words.

2

bi- (Latin)

biannual	biceps	biennium	binocular
bicameral	bicycle	bifocals	biplane
bicentenary	bidirectional	bifurcate	bipolar
bicentennial	biennial	bifurcation	

duo- (Latin)

dual	duality	duo	duopoly
dualism	duet	duologue	

di- (Greek)

dichromatic	diode	dipole
digraph	dioxide	

3

tri- (Latin/Greek)

triangle	triceratops	triennial	triplicate
triangular	tricycle	trigonometry	tripod

ter- (Latin)

tercentenary	tercentennial	tercet	tertiary

4

quadr-, quar- (Latin)

quadrangle	quadrennium	quart	quartile
quadrangular	quadruped	quarter	
quadrennial	quadruple	quartet	

tetra- (Greek)

tetracycline	tetragonal	tetrameter
tetragon	tetrahedron	

5

quint- (Latin)

quintet	quintile	quintuple	quintuplet

pent- (Greek)

pentadactyl	pentagonal	pentarchy
pentagon	pentameter	pentathlon

6

sex- (Latin)

sextant	sextet	sextuple

hex- (Greek)

hexagon	hexagram	hexameter	hexidecimal
hexagonal	hexahedron	hexane	

7

sept- (Latin)

September	septet	septilateral	septuagenarian

hept- (Greek)

heptagon	heptagonal	heptameter	heptarchy

8

octa-, *octo-* (Latin/Greek)

octagon	octet	octogenarian
octagonal	October	octopus

9

nona-, *nove-* (Latin)

nonagenarian	nonagonal	novena
nonagon	November	

10

dec-, deca-, deci- **(Latin/Greek)**

decade	decathlon	decennium	decimate
decagon	December	decigram	decimation
decagonal	decennial	decimal	decimeter

100

cent- **(Latin)**

cent	centennial	centigram	centipede
centenary	centigrade	centimeter	century

hect- **(Greek)**

hectare	hectogram	hectometer

1,000

mille- **(Latin)**

millenary	millennium	millipede
millennial	million	

kilo- **(Greek)**

kilobyte	kiloliter	kilowatt
kilogram	kilometer	

10,000

myria- **(Greek)**

myriad	myriameter

million

mega- **(Greek;** *mega* **also means** *large***)**

megabyte	megameter	megawatt

 See Appendix G for more *mega-* words.

billion

giga- (Greek)

gigabyte   gigacycle   gigahertz   gigameter

trillion

tera- (Greek)

terahertz   terameter

quadrillion

peta- (Greek)

petameter

quintillion

exa- (Greek)

exameter

BIBLIOGRAPHY

The American heritage dictionary (2nd ed.). (1982). Boston: Houghton Mifflin.
The American heritage dictionary (4th ed.). (2000). Boston: Houghton Mifflin.
Random House unabridged dictionary (2nd ed.). (1993). New York: Random House.

Suffixes

Suffixes are word parts added to the end of a base element that is usually of Anglo-Saxon or Latin origin. Some suffixes have specific meanings and usually place a word in a specific part of speech; other suffixes do not. Because suffixes are usually unstressed, the vowel sound is likely to be schwa. The suffixes listed in this appendix appear in thousands of words and are of Latin origin unless noted otherwise. The meaning and/or part of speech is given for each suffix. The suffixes appear in alphabetical order, not in order of presentation. See Chapter 7 for a logical sequence of presentation. Students need to learn suffixes for both reading and spelling. Prefixes and additional suffixes can be added to some of the words in this appendix.

-able (able, can do; adjective; generally used with Anglo-Saxon base words)

allowable	charitable	drinkable	flammable
answerable	comfortable	eatable	floatable
approachable	creditable	employable	forgivable
approvable	deceivable	enjoyable	honorable
arguable	definable	excitable	hospitable
bearable	desirable	explainable	improvable
believable	disputable	exportable	jumpable
buyable	dissolvable	fixable	kissable

likable	readable	retractable	swimmable
lovable	realizable	retrievable	tastable
mendable	reasonable	returnable	taxable
movable	receivable	sailable	teachable
notable	recognizable	sinkable	testable
observable	regrettable	sizable	trainable
organizable	remarkable	smellable	valuable
passable	removable	solvable	weavable
payable	repairable	storable	workable
portable	repayable	suitable	
preservable	respectable	supportable	

The related suffix -*ability* (-*able* + -*ity*) can be added to many of the same base elements to make nouns (e.g., *teachable, teachability; floatable, floatability; remarkable, remarkability*).

Variant of -*able*
  -*ible* (*able, can do;* **adjective; primarily used with Latin roots**)

accessible	credible	forcible	reprehensible
collapsible	destructible	illegible	repressible
compatible	edible	intelligible	resistible
comprehensible	eligible	legible	responsible
convertible	expressible	perceptible	reversible
corrigible	extendible	possible	sensible
corruptible	flexible	reducible	terrible

The related suffix -*ibility* can be added to many of the same base elements to make nouns (e.g., *credible, credibility; responsible, responsibility; possible, possibility*).

-*ade* (*result of action;* **noun**)

accolade	cascade	escapade	masquerade
ambuscade	cavalcade	esplanade	palisade
balustrade	charade	gallopade	promenade
barricade	colonnade	lemonade	renegade
blockade	crusade	marinade	serenade
brigade	escalade	marmalade	stockade

-age (collection, mass, relationship; noun)

acreage	foliage	parsonage	shrinkage
anchorage	herbage	passage	soakage
appendage	leafage	personage	steerage
baggage	leakage	pilgrimage	stoppage
bandage	leverage	plumage	storage
beverage	lineage	postage	trackage
brokerage	linkage	poundage	truckage
coinage	luggage	ravage	vicarage
cooperage	mileage	salvage	village
courage	moorage	savage	voyage
dockage	package	selvage	wreckage
drainage	parentage	sewage	

-al, -ial (relating to or characterized by; adjective)

abdominal	dermal	horizontal	mortal
acquittal	developmental	hymnal	nasal
adverbial	devotional	institutional	national
alluvial	diagonal	internal	natural
ancestral	disposal	intestinal	nocturnal
baptismal	doctoral	journal	nominal
baronial	editorial	labial	normal
betrayal	educational	liberal	occasional
biennial	elemental	literal	octagonal
binomial	emotional	manual	optional
cardinal	eternal	marginal	ordinal
causal	external	marital	original
centennial	federal	maternal	ornamental
collegial	final	mayoral	parochial
colloquial	formal	medical	pastoral
colonial	fractional	medicinal	paternal
confessional	frontal	menial	perennial
conjugal	functional	mental	personal
correctional	funeral	millennial	pictorial
criminal	general	minimal	plural
denial	gradual	monarchal	polynomial
dental	guttural	moral	primordial

principal	retinal	spinal	territorial
professional	retrieval	spiritual	thermal
proportional	reversal	spousal	universal
rational	ritual	subliminal	visional
recessional	seasonal	supplemental	visual
recital	sensational	taxidermal	
regional	several	terminal	
remedial	skeletal	terrestrial	

Variants of -*ial*

-*cial* (used after a base element ending in *c*)

artificial	facial	judicial	racial
beneficial	financial	official	social
commercial	glacial	provincial	special

-*tial* (usually used after a base element ending in *t*)

celestial	differential	initial	prudential
circumstantial	experiential	martial	substantial
credential	inferential	potential	

-*an* (*relating to;* adjective or noun)

American	Cuban	Lutheran	suburban
Anglican	epicurean	Minnesotan	urban
cosmopolitan	European	Republican	veteran

Variant of -*an*
-*ian*

agrarian	Bostonian	humanitarian	Yugoslavian
Appalachian	Canadian	Italian	
Armenian	centenarian	Norwegian	
Australian	civilian	vegetarian	

-*ant* (*action* or *state;* noun)

accountant	consultant	informant	servant
adjutant	contestant	irritant	stimulant
annuitant	decongestant	lieutenant	supplicant
attendant	disinfectant	merchant	tenant
claimant	expectorant	peasant	
complainant	immigrant	Protestant	

-*ant* (adjective)

abundant	dominant	flippant	relevant
arrogant	dormant	gallant	tolerant
brilliant	elegant	hesitant	truant
buoyant	exorbitant	incessant	vibrant
discordant	expectant	intolerant	
distant	extravagant	militant	

The suffix -*ance* is related to the suffix -*ant* and can be added to many of the same base elements to form nouns (e.g., *tolerant, tolerance; brilliant, brilliance; dominant, dominance*). The related suffix -*ancy* also forms nouns (e.g., *militancy, accountancy, compliancy*).

-*ar* (adjective; used with Latin roots)

angular	molecular	rectangular	tubular
cellular	muscular	secular	vascular
circular	particular	singular	vehicular
familiar	peculiar	solar	vernacular
glandular	polar	spectacular	vestibular
globular	popular	stellar	vulgar

Some common nouns end in -*ar* (e.g., *beggar, molar, hangar, sugar, liar, burglar, cellar, pillar, collar, vinegar, cigar, scholar, registrar*), but note that these -*ar* spellings do not always denote the suffix -*ar*.

-*ard* (*one habitually or excessively in a specified condition;* Anglo-Saxon/ German; noun)

coward	drunkard	laggard

-*ary* (*relating to, place where;* noun)

anniversary	dictionary	granary	notary
apothecary	dispensary	infirmary	obituary
aviary	emissary	judiciary	plenipotentiary
beneficiary	estuary	mercenary	reliquary
boundary	formulary	missionary	secretary
commissary	glossary	mortuary	seminary

| statuary | summary | topiary | visionary |
| subsidiary | syllabary | tributary | vocabulary |

-ary (adjective)

arbitrary	elementary	ordinary	sanitary
binary	extraordinary	plenary	secondary
cautionary	fiduciary	preliminary	sedentary
confectionary	honorary	primary	sedimentary
contrary	imaginary	proprietary	stationary
coronary	literary	reactionary	temporary
customary	military	revolutionary	veterinary
dietary	momentary	rudimentary	voluntary
disciplinary	monetary	salivary	
documentary	necessary	salutary	

-ate (*cause* or *make;* verb)

affiliate	dictate	illustrate	repudiate
ambulate	dominate	infiltrate	retaliate
appropriate	enunciate	initiate	speculate
approximate	eradicate	mediate	stimulate
associate	estimate	mutilate	stipulate
coagulate	exfoliate	operate	substantiate
decimate	hesitate	percolate	vaccinate
dedicate	hibernate	radiate	vacillate
deviate	hydrate	relate	ventilate

-ate (adjective)

adequate	collegiate	desolate	moderate
alternate	compassionate	desperate	private
appellate	confederate	determinate	separate
appropriate	considerate	immediate	temperate
articulate	corporate	legitimate	ultimate

The vowel sound in the suffix -ate is usually long /ā/ when the affixed word is a verb (e.g., as in *appropriate,* meaning *to set aside*). When the affixed word is an adjective, the vowel sound in the suffix is usually schwa (e.g., as in *appropriate,* meaning *fitting the situation*).

-cide (*kill*; **noun**)

autocide	herbicide	matricide	sororicide
biopesticide	homicide	parenticide	suicide
fratricide	infanticide	patricide	uxoricide
fungicide	insecticide	pesticide	vermicide
germicide	liberticide	regicide	

 The suffix -*cide* and the root *cise*, meaning *to cut*, come from the same Latin root, *caedere*.

-cy (*state, condition,* or *quality*; **noun**)

bankruptcy	policy	secrecy

Variant of -*cy*
   -*acy*

accuracy	conspiracy	intimacy	papacy
adequacy	delicacy	legitimacy	pharmacy
advocacy	diplomacy	literacy	piracy
candidacy	efficacy	lunacy	privacy
celibacy	inaccuracy	obstinacy	supremacy

-dom (*quality, realm, office,* or *state*; **Anglo-Saxon; noun**)

boredom	dukedom	kingdom	stardom
chiefdom	earldom	martyrdom	wisdom
Christendom	freedom	popedom	
clerkdom	heirdom	serfdom	

-ed (**Anglo-Saxon; past participle of regular verb**)
   (**pronounced /əd/ after a base element ending in** *d* **or** *t*)

belted	fitted	herded	sighted
blasted	founded	inspected	stranded
blinded	fretted	knotted	stunted
bonded	funded	lifted	tinted
branded	gifted	minded	unfounded
disrupted	handed	pointed	vaulted
erupted	headed	ragged	
exploded	heated	sanded	

(pronounced /d/ after a base element ending in a voiced consonant)

armed	drowned	gleaned	stewed
called	famed	hinged	swelled
canned	fledged	opened	tailed
clubbed	frowned	rubbed	
curved	garbed	screamed	

(pronounced /t/ after a base element ending in an unvoiced consonant)

backed	fixed	hooked	mixed
boxed	fleeced	laughed	offed
cropped	flipped	locked	peaked
crushed	flounced	marked	voiced
cursed	forced	matched	
dished	helped	milked	

 The suffix -*ed* can be added to many hundreds of other words of Anglo-Saxon, Latin, and Greek origin.

-ee (*one who receives the action;* noun [person])

absentee	devotee	grantee	pledgee
addressee	divorcee	guarantee	referee
appointee	employee	internee	refugee
committee	endorsee	licensee	releasee
confirmee	escapee	nominee	trustee
deportee	examinee	payee	Yankee

-eer (*one associated with;* noun [person])

auctioneer	cameleer	mountaineer	privateer
balladeer	electioneer	musketeer	profiteer
buccaneer	engineer	mutineer	volunteer
charioteer	gazetteer	pioneer	

-en (*made of* or *to make;* Anglo-Saxon; verb; primarily used with Anglo-Saxon base words)

blacken	enliven	lighten	thicken
cheapen	flatten	loosen	tighten
dampen	freshen	ripen	toughen
darken	harden	roughen	waken
deepen	hasten	soften	weaken
enlighten	lengthen	strengthen	widen

-en (Anglo-Saxon; adjective)

barren	drunken	mistaken	spoken
broken	frozen	olden	sullen

-en (*made of;* Anglo-Saxon; adjective)

earthen	leaden	silken	woolen
golden	oaken	wooden	

-ence (*action, state,* or *quality;* noun)

circumference	confluence	dissidence	reference
conference	difference	independence	resilience
confidence	diffidence	interdependence	

-ency (*action, state,* or *quality;* noun)

deficiency	emergency	urgency
efficiency	fluency	

-ent (*referent;* noun)

accident	decedent	incident	resident
adolescent	delinquent	incumbent	student
agent	dependent	patient	
constituent	dissident	referent	

-ent (adjective)

absorbent	diligent	inconsistent	negligent
affluent	emergent	indulgent	obedient
beneficent	evident	innocent	resilient
candescent	excellent	intelligent	reticent
confident	exigent	latent	silent
convenient	existent	lenient	sufficient
convergent	fluent	magnificent	transparent
decadent	imminent	malevolent	urgent
dependent	incident	munificent	violent

The suffixes *-ence* and *-ency* are related to the suffix *-ent* and can be added to many of the same base elements to form nouns (e.g., *dependent, dependence, dependency; resident, residence, residency*).

-er (*one who; that which;* **noun; primarily used with Anglo-Saxon base words**)

archer	hanger	miner	splasher
baker	hauler	performer	sprinkler
banker	healer	picker	stationer
boxer	heater	pitcher	swimmer
catcher	helper	prowler	talker
clipper	informer	rancher	teller
counter	keeper	roaster	tracker
dancer	lodger	runner	walker
diner	logger	scribbler	washer
fiddler	looter	shipper	watcher
fighter	manager	skater	
financier	marker	skier	
gambler	milker	smoker	

-er (**adjective [comparative degree]; primarily used with Anglo-Saxon base words; see** *-est* **for superlative degree adjectives**)

bigger	earlier	older	smaller
blacker	fatter	redder	sweeter
bolder	flatter	safer	taller
clearer	greener	shorter	wetter
cloudier	happier	simpler	
colder	hotter	skinnier	
drier	muddier	slimmer	

-ery (*relating to, quality,* **or** *place where;* **noun**)

bakery	demagoguery	nunnery	stationery
bindery	embracery	nursery	stitchery
bravery	flattery	pottery	tannery
confectionery	hatchery	refinery	treachery
cookery	imagery	rookery	trickery
creamery	knavery	slavery	witchery
crockery	millinery	sorcery	

-ese (*related to;* **noun or adjective**)

Burmese	journalese	Portuguese	Vietnamese
Cantonese	legalese	Siamese	
Chinese	novelese	Taiwanese	
Japanese	Pekingese	Tonkinese	

-ess (*feminine;* **noun**)

actress	goddess	leopardess	sculptress
authoress	governess	lioness	songstress
countess	heiress	mayoress	tigress
duchess	hostess	murderess	waitress
empress	huntress	princess	

-est (**adjective [superlative degree]; see** **-er** **for comparative degree adjectives**)

biggest	fastest	hottest	reddest
cloudiest	fleetest	longest	slowest
deepest	greenest	muddiest	warmest

 The suffix *-est* can be added to most adjectives.

-ette (*small* **or** *diminutive;* **noun**)

banquette	dinette	navette	statuette
barrette	gazette	novelette	usherette
bassinette	layette	palette	wagonette
brunette	maisonette	pianette	
cigarette	marionette	rosette	

-fold (*related to a specified number or quantity;* **noun**)

fiftyfold	manyfold	tenfold	twofold
hundredfold	multifold	thousandfold	

-ful (*full of* **or** *full;* **Anglo-Saxon; adjective; primarily used with Anglo-Saxon base words**)

awful	forgetful	plateful	truthful
bashful	fretful	plentiful	useful
beautiful	frightful	restful	wasteful
boastful	gainful	rightful	willful
bountiful	grateful	shameful	wishful
careful	harmful	spiteful	wonderful
doubtful	helpful	tactful	wrongful
faithful	hopeful	tasteful	youthful
fitful	painful	thankful	

The suffix *-ful* can also be used as a noun.

armful	glassful	spadeful
bagful	mouthful	spoonful
bellyful	sackful	thimbleful

-fy, -ify (*make;* **verb**)

beautify	gentrify	notify	satisfy
certify	glorify	pacify	signify
classify	gratify	personify	simplify
deify	horrify	prettify	specify
dignify	identify	purify	stupefy
diversify	intensify	putrefy	terrify
edify	justify	qualify	testify
electrify	liquefy	quantify	unify
falsify	magnify	rarefy	vilify
fortify	modify	reify	

The Latin roots *fac, fact, fect,* and *fic* are related to the suffixes *-fy* and *-ify.*

-hood (*condition, state,* or *quality;* **Anglo-Saxon; noun**)

babyhood	fatherhood	livelihood	priesthood
boyhood	girlhood	manhood	sainthood
brotherhood	knighthood	motherhood	sisterhood
childhood	likelihood	neighborhood	womanhood

-ian (-cian) (*one having a certain skill or art;* **noun [person]**)

academician	magician	patrician	rhetorician
diagnostician	mathematician	Phoenician	statistician
electrician	metaphysician	phonetician	tactician
geometrician	musician	physician	theoretician
Grecian	obstetrician	politician	
logician	optician	practician	

In these words ending in *-cian*, *c* is the final letter of the base element and *-ian* is the suffix, but this pattern is often taught as *-cian*.

-ic (*of, pertaining to,* or *characterized by;* **adjective**)

academic	geometric	music	ritualistic
agnostic	gigantic	mystic	romantic
arithmetic	hectic	narcotic	rustic
automatic	historic	naturalistic	scientific
civic	hypnotic	optimistic	seismic
classic	hypothetic	Pacific	Slavic
diagnostic	impressionistic	parasitic	socialistic
diplomatic	linguistic	patriotic	solipsistic
eccentric	logarithmic	philharmonic	specific
egotistic	logistic	pluralistic	stoic
elastic	magic	poetic	stylistic
enthusiastic	materialistic	politic	symbolic
epileptic	microscopic	public	

-ile (*relating to, suited for,* or *capable of;* **noun**)

automobile	locomobile	quartile	textile
domicile	missile	quintile	
juvenile	percentile	reptile	

-ile (*relating to, suited for,* or *capable of;* **adjective**)

agile	fragile	mobile	versatile
ductile	futile	nubile	
facile	hostile	prehensile	
fertile	immobile	sterile	

-ine (*nature of;* **noun**)
(usually pronounced /ĭn/)

discipline	intestine	saccharine
heroine	medicine	

(pronounced /ēn/)

aquamarine	figurine	magazine	vaccine
chlorine	gasoline	mezzanine	wolverine
citrine	glassine	submarine	
citrulline	glycine	tambourine	

-ine (*nature of*; **adjective**)
   (usually pronounced /īn/)

alkaline	clandestine	feline	piscine
aquiline	divine	leonine	porcine
bovine	elephantine	murine	serpentine
canine	equine	ovine	taurine

   (usually pronounced /ĭn/)

| crystalline | genuine | peregrine |
| feminine | masculine | |

   (usually pronounced /ēn/)

| Benedictine | pristine |

-ing (*action, process,* or *art*; **noun**)

| dancing | gathering | swimming |
| drawing | skipping | swashbuckling |

-ing (**present participle of verb; adjective**)

| believing | seeing | thinking |

 Many hundreds of other words contain the suffix *-ing*.

-ion (-sion) (*act of, state of,* or *result of*; **noun**)
   (usually pronounced /shən/ when the final syllable of the base element has a short vowel sound)

admission	depression	mansion	recession
apprehension	expansion	pension	regression
concession	expression	possession	submission
confession	expulsion	procession	suspension
convulsion	extension	progression	tension

   (usually pronounced /zhən/ when the final syllable of the base element has a long vowel sound)

abrasion	erosion	intrusion	submersion
adhesion	exclusion	invasion	vision
cohesion	excursion	persuasion	
diversion	infusion	seclusion	

In these words ending in -*sion*, *s* is the final letter of the base element and -*ion* is the suffix, but this pattern is often taught as -*sion*.

-ion (-tion) (*act of, state of,* or *result of*; noun)
(pronounced /shən/)

abdication	declaration	explication	invitation
abstraction	dedication	exploration	invocation
acquisition	deduction	extraction	justification
adaptation	delegation	federation	location
addition	depletion	fertilization	lubrication
adoption	deportation	flirtation	mediation
ambition	derivation	flotation	medication
ammunition	description	formulation	meditation
appreciation	desolation	foundation	modernization
attention	devotion	frustration	modulation
authorization	diction	glorification	mortification
aviation	dislocation	gradation	nation
cancellation	disposition	graduation	navigation
causation	disruption	habitation	negotiation
celebration	distraction	identification	notification
certification	distribution	implication	numeration
circulation	domination	incubation	nutrition
citation	duplication	indication	objection
collection	edition	inflation	obstruction
commendation	education	inhalation	population
composition	elation	inhibition	position
condensation	election	injection	prediction
condition	elevation	insertion	preparation
congregation	equation	inspiration	preposition
construction	eructation	instruction	prescription
contention	evacuation	intention	presentation
continuation	examination	interruption	preservation
correlation	exception	intoxication	presumption
creation	exhalation	introduction	probation
decimation	expectation	investigation	projection

proportion	replication	sophistication	termination
provocation	reputation	stipulation	traction
qualification	reservation	strangulation	tradition
quotation	resignation	subjection	transition
radiation	revocation	subtraction	trepidation
recommendation	rotation	suffocation	vacation
recreation	salivation	susurration	validation
reduction	satisfaction	syllabication	variation
reflection	segregation	syndication	ventilation
regulation	sensation	tabulation	vibration
relation	situation	temptation	violation

 In these words ending in *-tion, t* is the final letter of the base element and *-ion* is the suffix, but this pattern is often taught as *-tion*.

(pronounced /chən/ after a base element ending in *-st*)

| combustion | digestion | ingestion |
| congestion | exhaustion | question |

-ish (*origin, nature,* **or** *resembling;* **Anglo-Saxon; adjective)**

amateurish	darkish	lavish	softish
babyish	devilish	longish	Spanish
biggish	dullish	loutish	strongish
bluish	foolish	reddish	stylish
bookish	fortyish	selfish	Swedish
boyish	freakish	sheepish	sweetish
British	frumpish	skittish	thickish
clownish	garish	sluggish	thinnish
dampish	girlish	smallish	youngish

-ism (*doctrine, system, manner, condition, act,* **or** *characteristic;* **noun)**

absenteeism	Catholicism	fatalism	idealism
altruism	classicism	feudalism	impressionism
atheism	criticism	heroism	industrialism
baptism	egoism	Hinduism	Judaism
Buddhism	egotism	humanism	materialism
capitalism	exorcism	hypnotism	mechanism

modernism
moralism
optimism
organism

pacifism
patriotism
pessimism
pluralism

positivism
radicalism
realism
ritualism

terrorism
ventriloquism
verbalism

-ist (*one who;* **noun [person]**)

abolitionist
accompanist
alarmist
allergist
archivist
artist
astrologist
Baptist
bassoonist
bicyclist
biologist
canoeist
cartoonist
cellist
chemist
clarinetist
colonist
communist
conformist

copyist
cosmologist
cyclist
dentist
dramatist
druggist
egoist
egotist
essayist
extortionist
extremist
federalist
florist
flutist
futurist
geologist
guitarist
harpist
herbalist

hobbyist
humorist
hypnotist
impressionist
jurist
linguist
lobbyist
loyalist
machinist
manicurist
modernist
moralist
motorist
oculist
opportunist
optimist
parachutist
pessimist
pharmacist

physicist
physiologist
pianist
positivist
psychologist
purist
reformist
reservist
revolutionist
scientist
socialist
taxidermist
terrorist
theorist
tourist
violinist

The suffix *-ize* is related to *-ism* and *-ist* and can be added to many of the same base elements to make nouns (e.g., *socialism, socialist, socialize; terrorism, terrorist, terrorize*).

-ite (*nature of, quality of,* or *mineral product;* **noun**)

alexandrite	dynamite	marcasite	sulfite
amazonite	favorite	meteorite	tanzanite
azurite	fluorite	Muscovite	trilobite
barite	graphite	parasite	Wisconsinite
calcite	hematite	satellite	
chlorite	Israelite	stalactite	
dolomite	malachite	stalagmite	

-ium (*chemical element* or *group;* **noun**)

ammonium	crematorium	lithium	sanatorium
aquarium	delirium	medium	sodium
atrium	emporium	millennium	solarium
auditorium	equilibrium	planetarium	stadium
biennium	helium	podium	tedium
cadmium	honorarium	premium	titanium
calcium	iridium	radium	uranium

The related plural noun suffix *-ia* can be added to some of the same base elements (e.g., *atria, honoraria, podia, media*).

-ive (*causing* or *making;* **adjective**)

abrasive	cursive	elusive	intrusive
active	decisive	eruptive	massive
assertive	defensive	evasive	medicative
attentive	depressive	excessive	native
cohesive	descriptive	exhaustive	negative
collective	destructive	expansive	offensive
comprehensive	diffusive	expensive	oppressive
congestive	dissuasive	explosive	passive
consecutive	divisive	extensive	perceptive
constructive	effective	furtive	positive
cooperative	effusive	imperative	primitive
corrosive	elaborative	impressive	progressive
creative	elective	instinctive	provocative

punitive	relative	speculative	superlative
receptive	revulsive	stimulative	
recessive	sensitive	submissive	

-ize (make; verb)

actualize	humanize	melodize	realize
apologize	hypnotize	memorize	scrutinize
colonize	idolize	minimize	sensitize
criticize	iodize	mobilize	socialize
dramatize	italicize	organize	standardize
economize	legalize	ostracize	tantalize
familiarize	liquidize	polarize	verbalize
fertilize	localize	politicize	vitalize
formalize	materialize	popularize	

The related suffixes -ism and -ist can be added to many of the same base elements to make nouns (e.g., formalize, formalism, formalist; realize, realism, realist).

-less (without; Anglo-Saxon; adjective; primarily used with Anglo-Saxon base words)

ageless	formless	moneyless	sleepless
blameless	groundless	nameless	sleeveless
breathless	hatless	noiseless	smokeless
breezeless	heedless	painless	soundless
careless	helpless	penniless	timeless
cheerless	homeless	pointless	tireless
childless	hopeless	priceless	tuneless
cloudless	joyless	restless	voiceless
endless	leafless	sailless	voteless
faceless	lifeless	senseless	wingless
faithless	loveless	shameless	wordless
faultless	matchless	shiftless	

-ling (*very small; diminutive;* Anglo-Saxon; noun)

cageling	fledgling	kindling	underling
changeling	foundling	sapling	wiseling
darling	gosling	seedling	yearling
duckling	kidling	starling	youngling

-logy (-ology) (*science* or *study of;* noun)

anthology	ecology	morphology	psychology
archaeology	ethnology	musicology	radiology
astrology	etiology	mythology	sociology
audiology	flaciology	neurology	technology
biology	geology	ophthalmology	terminology
cardiology	hydrology	ornithology	theology
chronology	immunology	paleontology	volcanology
cosmology	lexicology	pathology	zoology
criminology	meteorology	pharmacology	
dermatology	mineralogy	phonology	

The related forms *-ologist* (*-ology* + *-ist*), which denotes *one who deals with a specific topic* (e.g., *dermatologist, cosmologist, criminologist, audiologist*), and *-logue* can be added to many of the same base elements.

Note that *-logy* is often considered a Greek combining form. See Appendix H for a more extensive list of *-logy* words.

-ly (*like* or *manner of;* adverb)

absently	faintly	hoarsely	morbidly
badly	fearlessly	homely	namely
blindly	fervently	hurriedly	nicely
briskly	foolishly	jointedly	peacefully
broadly	forcedly	kingly	pleasantly
candidly	forcefully	likely	prettily
carefully	friendly	lonely	primely
cleanly	gladly	longingly	proudly
deadly	goodly	loudly	quickly
delightedly	grandly	madly	rarely
evasively	heatedly	maidenly	roundly

rudely	shakily	stiffly	vividly
ruggedly	smartly	swiftly	wisely
sadly	smilingly	validly	
sanely	sorely		

-ment (act of, state of, or result of an action; noun)

achievement	confinement	entertainment	payment
advertisement	derailment	excitement	postponement
agreement	detachment	government	punishment
amazement	disappointment	impeachment	refinement
amendment	employment	implement	replacement
announcement	encampment	infringement	resentment
argument	enchantment	instrument	retirement
arrangement	endorsement	integument	segment
basement	enforcement	management	sentiment
commandment	engagement	movement	settlement
commitment	enjoyment	nourishment	shipment
compliment	enlistment	ornament	statement
concealment	entanglement	pavement	testament

-most (most or nearest to; Anglo-Saxon; adjective [superlative])

bottommost	hindmost	middlemost	topmost
endmost	inmost	northernmost	undermost
farthermost	innermost	outermost	upmost
furthermost	lowermost	southernmost	uppermost

-ness (state of; Anglo-Saxon; noun; primarily used with Anglo-Saxon base words)

alertness	furiousness	promptness	strictness
ambitiousness	gladness	quaintness	sweetness
badness	greatness	quietness	swiftness
bigness	happiness	rightness	tightness
bluntness	hollowness	roundness	uproariousness
busyness	lightness	sadness	vastness
cautiousness	loudness	shortness	wellness
exactness	madness	shyness	wetness
expertness	neatness	sleeplessness	witness
fitness	newness	slowness	
flatness	politeness	smartness	
fleetness	prettiness	softness	

-or (*one who; that which;* noun; primarily used with Latin roots)

abdicator	confessor	fumigator	precursor
accelerator	contractor	generator	predecessor
actor	contributor	governor	predictor
adductor	creator	imitator	professor
advisor	creditor	impostor	projector
aggressor	curator	incinerator	prosecutor
agitator	defector	incisor	prospector
alternator	demonstrator	incubator	protector
ambassador	denominator	indicator	protractor
ancestor	depressor	instigator	radiator
arbitrator	detractor	instructor	reflector
auditor	dictator	interlocutor	refrigerator
aviator	director	inventor	respirator
bachelor	divisor	investigator	rotator
benefactor	donator	juror	senator
bettor	editor	legislator	solicitor
calculator	educator	lessor	spectator
capacitor	elevator	liberator	speculator
chancellor	erector	matador	supervisor
co-conspirator	escalator	mediator	survivor
collector	executor	moderator	tractor
communicator	extensor	narrator	transistor
competitor	exterminator	navigator	translator
compositor	fixator	numerator	ventilator
conductor	flexor	oppressor	visor

-ory (*relating to, quality,* or *place where;* noun)

allegory	directory	inventory	rectory
category	dormitory	laboratory	refectory
conservatory	factory	lavatory	reformatory
crematory	history	memory	territory

-ory (of, pertaining to, or characterized by; adjective)

accessory	cursory	manipulatory	satisfactory
advisory	declaratory	predatory	sensory
ambulatory	defamatory	proclamatory	signatory
auditory	exclamatory	promissory	speculatory
benedictory	exclusory	purgatory	supervisory
compulsory	inflammatory	reformatory	valedictory
contradictory	mandatory	salutatory	

-ous (full of or having; adjective; primarily used with Latin roots)

adventurous	fabulous	monstrous	simultaneous
anonymous	famous	mountainous	slanderous
calamitous	felicitous	murderous	solicitous
calciferous	fibrous	nervous	spontaneous
cavernous	frivolous	odorous	stupendous
coniferous	generous	poisonous	synonymous
conspicuous	gluttonous	pompous	thunderous
credulous	hazardous	populous	tremendous
cruciferous	horrendous	ravenous	unanimous
dangerous	humorous	ridiculous	vigorous
deciduous	igneous	rigorous	villainous
desirous	jealous	ruinous	viscous
dextrous	joyous	scandalous	vociferous
enormous	meticulous	scrupulous	
extraneous	miraculous	serous	

Variants of -ous
-cious

atrocious	judicious	pernicious	specious
audacious	loquacious	precocious	suspicious
auspicious	luscious	pugnacious	tenacious
delicious	malicious	sagacious	vicious
ferocious	officious	salacious	vivacious

-ious

amphibious	dubious	hilarious	notorious
anxious	fastidious	laborious	obvious
curious	furious	litigious	precarious
delirious	glorious	melodious	previous
devious	gregarious	mysterious	rebellious

-tious

ambitious	facetious	nutritious	scrumptious
conscientious	fictitious	pretentious	superstitious
contentious	flirtatious	propitious	vexatious
expeditious	infectious	repetitious	

 In words ending in *-tious*, *t* is the final letter of the base element and *-ious* is the suffix, but this pattern often is taught as *-tious*.

-s (noun [plural])
   (pronounced /s/ with a base element ending in an unvoiced consonant)

buckets	giraffes	traps
cats	graphs	trucks

   (pronounced /z/ with a base element ending in a vowel or a voiced consonant)

cars	halls	mountains	rings
cogs	knaves	news	trees
films	monkeys	reeds	

Variant of -s
   -es (noun [plural]; used with base words ending in s, x, ch, sh, and z)

boxes	gases	lunches
bushes	hutches	waltzes

 Many hundreds of other words contain plural suffixes.

-ship (*office, state, dignity, skill, quality, or profession;* **noun**)

authorship	companionship	horsemanship	relationship
captainship	courtship	kinship	scholarship
censorship	dictatorship	leadership	seamanship
chairmanship	ensignship	lordship	sponsorship
championship	fellowship	membership	township
chaplainship	friendship	ownership	workmanship
citizenship	guardianship	partnership	
clerkship	hardship	readership	

-some (*characterized by a specified quality, condition, or action;* **Anglo-Saxon;**
adjective; primarily used with Anglo-Saxon base words)

adventuresome	foursome	loathsome	twosome
awesome	frolicsome	lonesome	venturesome
bothersome	fulsome	meddlesome	wholesome
burdensome	gladsome	threesome	winsome
cumbersome	handsome	tiresome	
fearsome	irksome	toothsome	
flavorsome	lissome	troublesome	

-ster (*one who is associated with, participates in, makes, or does;* **noun**)

gangster	jokester	roadster	youngster
hipster	mobster	songster	
huckster	prankster	Teamster	

-tude (*condition, state,* **or** *quality of;* **noun**)

altitude	finitude	latitude	quietude
amplitude	fortitude	longitude	rectitude
aptitude	gratitude	magnitude	servitude
certitude	habitude	multitude	solitude
decrepitude	ineptitude	platitude	vicissitude
desuetude	infinitude	plentitude	
exactitude	lassitude	promptitude	

-ty, -ity (*state* **or** *quality of;* **noun**)

absurdity	felicity	negativity	sagacity
acidity	ferocity	ninety	scarcity
anxiety	finality	novelty	severity
automaticity	frailty	oddity	simplicity
calamity	frugality	paucity	solidarity
capacity	heredity	personality	solidity
captivity	humidity	perspicacity	specificity
commodity	integrity	plurality	stupidity
cruelty	legality	profanity	tenacity
domesticity	liberty	propriety	totality
eccentricity	liquidity	publicity	validity
elasticity	locality	quality	veracity
electricity	mentality	quantity	vivacity
entirety	multiplicity	reality	whimsicality
facility	nationality	rigidity	

-ure (*state of, process, function,* or *office;* noun)

censure	erasure	measure	seizure
closure	failure	pleasure	tenure
configure	figure	pressure	
disfigure	leisure	procedure	
enclosure	manure	secure	

Variant of -ure
    -ture

adventure	furniture	moisture	stricture
architecture	future	nature	structure
armature	gesture	overture	temperature
capture	indenture	pasture	texture
creature	juncture	picture	tincture
culture	lecture	portraiture	torture
curvature	legislature	posture	venture
expenditure	literature	puncture	vestiture
feature	mature	rupture	vulture
fixture	miniature	signature	
fracture	mixture	stature	

In these words ending in *-ture, t* is the final letter of the base element and *-ure* is the suffix, but this pattern is often taught as *-ture.*

-ward (*expressing direction;* Anglo-Saxon; adjective)

awkward	heavenward	onward	upward
backward	homeward	outward	wayward
earthward	inward	rearward	westward
eastward	leeward	seaward	windward
forward	northward	southward	

-y (*inclined to;* adjective; primarily used with Anglo-Saxon base words)

blotchy	creaky	eighty	flirty
brainy	creepy	fishy	floppy
brawny	dreary	flabby	foggy
bushy	dumpy	flaky	funny
cloudy	earthy	flashy	gawky

greedy	lucky	shaky	soggy
groggy	mighty	shifty	splotchy
gushy	milky	shiny	spooky
hairy	muddy	showy	stocky
heady	muggy	skimpy	tacky
healthy	musky	skinny	touchy
itchy	rainy	sleepy	tricky
jerky	scraggy	slimy	weedy
jumpy	scrappy	smoky	whiny
lengthy	scruffy	snappy	windy
loony	seedy	sneaky	wordy

BIBLIOGRAPHY

The American heritage dictionary (2nd ed.). (1982). Boston: Houghton Mifflin.

The American heritage dictionary (4th ed.). (2000). Boston: Houghton Mifflin.

Random House unabridged dictionary (2nd ed.). (1993). New York: Random House.

Latin Roots

Words of Latin origin come to English from the Latin language spoken in ancient Rome and in Latium, a country in ancient Italy. The Latin roots in English words carry specific meanings. The root syllables usually receive the stress in the word and therefore contain either a short or a long vowel sound. Most Latin roots are bound morphemes. They are affixed; that is, one adds prefixes and/or suffixes to them. Most roots form the basis of hundreds of associated words with the addition of numerous prefixes and suffixes.

The roots in this appendix are given in alphabetical order, with rarer variants in parentheses. The meaning of each root family is also listed in parentheses. The teacher should introduce the most common word roots used in common words first. See Chapter 7 for a logical order of presentation. See Chapter 8 for a sequence of presentation of some less common Latin roots. The lists in this appendix are not complete but contain the most frequently found words containing the targeted roots.

When presenting a new root, the teacher can show the root on an index card and have students write the root on paper. The teacher can ask students to generate words containing the root on the board or on paper. The teacher can observe whether students pick up the meaning of the root from the words generated.

After presenting the roots, the teacher should have word lists ready for students to read. In addition, words can be dictated for spelling. The class can discuss the meanings of the words as these meanings relate to specific roots. See Chapters 7 and 8 for additional activities involving Latin roots.

anni, annu, enni (year)

annals	bicentennial	interannual	sesquicentennial
anniversary	biennial	millennial	superannuate
annual	biennium	millennium	tercentenary
annualize	centenary	plurannual	tercentennial
annuitant	centennial	quadrennial	triennial
annuity	decennial	quadrennium	
biannual	decennium	quinquennial	
bicentenary	exannual	semiannual	

aud (to hear or listen)

audibility	audiogram	audiovisual	auditory
audible	audiologist	audiphone	audivision
audience	audiology	audit	inaudible
audio	audiometer	audition	subaudible
audioanalgesia	audiophiliac	auditor	
audiofrequency	audiospectogram	auditorium	

cad, cas, cid (to fall or befall)

accident	casual	decadent	occident
accidental	casualty	decay	Occident
cadaver	coincide	deciduous	occidental
cadaverous	coincidence	incidence	recidivism
cadence	coincident	incident	recidivist
cadenza	coincidental	incidental	
cascade	decadence	occasion	

cap, ceit, ceive, cep, cept, cip (to take, catch, seize, hold, or receive)

accept	capsule	conceptual	exception
acceptable	caption	deceit	exceptional
acceptance	captious	deceitful	forceps
anticipate	captivate	deceitfulness	incapable
anticipation	captive	deceive	inconceivable
anticipatory	captivity	deception	intercept
capability	captor	emancipate	interception
capable	capture	emancipation	interceptor
capacious	conceit	emancipator	municipal
capacitor	conceive	encapsulate	municipality
capacity	concept	encapsulation	participant
capstan	conception	except	participate

participation
perceive
percept
perceptible
perception

perceptive
principal
principle
receipt
receivable

receive
receptacle
reception
recipe
recipient

susceptibility
susceptible
unacceptable

capit, capt (chie, cip) (head or chief)

achieve
achievement
achiever
capital
capitalism
capitalist
capitalize
capitate
capitation
Capitol
capitular
capitulate
capitulation

caprice
capricious
captain
captaincy
chapter
chief
chieftain
decapitate
decapitation
handkerchief
kerchief
mischief
mischievous

occiput
overachiever
per capita
precipice
precipitate
precipitation
precipitous
recapitulate
recapitulation
underachiever
undercapitalization

cause, cuse, cus (to cause; motive)

accusation
accusative
accuse
accuser

because
causal
causality
causation

cause
causeless
excusable
excuse

inexcusable

cede, ceed, cess (to go, yield, or surrender)

abscess
accede
access
accessible
accession
accessory
ancestor
antecedent
cease
cessation
concede
concession

decease
decedent
exceed
excess
excessive
inaccessible
incessant
intercede
intercession
necessary
precede
precedent

precess
precession
predecessor
procedure
proceed
process
procession
recede
recess
recession
recessive
retrocede

secede
secession
secessionist
success
successful
succession
successive
supersede
unprecedented

cern (to separate), cert (to decide)

ascertain	certificate	concern
certain	certification	discern
certainty	certify	discernment

cise (to cut)

circumcise	decision	incision	precise
circumcision	decisive	incisive	precision
concise	excise	incisor	scissors
concision	excision	indecision	
decide	incise	indecisive	

 The root *cise* and the suffix *-cide,* meaning *to kill,* come from the same Latin root, *caedere.*

claim, clam (to declare, call out, or cry out)

acclaim	clamor	disclaim	misclaim
acclamation	clamorous	disclaimer	proclaim
claim	conclamant	exclaim	proclamation
claimant	counterclaim	exclamation	proclamatory
clamant	declaim	exclamatory	reclaim
clamatorial	declamation	irreclaimable	reclaimable

claus, clois, clos, clud, clus (to shut or close)

clause	conclusion	foreclose	occlusion
claustrophobia	conclusive	foreclosure	occlusive
claustrophobic	disclose	include	preclude
cloisonné	disclosure	inclusion	preclusion
cloister	enclose	inclusive	recluse
cloistral	enclosure	inclusiveness	reclusive
close	exclude	malocclusion	seclude
closet	exclusion	occlude	seclusion
conclude	exclusive	occlusal	

cred (to believe)

accredit	credible	credulity	incredible
accreditation	credit	credulous	incredulity
credence	creditable	creed	incredulous
credential	creditor	discredit	
credibility	credo	discreditable	

cur, curs (cours) (to run or go)

concourse	current	discursive	recourse
concur	curricular	excursion	recur
concurrent	curriculum	incur	recurrence
corridor	cursive	incursion	recurrent
courier	cursor	occur	succor
course	cursory	occurrence	
currency	discourse	precursor	

dent (tooth)

dental	dentilation	dentition	indent
dentation	dentin	dentofacial	indentation
denticulate	dentine	dentoid	indenture
dentiform	dentiphone	dentolingual	interdental
dentifrice	dentist	dentulous	labiodental
dentigerous	dentistry	denture	trident

dic, dict (to say or tell)

abdicant	dedicate	edict	predicament
abdicate	dedication	indicate	predicate
abdication	Dictaphone	indication	predication
addict	dictate	indicative	predict
addiction	dictation	indicator	prediction
addictive	dictator	indict	valedictorian
benediction	dictatorial	indictable	verdict
benedictory	dictatorship	indictment	vindicate
contradict	diction	interdict	vindication
contradiction	dictionary	interdiction	vindictive
contradictory	dictum	malediction	

duc, duce, duct (to lead)

abduce	deduct	induce	reducible
abduct	deductible	inductance	reduction
abduction	deduction	inductee	reproduce
abductor	deductive	induction	reproduction
adduction	ducal	inductive	seduce
adductor	duchess	introduce	seduction
aqueduct	duchy	introduction	traduce
conducive	duct	postproduction	transduce
conduct	ductile	producer	transduction
conductor	ductility	product	viaduct
conduit	educate	production	
deduce	education	reduce	

fac, fact, fect, fic (to make or do)

affair	defection	electrification	gratification
affect	defective	facile	identification
affection	defector	facilitate	imperfect
affectionate	deficient	facilitation	imperfection
artifact	deficit	facility	ineffective
artifice	deification	facsimile	infect
artificer	difficult	fact	infection
artificial	difficulty	faction	infectious
beautification	disaffected	factious	insignificant
benefactor	disinfect	factitious	intensification
beneficence	disinfectant	factor	justification
beneficent	disinfection	factory	magnification
beneficial	dissatisfaction	factotum	magnificent
beneficiary	diversification	facultative	maleficence
certificate	edification	faculty	maleficent
certification	edifice	falsification	manufacture
classification	effect	fiction	manufacturer
coefficient	effective	fictional	modification
confection	effectual	fictionalize	notification
confectionary	efficacious	fictitious	office
confectioner	efficacy	fortification	officer
confectionery	efficiency	gentrification	official
defect	efficient	glorification	officiant

officiate	profit	rubefacient	specification
officious	profiteer	sacrifice	stupefaction
pacification	purification	satisfaction	suffice
perfect	putrefaction	satisfactory	sufficient
personification	qualification	significant	unification
proficiency	quantification	signification	unsatisfactory
proficient	rarefaction	simplification	

 The Latin suffixes -*fy* and -*ify* are related to the roots *fac, fact, fect,* and *fic.*

feal, feder, fid, fide (*trust* or *faith*)

affiance	confidence	federacy	fiduciary
affidavit	confident	federal	infidel
bona fide	confidential	federalism	infidelity
confederacy	confidentiality	federalist	perfidious
confederate	diffidence	federation	perfidy
confidant	diffident	fidelity	Semper Fidelis
confide	fealty	fiducial	

fer (*to bear or yield*)

afferent	difference	insufferable	referendum
aquifer	different	interfere	referent
circumference	differential	interference	referential
confer	efferent	odoriferous	referral
conferee	ferriferous	offer	suffer
conference	ferry	prefer	sufferance
conifer	fertile	preferable	teleconference
coniferous	fertilization	preference	transfer
crucifer	fertilize	preferential	transferable
defer	fertilizer	proffer	transference
deference	floriferous	refer	transferrin
deferential	infer	referee	vociferant
differ	inference	reference	vociferous

fin, finis (*end*)

ad infinitum	finale	finish	paraffin
affinity	finalist	finisher	refine
confine	finalize	finite	refinement
confinement	finance	finitude	refinery
define	financial	indefinite	undefinable
definite	financier	infinite	
definitive	finial	infinitesimal	
final	finis	infinity	

fix (*to fix*)

affix	fixate	fixity	suffix
affixation	fixation	fixture	transfix
affixture	fixative	infix	transfixion
fix	fixator	prefix	

flect, flex (*to bend or curve*)

anteflexion	flexible	inflect	reflector
circumflex	flexile	inflection	reflectoscope
circumflexion	flexion	inflexible	reflex
deflect	flexor	nonreflective	reflexive
deflection	flexuous	reflect	retroflex
flex	genuflect	reflection	
flexibility	genuflection	reflective	

flu, fluc, fluv, flux (*flow*)

affluence	fluctuant	fluidimeter	influence
affluent	fluctuate	fluidity	influx
afflux	fluctuation	fluidize	mellifluous
circumfluent	flue	flume	reflux
confluence	fluency	flush	superfluity
confluent	fluent	fluvial	superfluous
effluence	fluid	fluviograph	
effluent	fluidic	fluviology	

form (to shape)

conform	format	informant	performer
conformist	formation	information	reform
conformity	formless	informative	reformation
deform	formlessness	informer	reformer
deformity	formula	misinform	transform
disinformation	formulaic	misinformation	transformation
form	formulary	nonconformist	transformer
formal	formulate	nonconformity	uniform
formality	inform	perform	uniformity
formalize	informal	performance	

gen, genus (race, kind, or species; birth)

agenesis	genealogy	genocide	monogenesis
congenial	generable	genre	nitrogen
congeniality	general	gentile	photogenic
congenital	generate	gentility	primogeniture
degenerate	generation	genuine	progenitor
degeneration	generative	genus	progeny
degenerative	generator	heterogeneous	regenerate
disingenuous	generic	homogeneous	regeneration
eugenics	generosity	homogenize	telegenic
gendarme	generous	hydrogen	transgenic
gender	genesis	indigenous	
gene	genetics	ingenuous	

grad, gred, gress (step, degree; to walk)

aggradation	degree	gradual	regress
aggression	digress	graduate	regression
aggressive	digression	graduation	retrograde
aggressor	downgrade	gressorial	retrogress
biodegradable	egress	ingredient	transgress
centigrade	gradate	ingress	transgression
congress	gradation	postgraduate	upgrade
congressional	grade	progress	
degradation	gradient	progression	
degrade	gradiometer	progressive	

grat, gre (*thanks; pleasing*)

agree	disagreeable	gratification	gratulant
agreeable	disagreement	gratify	gratulatory
agreement	disgrace	gratis	ingrate
congratulate	disgraceful	gratitude	ingratiate
congratulation	grace	gratuitant	ingratitude
congratulatory	graceless	gratuitous	
disagree	grateful	gratuity	

greg (*crowd, group, flock,* **or** *herd; to assemble*)

aggregate	congregation	desegregation	segregate
aggregation	congregational	egregious	segregation
congregate	desegregate	gregarious	segregationist

jac, jec, ject (*to throw or lie*)

abject	eject	object	projective
abjectness	ejection	objection	projector
adjacent	inject	objective	reject
adjectival	injection	objectivity	rejection
adjective	interject	project	subject
conjecture	interjection	projectile	subjective
deject	introject	projection	subjectivity
dejection	introjection	projectionist	trajectory

jud, judi, judic (*judge*)

adjudge	judge	judicature	prejudge
adjudicate	judgment	judicial	prejudice
adjudicative	judicator	judiciary	prejudicial
injudicious	judicatory	judicious	unprejudicial

jur, jus (*law or right*)

abjuration	conjure	juror	justification
abjure	conjurer	jury	justify
adjure	jurisdiction	juryman	readjust
adjust	jurisprudence	just	readjustment
adjustive	jurist	justice	
adjustment	juristic	justifiable	

lect, leg, lig (to choose, pick, read, or speak)

acrolect	electable	intelligible	neglectful
basilect	elector	lectern	negligent
collect	electorate	lecture	prelect
collection	elegant	legend	sacrilege
collective	idiolect	legendary	sacrilegious
delegate	illegibility	legibility	select
delegation	illegible	legible	selection
dialect	intellect	legion	selective
diligence	intellectual	Legionnaire's	
diligent	intelligence	mesolect	
elect	intelligent	neglect	

The roots *lect, leg,* and *lig* are related to the Greek combining form *logos,* meaning *speech* or *word.*

leg (law)

illegal	legal	legalize	legislature
illegality	legalese	legislate	legitimate
illegitimate	legalism	legislative	privilege
legacy	legalistic	legislator	
		legislative	

lit, liter, litera (letters)

alliterate	illiterate	literalism	obliterate
alliteration	litany	literary	obliteration
alliterative	literacy	literate	transliterate
illiteracy	literal	literatim	transliteration

loc, loqu (to speak, talk, or say)

ambiloquent	elocution	loquacious	soliloquist
circumlocute	eloquence	loquacity	soliloquy
circumlocution	eloquent	magniloquence	somniloquent
colloquial	grandiloquence	magniloquent	somniloquy
colloquialism	grandiloquent	obloquious	uneloquent
colloquy	interlocution	obloquy	ventriloquist
elocute	interlocutor	omniloquent	ventriloquy

magna, magni (great)

magnanimity	magnification	magnifico	magniloquent
magnanimous	magnificence	magnify	magnitude
magnascope	magnificent	magniloquence	magnum
magnate			

matr, matri (mother)

alma mater	matricide	matrilineal	matrix
maternal	matriculant	matrimonial	matron
maternity	matriculate	matrimony	matronymic
matriarch			

mit, miss (to send)

admission	emission	omit	remittance
admit	emit	permissible	subcommittee
commission	inadmissible	permission	submission
commit	intermission	permissive	submit
committee	intermittent	permit	transmission
compromise	intromission	premise	transmit
dismiss	mission	promise	transmitter
dismissal	missionary	remiss	
emissary	omission	remit	

mob, mot, mov (to move)

automobile	immovable	motivation	move
commotion	locomotion	motivational	movement
countermove	mob	motive	movie
demobilization	mobile	motor	promote
demote	mobility	motorbike	promoter
demotion	mobilization	motorboat	promotion
emote	mobilize	motorcade	remote
emotion	mobster	motorcycle	removal
emotional	motion	motordrome	remove
immobile	motionless	motorist	
immobilization	motivate	movable	

patr, pater (father)

compatriot	paternity	patriot	patroon
depatriate	patriarch	patriotic	patrophile
expatriate	patriarchy	patriotism	philopatric
expatriation	patrician	patron	repatriate
paterfamilias	patricide	patronage	repatriation
paternal	patrilineal	patronize	unpatriotic
paternalism	patrimony	patronymic	

ped (foot)

aliped	expeditious	pedal	pedomotive
biped	expeditiousness	pedestal	peduncle
carpopedal	impede	pedestrian	pinniped
centipede	impediment	pedicure	quadruped
depeditate	millipede	pediment	uniped
expedite	multiped	pedogram	velocipede
expedition	octoped	pedometer	

The Latin root *ped* is different from the Greek combining forms *ped* (meaning *child*) and *ped* (meaning *soil*).

pel, puls (to drive or push)

compel	expulsion	propeller	repellent
compulsion	impel	propulsion	repulse
compulsive	impulse	pulsate	repulsion
compulsory	impulsive	pulsation	repulsive
dispel	propel	pulse	
expel	propellant	repel	

pend, pens (to hang or weigh)

appendage	dispensary	independent	pension
appendectomy	dispensation	interdependence	pensive
appendix	dispense	interdependent	penthouse
compensate	dispenser	pendant	perpendicular
depend	expend	pending	suspend
dependability	expense	pendulate	suspenders
dependable	expensive	pendule	suspense
dependence	impending	pendulous	suspenseful
dependent	independence	pendulum	suspension
dispensable			

plic, ply (*to fold*)

accomplice	complication	explicitly	multiplication
applicability	complicity	explicitness	multiplicity
applicable	duplicate	implicate	multiply
applicant	duplication	implicit	plywood
application	duplicitous	imply	replica
applicator	duplicity	inapplicable	replicate
apply	explicable	inexplicable	simplicity
complicate	explicit	misapplication	uncomplicated

pos, pon, pound (*to put, place, or set*)

component	disposition	opposite	prepositional
compose	exponent	opposition	proponent
composer	exponential	ponder	proposal
composite	expose	ponderous	propose
composition	exposition	pose	proposition
compositor	exposure	posit	propound
composure	expound	position	purpose
compound	impose	positive	purposeful
counter-proposal	imposition	positor	purposeless
	impostor	post	superimpose
depose	impound	poster	suppose
deposit	interpose	postpone	supposition
deposition	interposition	postural	transpose
disposal	opponent	posture	transposition
dispose	oppose	preposition	

port (*to carry*)

airport	exporter	portage	reportage
apportable	import	portal	reporter
carport	important	portamento	support
comportment	importer	porter	supportive
deport	insupportable	portfolio	teleportation
deportation	opportune	porthole	transport
deportee	opportunity	portmanteau	transportable
deportment	passport	purport	transportation
export	port	rapport	transporter
exportation	portable	report	unimportant

put (*to think*)

computable	deputize	disputatious	reputable
computation	deputy	dispute	reputation
compute	disputable	imputation	repute
computer	disputants	impute	
depute	disputation	putative	

rect, recti (*straight* or *right*)

correct	erect	rectangular	regimental
correctable	erector	rectifiable	region
correction	incorrect	rectify	regional
corrective	indirect	rectilinear	regionalism
corrigible	indirectness	rectitude	regular
direct	irregular	rector	regularity
direction	irregularity	rectory	regulate
directive	reckon	redirect	regulation
directness	reckoning	regal	
director	rectangle	regiment	

rupt (*to break or burst*)

abrupt	corruptible	eruption	irrupt
abruption	disrupt	incorrupt	irruption
bankrupt	disruption	incorruptible	rupture
bankruptcy	disruptive	interrupt	
corrupt	erupt	interruption	

scrib, script (*to write*)

ascribe	inscription	scribable	subscriber
ascription	interscribe	scribacious	subscription
circumscribe	manuscript	scribble	superscription
conscript	nondescript	scribblemania	transcribe
conscription	postscript	scribe	transcriber
describe	prescribe	scribophobia	transcript
description	prescription	script	transcription
descriptive	proscribe	Scripture	
indescribable	proscription	scrivener	
inscribe	rescript	subscribe	

Verbs usually use *scribe,* as in *prescribe;* nouns usually use *script,* as in *prescription.*

sec, sect (*to cut*)

dissect	intersection	sectile	segment
dissection	resect	section	segmental
insect	resection	sectional	transect
intersect	secant	sector	

spec, spect, spic (*to see, watch, or observe*)

aspect	prospect	spectrogram
auspicious	prospector	spectroheliograph
circumspect	respect	spectrohelioscope
conspicuous	respectful	spectrology
despicable	respective	spectrometry
despise	retrospective	spectrophobia
disrespect	special	spectrophone
disrespectful	specialist	spectroscope
expect	species	spectrum
expectation	specify	speculate
inconspicuous	specimen	speculation
inspect	specious	speculator
inspection	spectacle	speculum
inspector	spectacular	suspect
introspection	spectator	suspicion
introspective	specter	suspicious
perspective	spectral	

spir, spire (*to breathe*)

aspiration	disspirited	perspiration	spirit
aspire	expiration	perspire	spiritual
co-conspirator	expire	respiration	spiritualism
conspiracy	inspiration	respirator	transpire
conspire	inspire	respire	uninspiring

sta, sist, stat, stit (*to stand*)

assist	ecstasy	persistence	stationary
assistant	ecstatic	persistent	stationer
assistive	establish	reconstitute	stationery
circumstance	establishment	reconstitution	statistic
circumstantial	estate	resist	status
consist	insist	resistant	subsist
consistency	insistence	restitution	subsistence
consistent	insistent	stamina	subsistent
constancy	instance	stance	substance
constant	instant	stanch	substandard
constitute	instantaneous	stanchion	substantial
constitution	instantiate	stand	substantiate
constitutional	insubstantiate	standard	substantive
desist	interstice	standardization	substitute
destitute	irresistible	standardize	superstition
destitution	obstacle	stanza	superstitious
distance	obstinate	static	transistor
distant	persist	station	

stru, struct (*stry*) (*to build*)

construct	industrious	instrument	reconstruction-
constructive	industry	instrumental	ist
construe	infrastructure	instrumentalist	restructure
destruction	instruct	obstruct	structural
destructive	instruction	obstruction	structure
indestructible	instructive	obstructionist	superstructure
industrial	instructor	reconstruction	

tact, tag, tang, tig, ting (*to touch*)

contact	intact	tactfulness	tangential
contagion	intangibility	tactile	tangibility
contiguous	intangible	tactless	tangible
contingency	tact	tactlessness	
contingent	tactful	tangent	

ten, tain, tin, tinu (to hold)

abstain	continuous	lieutenant	sustain
abstainer	detain	maintain	sustainer
abstinence	detainee	maintainer	sustenance
attain	detainment	maintenance	sustentation
attainment	detention	obtain	tenable
contain	discontent	obtainable	tenacious
container	discontented-	pertain	tenacity
containment	ness	pertinence	tenant
content	discontinuation	pertinent	tenement
contentment	discontinue	retain	tenet
continual	entertain	retainer	tenure
continuation	entertainer	retention	unattainable
continue	entertainment	retentive	untenable

tend, tens, tent (to stretch or strain)

antenna	extend	intensity	pretension
attempt	extension	intensive	pretentious
attend	extensive	intent	pretentiousness
attendance	extensor	intention	superintendent
attention	hyperextend	intentional	tendinitis
attentive	hyperextension	ostensible	tendon
attentiveness	hypertension	ostentation	tenotomy
contend	hypotension	ostentatious	tense
contender	inattention	ostentatious-	tension
contention	inattentive	ness	tent
contentious	inattentiveness	portend	tenuous
contentiousness	intend	portentous	unintentional
distend	intense	pretend	
distention	intensify	pretense	

tract (to draw or pull)

abstract	contract	detractor	extraction
abstraction	contractor	distract	intractable
attract	contractual	distractible	protract
attraction	detract	distraction	protractor
attractive	detraction	extract	retract

retraction	tract	tractile	tractor
subtract	tractable	traction	
subtraction	tractibility	tractive	

ven, veni, vent (to come)

advent	avenue	eventuality	preventable
adventitious	circumvent	inconvenience	prevention
adventitious-ness	contravene	inconvenient	preventive
	convene	intervene	revenue
adventure	convenient	intervention	souvenir
adventurer	convent	invent	unconventional
adventuresome	convention	invention	uneventful
adventuress	covenant	inventor	unpreventable
adventurous	event	inventory	venture
adventurous-ness	eventful	misadventure	venturesome
	eventual	prevent	

ver, veri (true or genuine)

veracious	verify	veritable
veracity	verisimilitude	verity
verdict	verism	very

vers, vert (to turn)

adversarial	conversant	inverse	varsity
adversary	conversation	inversion	versatile
adverse	converse	invert	versatility
advertise	convert	obverse	verse
advertisement	convertible	reverse	version
advertiser	diverse	reversible	versus
averse	diversification	reversion	vertebra
aversion	diversify	revert	vertebrate
aversive	diversion	subversion	vertex
avert	divert	subversive	vertical
controversial	extroversion	subvert	vertiginous
controversy	extrovert	universal	vertigo
converge	introversion	universe	vortex
convergent	introvert	university	

vid, vis (*to see*)

advise	individual	supervision	visionary
adviser	indivisible	supervisor	visit
advisor	invisible	supervisory	visitation
divide	nonvisual	televise	visitor
division	provide	television	visor
divisor	providence	video	vista
envision	provider	visa	visual
evidence	provision	visage	visualization
evident	revise	visibility	visualize
improvisation	revision	visible	
improvise	supervise	vision	

The Middle English term *vewe*, which became *view*, came from Latin *videre*, meaning *to see*.

interview	review	viewfinder
preview	view	

vit, vita, viv, vivi (to live)

antivivisectionist	survive	vivace	vividness
revitalize	vital	vivacious	viviparous
revival	vitality	vivacity	vivisection
revive	vitamin	vivarium	
survival	vitaminology	vivid	

voc, vok, voke (*to call*)

advocacy	evocative	provoke	vocalic
advocate	evoke	revocable	vocalization
avocation	invocation	revocation	vocalize
convocation	invoke	revoke	vocation
equivocal	irrevocable	vocabulary	vocational
equivocate	provocation	vocabulist	vociferant
equivocation	provocative	vocal	vociferous

BIBLIOGRAPHY

The American heritage dictionary (2nd ed.). (1982). Boston: Houghton Mifflin.

The American heritage dictionary (4th ed.). (2000). Boston: Houghton Mifflin.

Random House unabridged dictionary (2nd ed.). (1993). New York: Random House.

Greek Combining Forms

The word parts in this appendix come to us from the Greek language and usually appear in specialized words used in science and mathematics. Greek word parts are usually compounded—that is, two word parts are combined, as in *photograph* and *psychology*—and are thus called *combining forms* in many dictionaries. Suffixes are often added, as in *photographic* and *psychologist*. Some specific letter–sound correspondences are typically found in Greek words. Most common are *ph* as in *phonograph; ch* as in chemistry; and /ĭ/ or /ī/ as in *synonym* and *hydrogen*, respectively. Less common orthographic patterns include *ps* as in *psychiatry, mn* as in *mnemonics, pn* as in *pneumonia, rh* as in *rhinoceros*, and *pt* as in *pterodactyl*.

Students may not know the meanings of many of these words and are encouraged to predict the meanings based on the combining forms and to follow up by looking in a dictionary. Although the following combining forms are listed in alphabetical order, teach the most common first. See Chapter 7 for a logical sequence of presentation. See Chapter 8 for a sequence of presentation of some less common Greek combining forms. These lists are not complete but include the most frequently found words containing the targeted combining forms.

andr, anthr (*man*)

andragogy	andromorphic	anthroponym
andranatomy	androphobia	philander
androcentric	anthropoid	philanderer
androcracy	anthropologist	philanthropic
androgynous	anthropology	philanthropist
android	anthropomorphic	philanthropy
andrology	anthropomorphism	polyandry

arch (*chief* or *ruler*)

anarchy	archimorphic	autarchy	monarchy
archangel	architect	biarch	myriarch
archbishop	architectonic	ecclesiarch	oligarchy
archconservative	architectural	endarchy	panarchy
archdeacon	architecture	hierarchy	patriarch
archduke	archthief	matriarch	patriarchy
archenemy	archvillain	matriarchy	pentarchy
archetype	autarch	monarch	polyarchy

archae, arche, archi (*primitive* or *ancient*)

archaeoastronomer	Archaeozoic	archetype
archaeological	archaic	archilithic
archaeologist	archaism	archimorphic
archaeology	archecentric	archives
archaeopteryx	archegenesis	archivist

ast, astro (*star*)

archaeoastronomer	astrological	astrophobia
asterisk	astrologue	astrophotograph
asteroid	astrology	astrophysics
asterozoa	astrometeorologist	Astros
astrobiology	astrometeorology	astrosphere
astrobotanist	astrometry	astrotheology
astrochemistry	astronaut	bioastronautics
astrograph	astronomer	disaster
astrokinetic	astronomical	disastrous
astrolabe	astronomy	radioastronomy
astrologer	Astrophil	

auto (*self;* usually used as a prefix)

autarchy	autocracy	Automat	autophobia
autism	autocrat	automatic	autopsy
autoantibody	autocratic	automation	autoscope
autobiographi-cal	autodermic	automaton	autosuggestion
	autogenesis	automobile	autotelic
autobiography	autograph	automotive	autotherapy
autochthon	autohypnosis	autonomous	semiautomatic
autocide	autoimmune	autonomy	
autoclave	autoinfection	autonym	

biblio (*book*)

bible	bibliography	bibliophobia
biblical	biblioklept	bibliopole
biblioclast	bibliolatry	bibliosoph
bibliofilm	bibliology	bibliotheca
bibliogenesis	bibliomania	bibliotherapy
bibliographer	bibliophile	bibliotics
bibliographic	bibliophobe	photobibliography

bio (*life*)

abiosis	bioecology	biomaterial
aerobiology	bioengineering	biome
amphibious	bioethics	biomechanics
antibiotics	biofeedback	biomedicine
astrobiology	biogeographic	biometeorology
autobiographical	biogeographical	biometer
autobiography	biogeography	biometrics
bioactive	biogeosphere	biomicroscope
bioastronautics	biographer	biomotor
biochemistry	biographic	bionavigation
biocompatible	biographical	bionic
biocracy	biography	biopesticide
biocrat	biological	biophile
biodegradable	biologist	biophysics
biodiversity	biology	biopsy
biodynamic	biomagnetism	bioregion
bioecologist	biomarker	bioscope

biosphere
biotechnics
biotechnology
bioterrorism
chronobiology

ecobiology
hydrobiology
macrobiotic
microbiology
parabiosis

photobiotic
phyllobiology
psychobiography
symbiosis
zoobiotic

chrom (*color*)

achromachia
achromatic
achromoderma
chromatic
chromatid
chromatin
chromatogram
chromatology
chromatolysis
chrome
chromium

chromogenesis
chromogenic
chromophobic
chromoscope
chromosomal
chromosome
chromospheres
ferrochrome
heliochrome
heliochromoscope
hemochrome

hyperchromatic
hyperchromia
hypochromic
monochromatic
monochrome
orthochromatic
parachromatism
photochrome
polychromatic
polychrome

chron, chrono (*time*)

achroniasm
anachronistic
chronal
chronic
chronicle
chronicler
chronobarometer
chronobiology
chronognosis
chronogram
chronograph
chronographic

chronologer
chronological
chronologist
chronologize
chronology
chronometer
chronometric
chronometry
chronophobia
chronophotograph
chronoscope
chronotherapy

chronothermal
desynchronize
diachronic
diachronous
geochronic
geosynchronous
monochronic
parachronism
psychochronometry
synchronicity
synchronize
synchronous

cracy, crat (*rule, strength,* **or** *power;* **often used as a suffix**)

androcracy
aristocracy
aristocrat
aristocratic
autocracy
autocrat

autocratic
biocrat
bureaucracy
bureaucrat
bureaucratic
democracy

democrat
democratic
mediocracy
mobocracy
pancratic
plutocracy

plutocrat
plutocratic
technocracy
technocrat
technocratic
theocrat

cycl, cyclo (*wheel* or *circle; circular*)

bicycle	cyclomania	cyclorama	monocycle
bicyclist	cyclometer	cyclosporine	motorcycle
cyclamen	cyclometry	cyclotron	pericycle
cycle	cyclone	encyclopedia	recycle
cyclic	cyclonology	encyclopedic	tricycle
cyclical	cyclopedia	epicycle	unicycle
cycling	cyclopedist	geocyclic	
cyclist	cyclophobia	kilocycle	
cyclograph	Cyclops	megacycle	

dem, demo (*people*)

antidemocratic	democratism	demophile	endemic
demagogue	demographer	demophobe	pandemic
democracy	demographics	demophobia	philodemic
democrat	demographist	demotic	polydemic
democratic	demography	demotics	

derm (*skin*)

achromoderma	dermato-glyphics	dermatosis	hypodermis
adermia		dermatotherapy	intradermal
autodermic	dermatoid	dermis	megaderm
blastoderm	dermatologist	ectoderm	pachyderm
dermabrasion	dermatology	epidermis	pneumoderma
dermal	dermatome	hyperdermic	taxidermist
dermatitis	dermatoplasty	hypodermic	taxidermy

drome, dromos (*course* or *running*)

acrodrome	dromomania	dromotropic	palindrome
aerodrome	dromometer	hippodrome	paradromic
airdrome	dromophobia	hydrodrome	prodrome
dromedary	dromos	motordrome	syndrome
dromograph			

dyn, dynamo (*power, strength*, or *force*)

aerodynamics	dynamic	dynamoelectric	dynamoscope
biodynamic	dynamism	dynamogenesis	dynamotor
dynagraph	dynamite	dynamometer	dynastic
dynameter	dynamo	dynamometry	dynasty

dynatron   geodynamics   megadynamics   thermo-
dyne   hemodynamics   monodynamic   dynamics
dynode   hydrodynamic   photodynamic   toxicodynamic
electrodynamic

eco (*house* or *home*)

bioecologist   ecology   economy   ecotone
bioecology   ecomanage-   ecophobia   ecotourism
ecoactivist   ment   ecophysics   ecotype
ecobiology   ecomania   ecophysiology   macro-
ecogeographic   econometrics   ecospecies   economics
ecogeography   economical   ecosphere   microecology
ecological   economics   ecosystem   microeconomics
ecologist   economist   ecoterrorism

ecto (*outside, external,* or *beyond*)

appendectomy   ectoderm   ectomorphic   ectoplasm
ectoblast   ectogenous   ectoparasite   ectosuggestion
ectocardia   ectoglobular   ectopia   ectoterm
ectocommensal   ectomorph   ectopic   ectothermic

ectomy (*cut out;* often used as a suffix)

appendectomy   cystectomy   mastectomy   pneumectomy
bursectomy   hysterectomy   pneumatec-   splenectomy
cardiectomy   lumpectomy   tomy   tonsillectomy

geo (*earth*)

biogeographical   geodesic   geologist   geophysics
biogeography   geodynamics   geology   geopolitical
biogeosphere   geoglyphic   geometric   geopolitics
ecogeographic   geognosy   geometry   geosphere
ecogeography   geographer   geomorphic   geosynchro-
geocentric   geographic   geophagia   nous
geochemistry   geography   geophilous   geotechnics
geochronic   geohydrology   geophone   geothermal
geocyclic   geological   geophysical

gno, gnosi (to know)

agnosia	diagnosis	ignorant	prognosticator
agnostic	diagnostician	prognosis	telegnosis
agnostician	geognosy	prognosticable	
chronognosis	ignorance	prognosticate	

gon (angle)

diagonal	hexagonal	octagonal	polygon
goniometer	isogon	orthogonal	tetragon
heptagon	nonagon	pentagon	tetragonal
heptagonal	nonagonal	pentagonal	trigonometric
hexagon	octagon	perigon	trigonometry

gram, graph (written or drawn)

anagram	chronographic	grapheme
astrograph	chronophotograph	graphic
astrophotograph	cinematographer	graphite
autobiographical	cinematographic	graphology
autobiography	cinematography	graphomania
autograph	cyclograph	graphometer
bibliographer	demographer	graphomotor
bibliographic	demographics	graphophonemic
bibliography	demographist	heliograph
biogeographic	demography	hologram
biogeographical	dromograph	holograph
biogeography	dynagraph	holographic
biographer	dysgraphia	homograph
biographic	ecogeographic	homographic
biographical	ecogeography	hydrograph
biography	electrocardiogram	hydrographer
calligrapher	electroencephalogram	ideogram
calligraphic	epigram	isogram
calligraphy	epigraph	kinematograph
choreographer	ethnography	lexicographer
choreographic	geographer	lexicography
choreography	geographic	lexigraphy
chronogram	geography	limnograph
chronograph	graph	lithograph

lithographer
lithographic
lithography
lithostratigraphy
logogram
logograph
logographer
logographic
macrograph
macrophotography
megagram
microlithography
mimeograph
mimeographic
monogram
monograph
morphography
myelogram
oceanographer
oceanographic
oceanography
orthographic
orthography
pangram

pantograph
paragraph
parallelogram
pathography
petrograph
petrographic
phonocardiograph
phonogram
phonograph
photobibliography
photogram
photogrammetry
photograph
photographer
photographic
photography
photoheliograph
physiograph
physiographic
pictogram
pictograph
pneumatogram
pneumograph
polygraph

polygraphy
psychobiography
psychograph
radiograph
radiographic
seismograph
sonogram
spectrogram
spectroheliograph
stenographer
stenographic
stenography
stereogram
stereographic
stereography
tangram
telegram
telegraph
telegraphic
telephotography
thermograph
zoography

helio (*sun*)

aphelion
heliocentric
heliochrome
heliochromoscope
heliofugal
heliogram
heliograph
heliomania
heliometer

heliophilous
heliophobia
heliophobic
heliophyte
Heliopolis
helioscope
heliosphere
heliostat
heliotherapy

heliotherm
heliothermometer
heliotrope
helium
perihelion
photoheliograph
spectroheliograph
spectrohelioscope

hema, hemo (*blood*)

hematic	hemodynamics	hemorrhoids
hematite	hemogastric	hemospasia
hematologist	hemoglobin	hemostat
hematology	hemolysis	hemotose
hematoma	hemophilia	hemotoxic
hemochrome	hemophobia	hemotropic
hemocyte	hemorrhage	pseudohemophilia

hemi, demi, semi (*half;* **usually used as a prefix**)

demigod	hemihedron	semicircle	semiliterate
demigoddess	hemiplegia	semicircular	semimonthly
demimillionaire	hemisphere	semicivilized	semiprecious
demirelief	hemispherical	semiclassical	semipublic
demisuit	semiannual	semicolon	semirigid
demitasse	semiarid	semicoma	semiskilled
demitone	semiattached	semiconscious	semitrailer
hemialgia	semiautomatic	semifinal	
hemihedral	semicentennial	semifinalist	

hydr, hydra, hydro (*water*)

anhydride	hydraulic	hydroelectric	hydrophobia
anhydrous	hydrobiology	hydrofoil	hydrophone
dehydrate	hydrocarbon	hydrogen	hydroplane
dehydration	hydrocast	hydrogenated	hydroponic
geohydrology	hydrocephalus	hydrograph	hydroscope
hydrangea	hydrochloride	hydrographer	hydrosphere
hydrant	hydrodrome	hydrologist	hydrostat
hydrate	hydrodynamic	hydrology	hydrotherapy

hyper (*over, above,* **or** *excessive;* **usually used as a prefix**)

hyperacidity	hyperconscious	hyperlogia	hyperthermal
hyperactive	hypercritical	hypermetric	hyperthermia
hyperbola	hyperextension	hypersensitive	hyperthermic
hyperbole	hyperglycemia	hypersonic	hyperventilate
hyperbolic	hyperkinesia	hypertelic	hyperventi-lation
hyperbolize	hyperkinetic	hypertension	
hyperchromatic	hyperlexia	hypertensive	
hyperchromia	hyperlexic	hypertext	

hypn, hypno (*sleep*)

aphypnia	hypnoanalysis	hypnopathy	hypnotherapy
autohypnosis	hypnogenesis	hypnopedia	hypnotic
dyshypnia	hypnology	hypnophobia	hypnotism
hypnesthesia	hypnomania	hypnosis	hypnotize

hypo (*under;* **usually used as a prefix**)

acryhy- potphermy	hypocrisy	hypologia	hypothermia
hypoacidity	hypocrite	hypomania	hypothermic
hypoactive	hypocritical	hyposensitive	hypothesis
hypoallergenic	hypodermic	hyposomniac	hypothetical
hypochondria	hypodermis	hypotension	hypothyroidism
hypochromic	hypoglycemia	hypothermal	hypoventilation

kine, cine (*movement*)

akinesthetic	cinematography	kinematics	kinesthetic
astrokinetic	cinephile	kinematograph	kinetic
cinema	cinerama	kinescope	orthokinesis
cinemascope	dyskinesia	kinesiology	photokinesis
cinemascopic	electrokinetics	kinesiometer	photokinetic
cinemato- graphic	hyperkinesia	kinesis	telekinesia
	hyperkinetic	kinesthesia	telekinetic

lex (*word*)

alexia	hyperlexic	lexicography	lexigraphy
alexithymia	lexeme	lexicologist	lexis
dyslexia	lexical	lexicology	paralexia
dyslexic	lexicalize	lexicon	
hyperlexia	lexicographer	lexiconophonist	

lith, litho (*stone*)

archilithic	lithographer	lithophyll
cystolith	lithographic	lithophyte
endolithic	lithography	lithosphere
lithic	lithologist	lithostratigraphy
lithium	lithology	lithotomy
lithogenesis	lithometer	megalith
lithograph	lithophile	megalithic

microlith	monolithic	protolithic
microlithography	Neolithic	xenolith
monolith	Paleolithic	zoolithic

log, logo, logue (*speech* or *word*)

alogia	logical	logogogue	logometric
catalogue	logicaster	logogram	logopedics
dialogue	logician	logograph	logophasia
eclogue	logistical	logographer	logorrhea
eulogy	logistics	logographic	monologue
hyperlogia	logocentric	logomachy	syllogism
hypologia	logocentrism	logomania	travelogue
logic			

logy (ology) (*science* or *study of*; usually used as a suffix; derived from *logos, logue: speech, word*)

aerobiology	dermatology	lexicology
andrology	doxology	lithology
anthropology	ecobiology	metrology
archaeology	ecology	microbiology
astrobiology	ecophysiology	microecology
astrology	ectobiology	micrology
astrometeorology	endocrinology	mineralogy
astrotheology	epidemiology	morphology
bacteriology	ethnology	musicology
bibliology	ethology	neology
bioecology	etiology	neurology
biology	etymology	neuropathology
biometeorology	geohydrology	ophthalmology
biotechnology	geology	paleontology
cardiology	gerontology	parapsychology
chromatology	graphology	pathology
chronobiology	hematology	pathophysiology
chronology	hydrobiology	pedology
climatology	hydrology	pharmacology
criminology	hypnology	philology
cyclonology	ideology	phobiology
demonology	kinesiology	phonology

photology   psychopathology   technology
phrenology   Scientology   teleology
phyllobiology   seismology   theology
physiology   sophiology   zoology
pneumatology   spectrology   zoopathology
protozoology   stereology   zoophysiology
psychology

macro (*large, long,* or *great;* **usually used as a prefix; opposite of** *micro*)

macrobiotic   macroeconomics   macronutrient
macrocephaly   macrofossil   macrophage
macrochemistry   macrograph   macrophotography
macroclimate   macroinstruction   macrophysics
macrocosm   macromania   macrophyte
macrocosmic   macrometer   macroscopic
macrocyte   macromolecule
macrodont   macronucleus

mania (*madness, frenzy, abnormal desire,* or *obsession*)

balletomania   hypnomania   maniacal   pyromania
bibliomania   hypomania   maniaphobia   schizomania
cyclomania   kleptomania   megalomania   scribblemania
dromomania   logomania   micromania   sophomania
ecomania   macromania   mythomania   technomania
egomania   mania   phonomania   theomania
graphomania   maniac   photomania   zoomania
heliomania

mechan, mechano (*machine*)

mechanic   mechanism   mechanize   mechanogym-
mechanical   mechanisms   mechanized   nastics
mechanically   mechanistic   mechanizing   mechano-
mechanician   mechanistically mechanother-   thermy
mechanics   mechanization   apy

mega (*large* or *great;* **usually used as a prefix)**

acromegaly	megafog	megalosaur	megatechnics
hepatomegaly	megagram	megameter	megatherm
megabit	megahertz	megaphone	megaton
megabyte	megalith	megapod	Megatron
megacycle	megalithic	megapode	megavolt
megadactyl	megalomania	megascope	megawatt
megaderm	megalophonous	megascopic	omega
megadont	megalopolis	megasecond	splenomegaly
megadynamics			

meta (*beside, after, later,* or *beyond;* **usually used as a prefix)**

meta-analysis	metacognitive	metamorphism	metaphysics
metabolic	metaethics	metamorphosis	metaplasm
metabolism	metalanguage	metaphor	metatarsal
metabolize	metalinguistics	metaphrase	metazoa
metacarpal	metamorphic	metaphysical	metazoan
metacognition			

meter, metr (*measure*)

altimeter	dynamometry	logometric
anemometer	econometrics	macrometer
astrometry	geometric	medimeter
barometer	geometry	megameter
biometer	goniometer	meter
biometrics	graphometer	metric
chronobarometer	gravimeter	metrical
chronometer	heliometer	metrication
chronometric	heliothermometer	metrology
chronometry	heptameter	metronome
cyclometer	hexameter	micrometer
cyclometry	hypermetric	morphometric
diameter	interferometer	odometer
dimeter	interferometry	parameter
dromometer	isometric	parametric
dynameter	kinesiometer	pedometer
dynamometer	lithometer	pentameter

perimeter	psychometrics	symmetric
perimetric	quadrimeter	symmetry
photogrammetry	seismometer	telemetry
photometer	sonometer	thermometer
physiometry	spectrometer	trigonometric
pneumatometer	speedometer	trigonometry
psychochronometry	spherometer	trimeter
psychometrician	stereometry	zoometry

metro (*mother city*)

Metro	metropolis	metropolitans
metronymic	metropolitan	metropolitics

micro (*small* or *minute;* **usually used as a prefix; opposite of** *macro*)

biomicroscope	microculture	micromechanics
microacoustics	microdont	micrometer
microanalysis	microdot	microorganism
microbar	microecology	microphone
microbe	microeconomics	microphysics
microbiology	microenvironment	microplankton
microbrewery	microfiber	microprocessor
microburst	microfilm	microreader
microchemistry	micrograph	microscope
microcircuit	microlith	microscopic
microclimate	microlithography	microsurgery
microcomputer	micrology	microwave
microcopy	micromanage	photomicroscope
microcosm	micromania	stereomicroscope

mon, mono (*one*)

monarch	monocotyledon	monodynamic	monolithic
monastery	monocracy	monogamy	monologue
monocellular	monocrat	monogenesis	mononucleosis
monochord	monocular	monoglot	monophobia
monochromatic	monoculture	monogram	monophonic
monochrome	monocycle	monograph	monopoly
monochronic	monodactyl	monogyny	monosyllabic
monocle	monodrama	monolith	monosyllable

| monotheism | monotone | monotony | monounsatu- |
| monotheistic | monotonous | monotreme | rated |

morph (form, shape, or structure)

allomorph	geomorphic	morphometric
andromorphic	metamorphic	morphophonemics
anthropomorphic	metamorphism	morphosis
anthropomorphism	metamorphosis	morphosyntax
archimorphic	morpheme	perimorph
ectomorph	morphemics	polymorphic
ectomorphic	morphic	polymorphous
endomorph	morphogenesis	protomorphic
endomorphic	morphography	theomorphism
exomorphic	morphology	zoomorphism

neo (new or recent)

neoblastic	neoexpressionism	neology
neoclassical	neogenesis	neomodern
neoconservatism	neoimpressionism	neomodernism
neocortex	neoliberation	neonatal
neocosmic	Neolithic	neonate
neocritical	neologism	neophyte

nym, onym (name or word)

acronym	autonym	homonymous	patronymic
allonym	characternym	matronymic	pseudonym
anonymity	eponym	metonym	synonym
anonymous	euonymus	metonymy	synonymous
anthroponym	heteronym	numeronym	synonymy
antonym	heteronymous	paronym	tautonym
antonymous	homonym	paronymous	toponym

ortho (straight, correct, or upright)

orthocenter	orthoepy	orthokinesis	orthoscopic
orthochromatic	orthogenesis	orthomolecular	orthostatic
orthodontia	orthogenic	orthopedics	orthotics
orthodontics	orthogonal	orthopedist	orthotist
orthodontist	orthographic	orthopod	
orthodox	orthography	orthopsychiatry	

pan (panto) (all)

panacea	panegyric	panoply	pantheistic
panarchy	pangenesis	panoptic	pantheon
pancratic	pangram	panorama	pantograph
pandemic	panharmonic	pansophy	pantomime
pandemonium	panhuman	pantheism	

para (beside, alongside, or position; **usually used as a prefix)**

parabiosis	paradox	parallelism	paraphernalia
parable	paradoxical	parallelogram	paraphrase
parabola	paradromic	paralysis	paraprofes- sional
parabolic	paragon	paralytic	
paracentral	paragraph	paralyze	parapsychology
parachromatism	parajournalism	paramedic	parasensory
parachronism	paralegal	parameter	parasite
parachute	paralexia	parametric	parasympathetic
paradental	parallax	paranoia	parathyroid
paradigm	parallel	paranormal	paratroopers

path (feeling, suffering, or disease)

antipathy	neuropathy	pathology	somnipathy
apathetic	parasympathetic	pathophobia	sympathetic
apathy	pathetic	pathophysiology	sympathomimetic
empathize	pathogen	photopathy	sympathy
empathy	pathogenesis	protopathic	telepathic
homeopathy	pathogenic	psychopath	telepathy
hypnopathy	pathography	psychopathic	theopathy
neuropathologist	pathological	psychopathology	unsympathetic
neuropathology	pathologist	sociopath	zoopathology

ped (child)

hypnopedia	pedagogic	pedantic	pedocracy
orthopedics	pedagogue	pediatrician	pedodontics
orthopedist	pedagogy	pediatrics	pedodontist
pedagog	pedant	pediophobia	pedology

ped (soil)

pedalfer	pedocal	pedogenesis	pedology

The Greek combining forms *ped* (meaning *child*) and *ped* (meaning *soil*) are different from the Latin root *ped,* which means *foot.*

peri (*around* or *near;* **usually used as a prefix**)

pericardiac	perigon	periodic	periscope
pericardium	perihelion	periodical	periscopic
pericentric	perimeter	periodontal	peritoneum
pericranium	perimetric	peripatetic	
pericycle	perimorph	peripheral	
perigee	period	periphery	

phil, phila, phile, philo (*love* or *affinity for*)

Anglophile	Philadelphia	philogynist
audiophile	philander	philologist
bibliophile	philanderer	philology
biophile	philanthropic	philomath
cinephile	philanthropist	philomuse
demophile	philanthropy	philophobia
Francophile	philatelist	philosopher
gastrophile	philately	philosophize
geophilous	philharmonic	philosophy
hemophilia	philhippic	philotechnic
hemophiliac	philodemic	philotechnicist
lithophile	philodendron	pseudohemophilia
logophile	philodox	

phobia, phobic; phobe (*irrational fear or hatred; one who fears/hates*)

acousticophobia	chronophobia	heliophobic	photophobia
acrophobia	claustrophobia	hemophobia	polyphobia
aerophobia	claustrophobic	hydrophobia	psychophobia
agoraphobia	cyclophobia	hypnophobia	pyrophobia
androphobia	demophobe	monophobia	spectrophobia
Anglophobe	demophobia	noctiphobia	technophobe
aquaphobia	dromophobia	ornithophobia	technophobia
astrophobia	ecophobia	pathophobia	thermophobia
autophobia	Francophobe	philophobia	xenophobia
bibliophobe	heliophobia	phobiology	zoophobia
bibliophobia			

There are names for more than 500 phobias, most of which come from the field of medicine. See http://www .phobialist.com for a larger list of phobias compiled by Fredd Culbertson.

phon, phono (*sound*)

allophone	lexicophonist	phonology
Anglophone	megaphone	phonoscope
antiphonal	microphone	phonostethoscope
cacophony	monophonic	phonotype
diplophonia	morphophonemics	spectrophone
euphonious	phoneme	stereophonic
euphony	phonemic	symphonic
Francophone	phonetic	symphony
geophone	phonetician	techniphone
gramophone	phonic	telephone
graphophonemic	phonics	vibraphone
heterophony	phonocardiograph	xylophone
homophone	phonogram	
hydrophone	phonograph	

photo (*light*)

aphototropic	photogram	photopathy
astrophotograph	photogrammetry	photophilia
chronophotograph	photograph	photophobia
macrophotography	photographer	photosensitive
photoallergy	photography	photosensitivity
photobiotic	photoheliograph	photosphere
photochrome	photojournalism	photosynthesis
photocopy	photokinesis	phototherapy
photodynamic	photokinetic	photothermic
photoelectric	photology	photothermy
photoengrave	photometer	phototropic
photoengraving	photomicroscope	telephoto
photogenic	photon	telephotography

phyll (*leaf* or *leaves*)

aphyllus	lithophyll	phyllode	phyllopod
chlorophyll	phyllo	phylloid	phyllotaxy
gamophyll	phyllobiology	phyllome	sporophyll
heterophyllus			

phys (*nature*)

astrophysics	microphysics	physiocrat	physiology
biophysics	pathophysiology	physiogenesis	physiometry
ecophysics	physical	physiognomy	physiosophic
geophysical	physician	physiograph	physiotherapy
geophysics	physicist	physiographic	physiotype
macrophysics	physicotherapeu-tics	physiological	physique
metaphysical		physiologist	zoophysiology
metaphysics	physics		

pneumo, pneumon (*breath* or *lung*)

bronchopneumonia	pneumectomy	pneumograph
pneumatic	pneumocardial	pneumonectomy
pneumatogram	pneumococus	pneumonia
pneumatology	pneumocystis	pneumonitis
pneumatometer	pneumoderma	pneumotherapy
pneumatoscope	pneumogastric	postpneumonia
pneumatosis		

pod (*foot*)

megapod	podiatrist	podium
monopod	podiatry	tripod

poly (*many;* usually used as a prefix)

duopoly	polyclinic	polygraphy	polypharmacy
monopolize	polydactyl	polygyny	polyphony
monopoly	polydemic	polyhedron	polypod
polyandry	polyester	polymath	polysyllabic
polyarchy	polyethnic	polymorphic	polytechnic
polyarthritis	polygamy	polymorphous	polytendinitis
polycentric	polyglot	polymyxin	polytheism
polychord	polygon	polyneuritis	polytheistic
polychromatic	polygraph	polynomial	polyunsaturated
polychrome			

proto (*earliest, original,* or *first in time;* **used as a prefix**)

protocol	protolanguage	protoplasm	protozoa
protogalaxy	protolithic	protoplasmic	protozoan
protogyny	protomorphic	prototrophic	protozoic
protohistory	protopathic	prototype	protozoology
protohuman	protophyte		

psych (*mind* **or** *soul*)

orthopsychiatry	psychochronometry	psychomotor
parapsychology	psychodrama	psychoneurosis
psyche	psychodynamics	psychopath
psychedelic	psychogenesis	psychopathic
psychiatric	psychogeriatrics	psychophobia
psychiatrist	psychograph	psychosis
psychiatry	psychohistory	psychosocial
psychic	psycholinguistics	psychotechnics
psychoacoustics	psychologist	psychotherapist
psychoallergy	psychologize	psychotherapy
psychoanalysis	psychology	psychotic
psychobabble	psychometrician	psychotraumatic
psychobiography	psychometrics	psychotropic

saur (*lizard* **or** *serpent*)

brontosaurus	megalosaur	saurischian	stegosaurus
dinosaur	paleosaurid	sauropod	teleosaurus
dinosaurian	pterosaur	saury	titanosaurus
ichthyosaur	saurian	secnosaurus	tyrannosaur
lepidosaur	sauries	sinosaurus	tyrannosaurus

scope (*to watch or see*)

abdominoscope	cinemascopic	hydroscope
autoscope	dynamoscope	kaleidoscope
baroscope	endoscope	kinescope
biomicroscope	endoscopic	macroscopic
bioscope	gyroscope	megascope
bronchoscope	gyroscopic	megascopic
chromoscope	heliochromoscope	microscope
chronoscope	helioscope	microscopic
cinemascope	horoscope	ophthalmoscope

orthoscopic

otoscope

periscope

periscopic

phonoscope

phonostethoscope

photomicroscope

photoscope

pneumatoscope

polariscope

radioscope

seismoscope

spectrohelioscope

spectroscope

stereoscope

stereoscopic

stethoscope

telescope

telescopic

thermascope

soph (*wisdom* or *cleverness*)

bibliosoph	philosophy	sophisticated	sophomania
pansophic	physiosophic	sophistication	sophomore
philosopher	sophic	sophisticator	sophomoric
philosophical	sophiology	sophistry	theosophic
philosophism	sophism	Sophocles	unsophisticated
philosophize			

sphere (*circle*)

astrosphere	geosphere	magnetosphere	spheriform
atmosphere	heliosphere	mesosphere	spheroid
biogeosphere	hemisphere	petrosphere	spherometer
biosphere	hemispherical	photosphere	spheroplast
chemosphere	hydrosphere	pyrosphere	stratosphere
chromosphere	ionosphere	sphere	thermosphere
ecosphere	lithosphere	spherical	troposphere
exosphere			

stereo (*solid, firm,* or *hard*)

stereo	stereomatrix	stereoscopic
stereochemistry	stereometry	stereotaxis
stereogram	stereomicroscope	stereotomy
stereographic	stereophonic	stereotype
stereography	stereoplasm	stereotypical
stereological	stereoscope	stereovision
stereology		

techn (*skill, art,* or *craft*)

biotechnics	philotechnicist	Technicolor	technology
biotechnology	polytechnic	technicon	technomania
electrotechnics	psychotechnics	techniphone	technophile
eutechnics	pyrotechnic	technique	technophobe
geotechnics	technical	technobabble	technophobia
megatechnics	technicality	technocracy	technostructure
neotechnic	technician	technocrat	zootechnical
philotechnic	technicist	technologist	zootechny

tele (*distant;* usually used as a prefix)

autotelic	telekinesia	teleport
hypertelic	telekinetic	teleportation
telecast	telemarketing	teleprinter
telecommunication	telemedicine	telescope
telecommute	telemetry	telescopic
teleconference	teleology	teleshop
telecourse	telepathic	teletherapy
telegenesis	telepathy	telethon
telegnosis	telephone	teletranscription
telegram	telephoto	teletypist
telegraph	telephotography	television
telegraphic		

the, theo (*god*)

allotheism	pantheism	theocrat	theology
antitheism	pantheistic	theodicy	theomachy
astrotheology	pantheon	theogamy	theomania
atheism	philotheism	theogony	theomorphism
atheist	polytheism	theolatry	theopathy
atheological	polytheistic	theologian	theophany
monotheism	theocentric	theological	theophile
monotheistic	theocracy	theologize	

therm, thermo (heat or hot)

acrohypothermy	megatherm	thermogram
chronothermal	philothermic	thermograph
endothermic	photothermic	thermolysis
euthermia	photothermy	thermometer
exothermic	thermal	thermomotor
geothermal	thermascope	thermonuclear
heliotherm	thermic	thermophilic
heliothermometer	thermistor	thermophobia
hyperthermal	thermoacoustic	thermoreceptor
hyperthermia	thermochemistry	thermoregulate
hyperthermic	thermocouple	Thermos
hypothermal	thermodynamics	thermosphere
hypothermia	thermoelectric	thermostat
hypothermic	thermoelectron	thermotherapy
isothermal	thermogenesis	thermotoxin

zo, zoo (animal)

Archaeozoic	protozoan	zoolithic	zoophobia
asterozoa	protozoic	zoological	zoophysiology
azoic	protozoology	zoology	zoophyte
Cenozoic	Zodiac	zoomania	zooplankton
endozoic	zoobiotic	zoometry	zooplasty
Mesozoic	zoochore	zoomorphism	zoospore
metazoa	zoogenic	zoonosis	zoosterol
metazoan	zoogenous	zoonotic	zootechnical
Paleozoic	zooglea	zoopathology	zootechny
Phanerozoic	zoography	zoophile	zootomy
Proterozoic	zooid	zoophilic	zootoxin
protozoa	zoolatry		

BIBLIOGRAPHY

The American heritage dictionary (2nd ed.). (1982). Boston: Houghton Mifflin.

The American heritage dictionary (4th ed.). (2000). Boston: Houghton Mifflin.

Random House unabridged dictionary (2nd ed.). (1993). New York: Random House.

Words Commonly Found in Textbooks

Students must learn to read and spell many words found in content area textbooks and lectures as well as learn the meaning of these words. The words in this appendix are organized by subject area and grade level. The subject areas included are social studies (government, history, and psychology), mathematics, and science (biology, meteorology, physics, and chemistry). These lists are further subdivided according to topics that are often taught during the school year, such as the American Revolution, westward movement, state government, astronomy, physics, and so forth. Elementary grade lists are for third through sixth grades; secondary-grade lists are for 7th through 12th grades.

In addition to the spellings of the words listed, the meanings should be studied. Some terms have different meanings depending on the context. For example, *depression* has different meanings in psychology and geography, *conjunction* has different meanings in linguistics and astronomy, and *revolution* has different meanings in history and physics. In addition, students need to learn relationships among terms such as *legislative, judicial,* and *executive* when discussing government; *psychoanalyst, psychologist,* and *psychiatrist* when discussing psychology; and *recession* and *inflation* when discussing finance. Also note that many proper names of people and places appear in all content area texts and should be studied in addition to the words in this appendix.

The words in these lists may be used in many ways. Students may compare and contrast words such as *hurricane, earthquake,* and *tornado* or words such as *unicameral* and *bicameral*. Students may be asked to sort nouns, adjectives, and verbs within a group of words. Groups of students may draw webs of related words. See Chapters 7 and 8 for other possible activities using related and associated words.

WORDS FOUND IN SOCIAL STUDIES TEXTBOOKS

Teachers can make word lists for decoding and spelling practice using these topic lists and vocabulary taken directly from student textbooks. In addition to the words listed for the elementary grades, these words are found in many social studies textbooks.

Elementary Grades

Early Explorers

cape	explorer	passage	spice
discovery	navigation	route	trade
exchange	navigator	scurvy	trader
exploration	ocean		

Early America

barter	governor	Native American	Thanksgiving
celebration	hardship		treaty
charter	Indian	Pilgrim	winter
exchange	Mayflower Compact	pilgrimage	

Revolutionary War

assembly	freedom	monarchy	redcoat
boycott	indentured	musket	representation
colonist	independence	oppression	revolution
colony	loyalist	proclamation	servant
constitution	Minutemen	rebel	taxation
declaration	monarch	rebellion	Yankee

Civil War and Reconstruction

abolition	Confederacy	independence	secession
abolitionist	Confederate	massacre	siege
assassination	escape	reconstruction	slavery
autonomy	freedmen	revolt	Underground Railroad
battle	freedom	scalawag	Union
carpetbagger	Gilded Age	secede	
charge	hiding		

Westward Movement

covered wagon	hardship	Pacific	trail
expansion	homesteading	pioneer	westward
frontier	movement	territory	

Weather and Geography

anthropology	hemisphere	neighborhood	rain forest
community	hurricane	ocean	refinery
contour map	interdepend-ence	peninsula	relief map
desert		physical	rural
elevation	irrigation	plateau	satellite
equator	lake	political map	savannah
equatorial	latitude	pond	suburban
foothill	longitude	population	summit
geography	manufacturing	prairie	tide
glacier	meridian	precipitation	tornado
globe	meteorology	province	transportation
gulf	mountain		

Government and Citizenship

argumentative	emigrate	immigration	president
bicentennial	emigration	judicial	presidential
caricature	emigre	legislative	proletariat
centennial	government	oppressor	re-elect
democracy	governor	perpetuate	senator
dictatorship	hierarchy	politician	sequential
electoral	immigrant		

Secondary Grades

Teachers can make word lists for decoding and spelling practice using these topic lists and vocabulary taken directly from social studies textbooks. The following words are found in many secondary-grade social studies textbooks.

Ancient Cultures

acropolis	decode	mummification	ruin
amphitheater	delta	myth	sacrifice
ancient	gladiator	mythology	senator
aqueduct	god	offering	stadium
city-state	goddess	papyrus	tunic
civilization	hieroglyph	polytheism	valley
coliseum	immortal	pyramid	viaduct
constellation	irrigation	republic	ziggurat
cuneiform	mortal	Rosetta stone	zodiac

Middle Ages and Renaissance

archbishop	crusade	loyalty	Renaissance
armor	crusader	Magna Carta	schism
beheaded	Enlightenment	manuscript	scribe
bishop	fealty	medieval	scrivener
cathedral	feudal	monarch	serf
chain mail	fief	monarchy	serfdom
chivalry	illumination	monastery	simony
conquer	inquisition	pike	subjugation
conqueror	invasion	plate mail	sword
Constantinople	jousting	pope	vassal
convent	knighthood		

Pre–World War I

antitrust	muckraker	stockyards
bribery	muckraking	tenement
corporation	railroad	transcontinental
corruption	refinery	trustbusting
doctrine	sabotage	yellow journalism
monopoly		

World Wars I and II

aircraft
aircraft carrier
Allied
Allies
anti-aircraft
anti-Semitism
archduke
armistice
assassin
assassination
atomic
Axis
biplane
blackout
bomber
campaign

communism
concentration camp
debarkation
devastation
dictatorship
fallout
fascism
fascist
gunner
Holocaust
homeland
invade
invasion
isolationism
isolationist

liberation
Marxism
mustard gas
Nazism
nuclear
parachute
peacetime
socialism
totalitarian
totalitarianism
treaty
trench
triplane
warfare
Zionism

Cold War

agent
airlift
anti-American
ballistic
Berlin Wall
blackball
collectivization
commission
communism

communist
counterintelligence
crisis
detente
escalation
intelligence
intercontinental
investigation
Iron Curtain

McCarthyism
missile
nuclear
spy plane
surveillance
testify
testimony
treaty
warhead

Government and Citizenship

alien
ambassador
amendment
appeal
apportionment
assembly
ballot

bicameral
Bill of Rights
bureaucracy
campaign
campaign promise
capital
Capitol

caucus
checks and balances
citizen
citizenship
civil rights
Congress
congressional

constituent
Constitution
constitutionalist
debate
delegate
democracy
Democrat
demonstration
denaturalization
desegregation
desegregationist
diplomacy
diplomatic
discrimination
disobedience
dissolution
economic
embassy
entrepreneur
executive
extradition
federalism
federalist
feminism
feminist
filibuster
gerrymandering

inalienable
judge
judicial
jurisdiction
jury
justice
law
legal
legislation
legislative
legislator
lobbyist
multiculturalism
naturalization
naturalize
nomination
party
passport
petition
plank
platform
precinct
press
protest
racism
racist

referendum
religion
repeal
representation
representative
Republican
running mate
segregation
segregationist
Senate
senator
signature
sovereignty
speech
suffrage
suffragist
support
supremacist
supremacy
Supreme Court
television
unicameral
urbanization
voter registration
voting
Whig

Psychology

adolescence
afferent
agoraphobia
amygdala
antidepressant
anxiety
aphasia
axon

behaviorism
catatonic
central
cerebellum
cerebral
cerebrum
circadian
cognitive

conditioning
consciousness
cortex
cyclothymia
deindividualism
dendrite
dizygotic
dysthymia

echoic
eclecticism
efferent
electroconvulsive
electroencephalogram
electromyogram
electrooculogram
etiology
extrinsic
extroversion
frontal
functionalism
hallucination
heterosexuality
heuristic
hippocampus
homeostasis
homophobia
homosexuality
hyperphagia
hypochondria
hypothalamus
interdisciplinary
intrinsic

introspection
introversion
limbic
lobe
localization
microelectrode
monozygotic
nervous
neurotransmitter
occipital
oculomotor
olfactory
operant
overregularization
parasympathetic
parietal
perception
peripheral
phenomena
physiology
pituitary
prefrontal
pseudodialogue
pseudoinsomnia

pseudomemory
psychoanalysis
psychoanalyst
psychobiography
psychophysics
psychosocial
psychotherapy
psychotropic
schema
schizophrenia
seizure
self-actualization
sensorimotor
sexuality
sociobiology
somatosensory
spinal
structuralism
synapse
synaptic
technocrat
tomography
transformation
trichromatic

WORDS FOUND IN MATH TEXTBOOKS

Elementary Grades

Arithmetic and Place Value

addend
addition
borrowing
calculation
calculator
carrying

decimal
denominator
digit
dividend
division
divisor

even
fraction
hundreds
hundredths
multiplication
multiplier

numerator
odd
ones
operator
percentage
place

quotient   sign   tens   thousandths
reciprocal   subtraction   tenths   value
regrouping   symbol   thousands   zero
remainder

Geometry and Shapes

acute   hemisphere   opposite   reflection
adjacent   heptagon   parallelogram   rhombus
angle   heptagonal   pentagon   rotation
area   hexagon   pentagonal   scalene
axis   hexagonal   pentomino   sphere
circumference   horizontal   perimeter   square
congruent   intersection   perpendicular   surface area
cube   isosceles   polygon   symmetry
diagonal   linear   prism   trapezoid
diagonally   nonagon   protractor   triangle
diameter   nonagonal   pyramid   triangular
dimension   obtuse   radius   vertex
geometry   octagon   rectangle   vertical
graph   octagonal   rectangular   volume

Units of Measure

millimeter   yard   deciliter   milligram
centimeter   mile   centiliter   gram
decimeter   cubic centi-   kiloliter   decigram
kilometer   meter   ounce   centigram
inch   milliliter   pound   kilogram
foot   liter

Sampling, Statistics, and Problem Solving

algebra   deduce   extension
algorithm   deduction   formula
application   diagram   frequency
argument   distribution   greater than
average   equation   greater than or equal to
computation   equivalent   identity
cumulative   estimate   inequality

less than

median

statistics

less than or equal to

minimum

strategy

likelihood

permutation

surveyed

manipulative

prediction

transaction

mathematical

probability

validate

mathematician

solution

word problem

maximum

Secondary Grades

Algebra, Logic, and Sets

abscissa

disjunction

positive

absolute value

distributive

power

algebra

exponent

quadrant

associative

exponential

quadratic

asymptote

factorial

rational

asymptotic

factoring

real

base 10

formula

rise

binary

identity

run

binomial

imaginary

scientific notation

coefficient

integer

set

commutative

intersection

slope

conjunction

inverse

square

constant

irrational

square root

contrapositive

multiplicative

trinomial

converse

negative

union

coordinates

order of operations

variable

cube

ordinate

Venn diagram

cube root

polynomial

whole

Geometry and Trigonometry

arc

asymmetric

cone

dodecahedron

arccosecant

asymmetry

coplanar

eccentric

arccosine

chord

cosecant

eccentricity

arccotangent

collinear

cosine

ellipse

arcsecant

complementary

cotangent

elliptical

arcsine

concentric

cube

equidistant

arctangent

concentricity

degree

equilateral

exterior angle	line	proof	supplementary
foci	origin	pyramid	symmetric
focus	parabola	quadrilateral	symmetry
geometric	parabolic	radian	tangent
geometry	parallel	rhombus	tessellate
grad	parallelogram	right angle	tessellation
hyperbola	perpendicular	right triangle	theorem
hyperbolic	pi	scalene	transverse
hypotenuse	plane	secant	trigonometric
icosahedron	point	segment	trigonometry
interior angle	postulate	sine	vertex
isoceles	prism	square	vertices
leg			

Analysis and Calculus

calculus	*e*	logarithmic	minima
cardioid	integrate	matrices	multivariable
delta	integration	matrix	series
differential	logarithm	maxima	summation
discrete			

Statistics

bell curve	median	ratio
central tendency	mode	sample
confidence interval	outlier	sampling
distribution	percent	skew
error	percentile	standard deviation
histogram	population	subsample
mean	quartile	

WORDS FOUND IN SCIENCE TEXTBOOKS

Elementary Grades

Paleontology and Prehistory

ammonite	brontosaurus	Cretaceous
archaeopteryx	Cenozoic	dinosaurs

diplodocus	Precambrian	stegosaurus
extinction	pteranodon	Tertiary
glaciers	pterodactyl	Triassic
Jurassic	Quaternary	triceratops
mammoth	saber-toothed	trilobite
Mesozoic	skeleton	tyrannosaurus rex
Paleozoic		

Geology, Meteorology, and Astronomy

asteroids	cumulus	metamorphic	satellite
astronomy	earthquake	meteor	sediment
atmosphere	environment	meteorite	sedimentary
cirrocumulus	fault	meteorology	shuttle
cirrus	friction	moon	spacecraft
climate	granite	nimbus	telescope
comet	gravity	orbit	tide
constellation	igneous	planet	tornado
core	lava	polar	volcano
crust	magma	precipitation	weightless
cumulonimbus	mantle	rocket	weightlessness

Animals and Plants

adapt	cold-blooded	fibrous	pesticide
adaptation	community	habitat	photosynthesis
amphibian	coniferous	mammal	reptile
amphibious	deciduous	microorganism	warm-blooded
biology	development	nutrition	zoology
chlorophyll	ecosystem		

Experiments

adventure	equipment	interpretation	parallel
artificial	estimate	investigate	prediction
assumption	experience	measurement	production
calculation	experiment	microscope	requirement
classification	facsimile	neutral	sequence
communicate	hypotheses	numerical	spontaneous
complicated	hypothesis	observation	virtual
conclusion	instrument		

Chemistry

aluminum	element	oxygen
catalyst	hydrogen	petroleum
chemical	nitrogen	solution

Applied Physical Science

Celsius	megaphone	photograph	translucent
construction	molecular	prism	transparent
cylinder	opaque	spectrum	ultraviolet
Fahrenheit	percussion	temperature	vibration
infrared	periscope	thermometer	

Electricity and Magnetism

attraction	electricity	galvanometer	positive
battery	electromagnet	magnet	short-circuit
bulb	electronic	negative	transistor
circuit	filament	pole	

Technology

binary	invention	photocopy	technology
computer	microwave	refrigerator	telegraph
digital	patent	silicon	telephone

Secondary Grades

Scientific Method

analysis	discussion	observation	scientific
bias	double-blind	reliability	method
blind	empirical	replicate	scientist
conclusion	hypothesis	results	validity
control	literature	scientific	variable
data			

Biology

adenosine triphosphate	anaphase	bolus
aerobic	artery	botany
amino acid	asexual	capillary
amoeba	bile	carbon dioxide
anaerobic	biome	carbon-based

cell

centriole

chain

chemosynthesis

chromatid

chromatin

cytoplasm

cytosine

deoxyribonucleic acid

digestion

diploid

dissection

division

dizygotic

dominant

double helix

duodenum

dynamic equilibrium

enzyme

esophagus

evolution

evolve

genes

genetic

genome

genotype

genus

glucose

glycogen

Golgi apparatus

guanine

haploid

heterozygotic

homozygotic

insulin

interphase

islet

Krebs cycle

lactic acid

large intestine

meiosis

messenger RNA

metaphase

microorganism

mitochondria

mitosis

molecule

monozygotic

mutation

natural selection

nomenclature

nuclear membrane

nucleus

ontogeny

organ

organelle

organic

oxidative
   phosphorylation

oxygen

pancreas

paramecium

peristalsis

phenotype

phylogeny

prophase

protein

protozoa

recessive

reproduction

respiration

reticular

ribonucleic acid (RNA)

ribosome

sexual

small intestine

species

sphincter

spindle pole

stoma

stomach

taxonomy

telophase

thymine

transfer RNA

vein

zygote

Chemistry

absorption

acid

acidic

activation energy

adhere

adhesion

adhesive

adsorption

alkali

alkaline

alloy

anhydride

anhydrous

anion

aqueous

atom	ductility	malleability
atomic mass	electrolysis	malleable
atomic weight	electrolyte	mass number
Avogadro's number	element	meniscus
base	emulsifier	molar
basic	emulsion	molarity
beaker	endothermic	mole
boil	evaporate	molecular
bond	evaporation	molecular weight
buffer	exothermic	molecule
Bunsen burner	flask	noble gas
calorie	fluoresce	notation
catalyst	fluorescent	orbital
catalyze	formula	oxidation
cation	freeze	oxidize
caustic	gas	ozone
centrifuge	gaseous	period
chain	group	periodic table
cohere	half-life	pH
cohesion	heavy metal	phosphate
cohesive	humidity	pipette
colloid	hydrolysis	polymer
compound	hydrolyze	polymeric
concentrate	hydrophilic	precipitate
concentration	hydrophobic	radiation
condensation	inert	radioactivity
condense	inorganic	reaction
covalence	ion	relative humidity
covalency	ionic	ring
covalent	ionization	shell
crystal	isomer	solid
crystalline	isomeric	solution
decay	isotope	solvent
dewpoint	lanthanide	specific gravity
dilute	liquid	spin
dilution	luminance	state
dissolve	luminescence	stoichiometry
ductile	luminous	sublevel

subshell

substrate

surface tension

suspension

symbol

titrate

titration

univalent

valence

valency

vapor

viscosity

viscous

Physics[1]

absolute zero

acceleration

amperage

ampere

amplitude

angle

angstrom

angular momentum

applied

atmosphere

atmospheric

atom

atomic

axle

candela

capacitance

capacitor

centrifugal

centripetal

charge

coefficient

concave

conduction

conductor

conservation

constant

converge

convergent

convex

coulomb

current

cycle

differential

diffract

diffraction

dipole

dislocation

distance

diverge

divergent

dynamic

dyne

electromagnetic

electron

electrostatic

emission

energy

equilibrium

equipartition

exponential

farad

ferroelectricity

field

fission

fluctuation

fluid

fluid dynamics

force

frequency

friction

fulcrum

fusion

gravitation

gravity

harmonic

henry

hertz

horsepower

hydrostatic

ideal

illumination

image

inclined plane

inductance

inertia

infrared

ionic

irreversibility

irrotational

joule

kelvin

kinetic

kinetic energy

law

lens

lever

lift

[1]*Source:* Feynman, R.P., Leighton, R.B., & Sands, M. (1970). *The Feynman lectures on physics* (Vols. I–III). Reading, MA: Addison-Wesley.

lumen

magnet

magnetic

magnetism

magnitude

mass

mechanical advantage

mechanics

model

molecular

molecule

momentum

muon

neutrino

neutron

newton

nonlinear

nuclear

nuclei

nucleus

opacity

opaque

optics

oscillation

oxygen

parabola

parabolic

parity

particle

pendulum

period

periodic

periodicity

polarization

polarize

potential energy

power

pressure

principle

projectile

projectile motion

proton

pulley

quantum

quark

rate

real image

reflection

refraction

relativistic

relativity

resistance

resonance

resultant

screw

semiconductor

simple machine

slope

solenoid

spectrum

spring scale

static

superconductivity

superconductor

superposition

symmetry

synchrotron

tesla

theorem

theoretical

theory

thermal

thermodynamics

translucence

translucent

transparence

transparent

ultraviolet

vector

velocity

virtual image

volt

voltage

watt

wave

wavelength

weber

wedge

wheel

work

Astronomy

altitude

aphelion

arcminute

arcsecond

ascension

asteroid

astigmatism

astrology

aurora

autumnal

azimuth

binary

binoculars

black hole

celestial

comet

constellation

cosmic

declination

dwarf

eclipse
ecliptic
ellipse
elliptical
elongation
epoch
equinox
estival
event horizon
exosphere
galactic
galaxy
giant
gibbous
globular
gravitational
gravity
hibernal
infrared

interstellar
ionosphere
latitude
light-year
longitude
luminosity
lunar
magnetosphere
magnification
magnify
magnitude
matter
meridian
mesosphere
meteor
nebula
obliquity
observatory

occultation
opposition
optical
orbit
parallax
penumbra
perihelion
planet
planetarium
precession
radiation
recalibrate
recalibration
retrograde
revolution
rotation
sidereal
solar

solstice
spectral
spectrum
sphere
stratosphere
supernova
telescope
telescopic
terminal
  velocity
thermosphere
troposphere
ultraviolet
umbra
universe
vernal
zenith
zodiac

Geology

acid rain
aftershock
alluvial fan
alpine
anticline
aquiclude
aquifer
archipelago
artesian
atoll
basalt
batholith
bay
bedrock
bog
canyon

cape
clay
conservation
contour line
deforestation
delta
doldrums
dune
ebb
epicenter
erosion
estuary
fjord
gneiss
granite
groundwater

gypsum
hydrology
inlet
isobar
isobath
isotherm
isthmus
karst
kettle
lagoon
limestone
marsh
metal
mica
mineral
moraine

neap
oxbow
peat
permeable
petrified
phosphores-
  cence
pollution
preservation
reef
Richter scale
riverbed
runoff
sandbar
sandstone
scarp

sediment	slate	swamp	topsoil
sedimentation	slump	syncline	tsunami
shale	stalactite	tectonic	water cycle
silicate	stalagmite	terrace	watershed
silt	strait	tide pool	wetland
sinkhole			

Glossary

The key terms used in this book (in text in boldface type) are defined in this glossary. The definitions given are those that pertain to the study of language, reading, decoding, and spelling.

acronym   A word formed from the initial letters of a name, as in WAC from Women's Army Corps.

affix   A bound morpheme attached to the beginning or end of a base or root that creates a new word with a meaning or function that is different than that of the base or root. *See also* prefix; suffix.

allomorph   A variant form of a morpheme. For example, *-s* in *cats*, *-es* in *horses*, and *-en* in *oxen* are allomorphs of the English plural morpheme.

alphabetic code   Letter–sound relationships in an alphabetic writing system, the understanding of which is crucial to decoding and spelling in that system.

alphabetic principle   The representation of a phoneme by a graphic symbol, such as a letter or letters.

analytic phonics   An instructional approach in which students learn whole words and deduce the component parts, such as phonemes.

assimilated prefix   *See* chameleon prefix.

auditory discrimination   The ability to discriminate between similar-sounding phonemes, such as /p/ and /b/, /t/ and /d/, or /f/ and /v/.

automaticity   The immediate recognition of words while decoding.

base word A word, such as *spell*, to which prefixes and suffixes may be added to form related words, such *misspell* and *misspelling*.

blend *See* consonant blend.

blending The ability to say a word by fusing a sequence of sounds or syllables.

bound morpheme A prefix, suffix, or root that cannot stand alone, such as *re-*, *struct*, and *-ure* in *restructure*.

breve The diacritical marking (ˇ) appearing over a vowel grapheme that denotes a short, or lax, pronunciation of the vowel.

chameleon prefix A prefix in which the final letter of the prefix changes because of assimilation with the first letter of the base element (e.g., *con-* becomes a chameleon prefix in *collect, correct,* and *combine*). *Also called* assimilated prefix.

closed syllable A syllable containing a short vowel sound and ending with one or more consonants, as in *hot* or *plant*.

combining form In this book, word parts of Greek origin that can be combined with other combining forms or morphemes to form new words, such as *psych* and *ology*, which can be combined to make *psychology*.

compound word A word that is composed of two or more smaller words and whose meaning is related to that of the constituent words, such as *bookcase, lamp-post,* or *schoolhouse*.

consonant 1) A speech sound that is constricted or obstructed by the teeth, lips, roof of the mouth, and/or tongue during articulation; 2) a grapheme corresponding to a consonant sound.

consonant blend Two or three adjacent consonants before or after a vowel sound in a syllable, such as /spl/ in *split* or /nt/ in *font*. *Also called* consonant cluster.

consonant digraph Two adjacent consonants that represent one speech sound, such as *sh* in *ship* or *ch* in *church*.

consonant-*le* syllable A syllable ending in a consonant followed by *-le,* such as *-ble* in *table* or *-zle* in *puzzle*.

contraction A shortened word formed by omitting or combining some of the letters or sound as in *don't* from *do not*.

cursive writing Writing where the letters are joined together.

decoding The act of translating written words into vocal or subvocal speech. Decoding draws on certain linguistic skills and knowledge.

decoding–spelling continuum A recommended sequence for integrated decoding and spelling instruction across grade levels.

derivational morpheme A prefix or suffix added to a base or root that forms another word that is often a different part of speech than the base or root, such as *re-* in *return* or *-ful* in *hopeful*.

dialect A regional variety of a language distinguished by pronunciation, grammar, or vocabulary.

digraph   Two adjacent letters in a syllable that represent one speech sound, such as *th* for /th/ (as in *thin*) or *ai* for /ā/ (as in *rain*).

diphthong   1) A vowel in a syllable that produces two subtle sounds by gliding from one vowel sound to another, such as /oi/ in *boil* or /ô/ in *fawn*; 2) a grapheme corresponding to a diphthong sound. (*Note:* Some linguists disagree about how many diphthongs exist in English. Venezky, 1999, attributed this dispute to regional differences in vowel pronunciations. In this book, diphthongs are not distinguished from vowel digraphs.)

double-deficit hypothesis   The hypothesis that a child who has difficulty with both phonological processing and naming speed will have more difficulty with reading than a child with only one of those problems.

dyslexia   A specific learning disability that is neurological in origin. It is characterized by difficulties with accurate and/or fluent word recognition and by poor spelling and decoding abilities. These difficulties typically result from a deficit in the phonological component of language that is often unexpected in relation to other cognitive abilities and in the provision of effective classroom instruction. Secondary consequences may include problems with reading comprehension and reduced reading experience that can impede the growth of vocabulary and background knowledge (Hennessey, 2003; Hennessey was President of the International Dyslexia Association [IDA] and quoted the newly approved definition in the IDA newsletter *Perspectives*). *Also called* specific language disability; specific reading disability.

encoding   To change a spoken word into writing; another word for spelling.

etymology   The study of the history and origins of words by tracing their earliest use and changes in form and meaning.

fluency   Decoding speed that is gained as one masters the alphabetic code.

free morpheme   A base word or root that can stand alone as a whole word, such as *spell, script,* or *graph.*

grapheme   A written or printed letter or letters that represents a phoneme, such as *m* for /m/ or *oy* for /oi/.

high-frequency word   *See* sight word.

homograph   One of two or more words that have the same spelling but that sound different and differ in meaning, such as *polish* (to rub to make shiny, or a substance used while doing so) and *Polish* (the nationality).

homonym   One of two or more words that have the same sound and often the same spelling but that differ in meaning, such as *die* (to stop living), *die* (a device for cutting/stamping objects), and *dye* (color); *pail* and *pale;* or *bear* and *bare.* *Also called* homophone.

homophone   *See* homonym.

inflectional morpheme   "In English, a suffix that expresses plurality or possession when added to a noun [-*s* in *cats*], tense when added to a verb [-*ed* in *walked*], and comparison when added to an adjective [*-er* in *bigger*]" (Harris & Hodges, 1995, p. 116).

irregular word   A word that does not follow typical letter–sound correspondences, usually in the vowel sound(s), such as *there* or *cough*.

lax vowel sounds   *See* short vowel sounds.

long vowel sounds   The vowel sounds that are also letter names, such as /ā/ as in *pale*, /ē/ as in *demon*, /ī/ as in *pilot*, /ō/ as in *hobo*, and /o͞o/ as in *Cupid*. Some long vowel sounds are represented by vowel digraphs, such as *ai* as in *rain* and *ee* as in *feed*. Long vowel sounds have a longer duration relative to short vowel sounds. *Also called* tense vowel sounds.

macron   The diacritical marking symbol (‾) appearing over a vowel grapheme that denotes a long, or tense, pronunciation of the vowel.

manuscript writing   A form of handwriting in which letters are separate from one another, unlike in cursive writing. *Also called* printing.

metacognition   The act of reflecting on and monitoring cognitive activity.

metalanguage   The language used to talk about spoken and written language concepts.

metalinguistic awareness   The ability to think about and reflect on the nature and function of language.

morpheme   The smallest meaningful linguistic unit in a word.

morphology   "Study of the structure and forms of words, including derivation, inflection, and compounding" (Harris & Hodges, 1995, p. 158).

morphophonemic relations   The relationships between changing phonemic forms and constant written spellings, such as in *know* and *knowledge*.

multisensory instruction   Instruction using the simultaneous linking of visual, auditory, and kinesthetic–tactile modalities to enhance memory and learning.

neologism   A newly coined word, phrase, or expression.

open syllable   A syllable ending in a vowel sound, making the vowel sound long, as in me, hobo, and va cation. Open syllables may or may not have an initial consonant (e.g., the first syllable in the word *open* is an open syllable with no initial consonant).

orthography   The writing (spelling) system of a language.

phoneme   The smallest unit of sound that conveys a distinction in meaning, such as the /p/ of *pat* or the /m/ of *mat*.

phonemic awareness   An awareness of the sounds that make up spoken words *and* an ability to manipulate sounds in words.

phonestheme   A sound or sounds that because it appears in a number of words of similar meaning has a recognizable semantic association such as the gl in words that *glitter, glow,* and *gleam.*

phonetics 1) The nature and articulation of speech sounds and their representation by written symbols; 2) the systematic classification of speech sounds in a language.

phonics A teaching method that stresses letter–sound relationships in reading and spelling.

phonological awareness An awareness of various levels of the speech sound system, such as syllables, accent patterns, rhyme, and phonemes.

phonology 1) The science of speech sounds; 2) the sound system of a language.

portmanteau word A word formed by merging the sounds and meanings of two separate words, such as *brunch* (*breakfast* and *lunch*) or *smog* (*smoke* and *fog*). See "Word Wisdom: Portmanteau Words" in Chapter 8 for more information.

prefix A morpheme attached to the beginning of a base word or root, such as *dis-* in *disclaim,* that creates a new word with a changed meaning or function.

printing *See* manuscript writing.

rapid automatized naming (RAN) The rapid naming of colors, numbers, letters, and objects. RAN appears to be an important factor in later reading acquisition.

_r_-controlled vowel A vowel that immediately precedes, and whose sound is modified by, /r/ in the same syllable, as in *car, for, her, bird, curl, tear, berry,* or *marry.*

regular word A word that follows typical letter–sound correspondences in consonant and vowel sounds, such as *last* or *stump.*

root The main part of a word to which affixes are added to derive new words. For example, *struct* is the root of *destructive.* Roots are often, but not always, bound morphemes.

schwa The neutral vowel in unaccented or unstressed syllables in English words, such as the sound that corresponds to the grapheme *a-* in *asleep.* (The diacritical marking is /ə/.)

segmenting Separating a word into syllables or phonemes.

short vowel sounds The sounds of /ă/ in *map,* /ĕ/ in *bed,* /ĭ/ in *sip* or *gym,* /ŏ/ in *cot,* and /ŭ/ in *but.* Short vowel sounds have a relatively short duration. *Also called* lax vowel sounds.

sight word 1) A word that students know by sight without having to analyze it to pronounce it. Sight words may have regular (e.g., *jump, stop*) or irregular (e.g., *where, only*) spelling. *Also called* high-frequency word.

sound deletion The act of removing a specific sound from a syllable or word; doing so is more difficult when the sound is being deleted from a consonant blend.

specific language disability *See* dyslexia.

specific reading disability *See* dyslexia.

spelling pattern The letter or letter combinations representing specific phonemes. *See also* grapheme.

spelling rules   The principles guiding spelling, such as when to use *ck* instead of *c* or *k* to represent the /k/ sound.

suffix   A morpheme added to the end of a base or root that creates a new word with a changed meaning or grammatical function, such as *-or* added to the verb *instruct* to make the noun *instructor*.

syllabary   A writing system whose characters represent syllables.

syllabication   The process of dividing words into syllables.

syllable   A unit of sequential speech sounds containing a vowel and any consonants preceding or following that vowel, such as /ĭ/, /bĭ/, /ĭb/, and /bĭb/.

synthetic phonics   An instructional approach in which students learn letter–sound correspondences and blend parts to make whole words. *Also called* inductive phonics.

tense vowel sounds   *See* long vowel sounds.

unvoiced consonant   *See* voiceless consonant.

VCE syllable   *See* vowel-consonant-*e* syllable.

voiced consonant   A consonant articulated with vibration of the vocal cords.

voiceless consonant   A consonant articulated with no vibration of the vocal cords. *Also called* unvoiced consonant. (*Note:* /th/ in *this* is voiced; /th/ in *thin* is voiceless.)

vowel   1) A speech sound that is created by the free flow of breath through the vocal tract; 2) a grapheme corresponding to a vowel sound.

vowel-consonant-*e* (VCE) syllable   A syllable ending in a vowel, a consonant, and *e*, in that order, such as *made* or *cute*.

vowel digraph syllable   A syllable containing a vowel digraph, such as *meal* or *rain*. *Also called* vowel team syllable.

word identification   The pronunciation of unfamiliar words with such methods as the use of context clues, phonics, or structural analysis.

word recognition   The swift identification of a previously learned word and its meaning.

word sorting   A word-study activity in which students group words according to categories such as spelling patterns, sounds, language of origin, and/or meaning.

BIBLIOGRAPHY

This glossary was compiled using the following resources:

The American heritage dictionary (4th ed.). (2000). Boston: Houghton Mifflin.

Badian, N. (1997). Dyslexia and the double deficit hypothesis. *Annals of Dyslexia,* *47,* 69–87.

Harris, T.L., & Hodges, R.E. (1995). *The literacy dictionary: The vocabulary of reading and writing.* Newark, DE: International Reading Association.

Hennessey, N. (2003, Winter). President's letter. *Perspectives, 29*(1), 2.

Moats, L.C. (1995). *Spelling: Development, disability, and instruction.* Timonium, MD: York Press.

Moats, L.C. (2000). *Speech to print: Language essentials for teachers.* Baltimore: Paul H. Brookes Publishing Co.

Venezky, R.L. (1999). *The American way of spelling: The structure and origins of American English orthography.* New York: Guilford Press.

Index

Page numbers followed by *f* indicate figures and those followed by *t* indicate tables.